Riding the Tiger

ALSO BY LEON ARON

Roads to the Temple: Truth, Memory, Ideas, and Ideals in the Making of the Russian Revolution, 1987–1991

Russia's Revolution: Essays 1989–2006

Yeltsin: A Revolutionary Life

Riding the Tiger

Vladimir Putin's Russia and the Uses of War

Leon Aron

AEI PRESS

Publisher for the American Enterprise Institute

WASHINGTON, DC

ISBN-13: 978-0-8447-5054-5 (Hardback)
ISBN-13: 978-0-8447-5055-2 (Paperback)
ISBN-13: 978-0-8447-5056-9 (eBook)

Library of Congress Cataloging in Publication data have been applied for.

 PRESS

Publisher for the American Enterprise Institute for Public Policy Research
1789 Massachusetts Avenue, NW, Washington DC, 20036
www.aei.org

Printed in the United States of America

For Laure Berger

Contents

Я царствую! . . . Какой волшебный блеск!
Послушна мне, сильна моя держава;
В ней счастие, в ней честь моя и слава!

I reign! . . . What an enchanting luster!
Obedient to me, strong is my state;
In it my happiness, my honor and my glory!

—Alexander Pushkin, Скупой рыцарь
(*The Miserly Knight*)

His sentimentality frightened me. It was the
sentimentality of a man who could give himself
the best of reasons for doing strange things.

—V. S. Naipaul, *The Enigma of Arrival*

He had reached that moment in his life . . . when a
man abandons himself to his demons or to his genius,
following a mysterious law which bids him either to
destroy or outdo himself.

—Marguerite Yourcenar, *Memoirs of Hadrian*

Introduction

Two days before Russian tanks rolled into Ukraine, I was on Zoom, talking to the host of a news program in Asia. Earlier that day, as it had done for almost a month, the US government had issued yet another warning about Russia's imminent invasion.

It would be madness, I told the host, to start a war with a country of 44 million people—the second largest in Europe and one with a history of fierce guerrilla resistance to the Bolsheviks, the Nazis, and Stalin's Soviet Union. It would be irrational, absurd, improbable. Vladimir Putin was bluffing.

I'd been expecting Putin to go to war since his reelection to the presidency in 2018, I added. A small victorious war, the Russians called it. Not one with Ukraine.

The host looked skeptical. Before I could elaborate, he thanked me politely and said we were out of time.

Virtually all experts—inside and outside governments, in the West, Russia, and Ukraine—thought invading Ukraine would be a colossal mistake, in addition to being, standing Talleyrand on his head, a monstrous crime.[1] And so it proved to be, within weeks. We were wrong for the right reasons.

* * * *

Almost 120 years earlier, at the beginning of the Russo-Japanese War, in February 1904, Prime Minister Sergei Vitte overheard a conversation between the commander of the Russian troops in Manchuria, Alexei Kuropatkin, and the chief of the Russian police, Vyacheslav Pleve. Kuropatkin accused Pleve of joining a gang of bellicose "political adventurers." "Alexei Nikolaevich," Pleve replied, using Kuropatkin's patronymic, "you don't know Russia's internal situation. To thwart a revolution, we need a small victorious war."[2]

Putin, too, needed such a war. His reasons may not have been as urgent as Pleve's—no revolution was in sight—but they were, to Putin, no less compelling. He'd made war with the American-led West and his mission as the motherland's invincible defender the cornerstones of his regime's legitimacy. He'd saddled the tiger of militarized patriotism. But the animal required more and more meat and grew ever more difficult to dismount.

Putin was a most willing rider, though. Precisely because the assault on Ukraine seemed, from the outside, so irrational, this book's original purpose of clarifying and annotating the direction in which Putin propelled his country became all the more valid: to try and explain what sort of man was given to so seemingly senseless an impulse and, more important, what sort of country he's forged to support him, at least initially, in this insane war.

One way or another, sooner or later, the war in Ukraine will end. But the house that Putin built, his Russia, will remain. This book is a walk about its interior—not yet another biography or chronicle of Putin's rule, but a sketch of some key load-bearing structures in the edifice he erected.

We will have to live with this creation of his and the political and moral imperatives that drive this Russia to wars—as the one with Ukraine may not be the last.

1

The Vladimir Putin Story

On February 24, 2022, at six in the morning, Vladimir Putin addressed the Russian people. In somber tones, he charged the US and its NATO allies with, among other things, "spitting on other countries and their citizens," imposing their collective will on those who disagreed with them, and seeking to destroy Russia's values and corrupt the nation. NATO, he said, supported the extreme nationalists and neo-Nazis who had seized power in Kyiv in 2014.[1] These same henchmen had perpetrated genocide on ethnic Russians in Ukraine and were planning to slaughter innocents, just as the Ukrainian nationalists had done in the service of Hitler. And now they were trying to obtain nuclear weapons, he said, so they could use them when the time was right.

There was more. As Putin saw it, NATO's threat to Russia from Ukraine was not unlike the one that Nazi Germany posed to the Soviet Union in June 1941. Appeasement would cost millions of lives, as it had 81 years ago—and he, the Russian president, would not make the same mistake.

So bizarre was this diatribe even among his by now habitual vituperations of the West that to many stunned observers, Putin appeared unhinged.

Was it a symptom of Putin's not being "in touch with reality," as German Chancellor Angela Merkel concluded eight years before, after speaking to him in the wake of Russia's occupation and annexation of Crimea?[2]

"No one ever made a decision because of a number," said Daniel Kahneman, the only psychologist to win the Nobel Prize in economics for his work in cognitive psychology, judgment, and decision-making. "They need a story."[3]

I understand Kahneman to mean a kind of inner melody, a leitmotif that scores the orchestra of our lives—its themes, its volume, the pauses, and the crescendos. It explains something that utility theory cannot always account for. Cannot because, as Kahneman and his friend and colleague Amos Tversky argued, utility theory neglects cognitive biases they called "heuristics": "beliefs" and "attitudes" that account for the ostensibly "irrational" choices people make,[4] such as Putin's attempt to destroy Ukraine, which may cost him his power, or even his life.

What is Putin's "story"—the inspiration, the engine, the rudder?

* * * *

For over two decades now, Putin has positioned himself as a Russian patriot—and he may very well be one. But this is a relatively recent addition to his credo. The first 39 of his 70 years were spent in the Soviet Union. This is the time when we—or most of us—become adults, when our minds and souls are molded.

Putin is no exception. He is first and foremost an ardent Soviet patriot. "It would not be an exaggeration in the slightest to call me a successful result of the patriotic upbringing of the Soviet citizen," Putin told interviewers.[5] *Moy adres ne dom i ne ulitsa/Moy adres Sovetskiy Soyuz*! went a popular Soviet song of my youth, in the 1970s.[6] "My address is not a house or a street. My address is the Soviet Union!" Whether in the Kremlin, his Sochi villa, or the Novo-Ogaryovo dacha, the Soviet Union remains Putin's address.

And why shouldn't Putin be a Soviet patriot? The Soviet Union lifted him from the slums of postwar Leningrad—a communal apartment without hot water, with a kitchen sink shared by three families and a toilet on the staircase landing[7]—and placed him in the country's highest caste next only to the party *nomenklatura*—the KGB.

And what a country it was! Not the totalitarian police state that expelled Alexander Solzhenitsyn and tormented Andrei Sakharov but the ostensibly unstoppable winner in the global contest with the US: beating America in Angola, Ethiopia, Nicaragua, and Vietnam; achieving nuclear parity with the United States; and forcing the American president to come to Moscow and seek the truce of détente.

They were young, hungry, and hardworking—Putin and his KGB colleagues, majors and lieutenant colonels in their 30s, on their way up. Then

THE VLADIMIR PUTIN STORY 5

their boss, the KGB chairman Yuri Andropov, became general secretary, and, although in the Kremlin for only 15 months, he set the country's course: a cleaner socialism, jail or death to dissidents and thieves, patriotism, a steely grip on the Eastern and Central European holdings, continuing rearmament and modernization of the strategic nuclear arsenal, and not an inch conceded in the global duel with America.

And then this country was taken from them.

Yes, *taken*. Fatally weakened, the way they saw it, by traitors and incompetents within and enemies outside. "Mindless blabbers (*slovobludy*), timeservers (*konyukturshchiki*) are ready to betray not only the party but our country as well," Putin would tell the congress of the ruling United Russia party many years later. "This happened in our history, including our most recent history."[8] Instead of fighting to save the Soviet Union with necessary reforms—"consistently, insistently, and fearlessly"—the country's leaders "buried their heads in the sand and stuck their asses up in the air."[9]

Putin never bought the claim of the West and the Russian democrats that there were no winners and losers in the Cold War. Russia's "geopolitical enemies," surely, did not "stand idly by" as the Soviet Union was sinking: They "helped the process along," he averred.[10] It was "their" (the West's) victory—and theirs to celebrate.[11]

They more than merely "helped along"—far more, insisted Nikolai Patrushev, secretary of Russia's Security Council and likely the second most powerful man in Russia. With the hollow cheeks of a medieval ascetic, hooded eyes, and the beaky nose of a bird of prey; a veteran of Soviet counterintelligence; a general of the army; and a former head of the Federal Security Service (FSB), Patrushev makes Putin seem almost liberal by comparison. Putin's friend and confidant, Patrushev hails from the coterie of Leningrad KGB officers in the second half of the 1970s whom Putin would promote to key posts in national security, police, and the economy.[12]

It was all Zbigniew Brzezinski's fault. In the 1970s, Patrushev told a Russian newspaper, Brzezinski, President Jimmy Carter's national

Secretary of the State Security Council Nikolai Patrushev.

security adviser "of Polish descent," developed a strategy aimed at the Soviet Union's "weak spots."[13] The idea was to distract the Soviet Union from the "real struggle" with the United States by forcing Moscow to concentrate on its domestic problems.

The CIA, Patrushev continued, engaged leading economists and business leaders to work out the details. And they delivered: The economy was the Soviet Union's "weakest link," especially its dependence on oil and gas exports. A "collusion" between America and oil-producing countries followed, the price of oil fell dramatically, and the Soviet Union's income dropped with it.[14]

To further "provoke" an increase in the Kremlin's expenditures, the United States "drew" it into the war in Afghanistan, "ignited anti-government acts" in Poland and other states of the "socialist camp," and unleashed an arms race.[15]

The Americans did achieve their goals. Moscow's outlays exceeded its earnings, and a deep economic crisis followed, soon affecting the Soviet Union's politics and ideology. The "liquidation" of the USSR and the Warsaw Pact then became only a matter of time.[16]

Regardless of who bore the most blame for the fall of the Soviet Union, to Putin it was a calamity of unparalleled magnitude. Although swift and largely nonviolent—unlike, for instance, the disintegration of Yugoslavia, which unfolded at almost the same time—the end of the Soviet Union was to him "the greatest geopolitical catastrophe of the 20th century"[17]—the century of two world wars, Nazism, fascism, the Holocaust, the Gulag, the Cultural Revolution, and the Rwandan genocide. When asked which event in Russian history he would have changed if he could—the history of the Mongol and Nazi invasions, Ivan the Terrible's massacres, the civil war, the Gulag, and the man-made famines—Putin replied instantly: "The collapse of the Soviet Union."[18]

However many victors the end of the Cold War may have had, of the vanquished there was only one. To this history buff and Germanophile, his country's misfortune must have looked like Germany after the 1919 Versailles Treaty: the source of endless and deliberately inflicted indignities. Russia was rendered a character in Dostoevsky's *Humiliated and Insulted*.[19]

In linguistics, Russian is a "synthetic" language. Unlike in English, with its strict word order, Russian words are inflected by cases and genders, suffused with prefixes and suffixes, and thus may be arranged in any order, as in Latin. Not only does the word order change the meaning of the sentence, but it conveys the emotional tenor as well.

So when, in the annual state-of-Russia address, Putin said, "*A na nashikh vedushchikh predpriyatiyakh po obogashcheniyu uran sideli amerkanskie inspektora*," or, literally, "and on our leading uranium enrichment plants sat American inspectors," to the Russian ear the unmistakable connotation was that of a debased, even occupied, country.[20] (Putin likely was referring to the Megatons for Megawatts program, in which the United States paid Russia around $17 billion for 500 tons of weapons-grade uranium from missile warheads to be converted into fuel for American power plants.)[21] Later, Putin would add another layer of disgrace: In the same cursed 1990s, he averred, CIA agents were among "advisers" to the Russian government.[22]

* * * *

Most revolutions are followed by restorations. The latter are never complete; they never erase all the novelties entirely, even as they subvert and erode them. Those who don't regret the disintegration of the Soviet Union, Putin said, do not have a heart; those who want to resurrect it "as it was" don't have a head.[23] He made clear where his heart was, but his head was very much in control: The Putin restoration was patient, gradual, and selective.

There was no frontal attack on the core elements of the Mikhail Gorbachev–Boris Yeltsin revolution: a multiparty system, freedom of speech, and private property. No attempt was made to resurrect a thoroughly discredited Communist ideology. Instead, from the beginning, each institution was undermined and hollowed out, steadily and methodically. Putin never lost sight of his overarching goal: to recover for the Russian state most of the key economic, political, and geostrategic assets lost in the Soviet Union's demise.

In a key break with the previous decade and a half, when civil society appeared to have gained primacy over the state, Russia was again becoming synonymous with its state—and the state was again the foundation of its glory. To oppose the government was once more like opposing the nation. Putin claimed a "long historical tradition" of the Russians' "respect for the state" and chided the intelligentsia for pretending to do battle with the government when, in fact, they were against Russia.[24]

By the end of Putin's first presidency, in 2004, Russian politics, courts, television, and what Lenin called the "commanding heights" of the economy—first and foremost oil and natural gas—were repossessed or controlled by the state. Soon the Kremlin began to found its own corporations—all those with "Ros" (short for *Rossiya*) in their names: Rosatom, Rosnano, Rostekh. By the end of his second term in office, in 2007, the state was dominant in all "strategic sectors."[25] As a leading historian of Russia's post-Soviet economic transition put it, the state controlled whatever it wanted to control, leaving the rest in private hands.[26]

Plaque commemorating former Soviet leader Yuri Andropov in Lubyanka Square, Moscow.

Owners of larger companies were made to understand that they did not really own their businesses: They were merely managing them on behalf of the state. Those who disagreed could sell out and buy a mansion in "Londongrad's" Belgravia, Kensington Square Gardens, Highgate, or Surrey. For recalcitrants, there was a charge of tax evasion or embezzlement, a kangaroo court, and a long prison term. Mikhail Khodorkovsky—Russia's onetime richest man and the majority owner of the country's biggest private company, the oil giant Yukos—thought he was free to fund opposition parties, contemplate a private pipeline to China, and disparage government ministers in front of the president. When in 2005, after two years in pretrial detention, he was sentenced to nine years in a penal colony and Yukos was taken over by the state-owned Rosneft, the lesson was not lost on Russia's entrepreneurs, big and small.

Eleven days before he became acting president, on New Year's Eve 1999, Prime Minister Putin unveiled a memorial plaque to Andropov on the wall of the former KGB headquarters on Lubyanka Square in the center of Moscow. A few months later, he brought back the old Soviet anthem. It had new words, which no one knew, but everyone over the age of 20 could hum the tune—which was exactly the point.

* * * *

In the early 1970s, the perennial Soviet Foreign Minister Andrei Gromyko described the contemporary world as one in which there was "not a single problem of any significance" that could be "solved without the Soviet Union or against its wishes."[27] Once the Russian economy and politics were back under the state's ownership or control, it was the turn of geostrategic assets: the recovery of Russia's status in world affairs to correspond to Gromyko's encomium.

A foretaste of things to come was offered in early 2007 at the Munich Security Conference, when Putin shocked the international beau monde with a blistering attack on the post–Cold War world order. As the chancellor of Germany, the EU's foreign policy chief, NATO's secretary general, US senators, and foreign ministers from a dozen nations looked on, Putin adumbrated almost all the themes that would inform and justify his policies for years to come.

The first of these refrains was his fixation on the evils the US perpetrated. Having appointed itself the "only master of the world," America had sought to impose its political and economic order on other countries, including those of its alleged European allies. The result, Putin explained, was the erosion of justice and fairness in world affairs, the "hypertrophied" application of naked force in international affairs, and military adventures that precipitated one crisis after another.[28]

Another consequence of America's unrestrained thirst for dominance was the admission of Central and Eastern European nations into NATO. At whom was the expansion aimed? It was a rhetorical question, of course: Russia was the target.

Or take the missile defense that, Putin averred, was being "actively developed" by the US. Whether it would work was another question, but in theory it could "completely neutralize" Russia's nuclear arsenal and enable America to feel invulnerable in local or perhaps even global military conflicts. Yes, the US and Russia were bound by strategic arms control agreements. But while Russia scrupulously and "transparently" adhered to its obligations, the US was hiding at least a "couple hundred" nuclear warheads "under a blanket."[29]

Russian internal affairs were another target of the America-led aggression. Pretending to promote human rights—a goal that he welcomed—"foreign states" sought to influence the country's politics. When nongovernmental organizations (NGOs) were "secretly financed" from abroad, they were by definition also ruled from abroad, becoming an instrument in the hands of those who fund them. This was not democracy. This was one state influencing another, and it was unacceptable.

Putin was enjoying himself. After half an hour of prepared remarks, he spent almost an hour on questions and answers. "I wished I could have a separate discussion with every questioner!" he exclaimed.[30] He was animated, preening, and showing off his excellent memory for facts and figures.

The reaction ranged from deep disappointment to anxiety and fear. "I do not see how we can negotiate a new partnership pact with Russia," said a member of European Parliament from the German Green Party. "He's gone over the top."[31] The Czech foreign minister became still more convinced of the wisdom of NATO's expansion,[32] and his Swedish counterpart concluded that "this was the real Russia of now and possibly in four or five years' time it could go further in this direction."[33] "As Putin spoke . . . the atmosphere in the ballroom changed palpably," recalled two former State Department officials.[34]

Having initially offered Putin a polite welcome, the audience—
even those who shared Putin's criticism of the Iraq war—
reacted with shock, concern and even offense. Contrary to the
qualified optimism that still prevailed about Russia, it sounded
as if Putin was driving toward a new Cold War.[35]

Quite a different response had greeted Putin six years earlier when he
spoke to the German Bundestag, the first Russian head of state to have
done so. Speaking German—the "language of Kant, Schiller, Goethe," he
reminded the deputies—Putin extolled a united Europe and the indivisi-
bility of European culture. Russia had broken with "totalitarian Stalinism,"
he declared, and this irreversible choice of the Russian people led to the
razing of the Berlin Wall. Development of democracy was his government's paramount goal. Russians had learned the lessons of the Cold War
and the "ideology of occupation," and no one would ever be able to return
Russia to that past. The "mighty and vigorous heart of Russia" was open to
a genuine partnership with Germany in the cause of the construction of a
"common European home."[36] He received a standing ovation.

Where was Putin sincere: in Munich or Berlin? Or was he genuine on
both occasions? Like the course of big ships, large states' behavior in the
world is propelled by the momentum of previously made choices; they
are not easy to turn around abruptly. In almost every regime change,
foreign policy is the last area to be altered. In following Gorbachev and
Yeltsin in Berlin, did Putin make conviction out of necessity as politicians often do—only to reverse the direction when he was firmly in
charge and could indulge the revenge-and-recovery sensibility of a
Soviet patriot humiliated by the demise of the superpower motherland
and America's victory in the Cold War? As Alexander Pushkin wrote in
his beautiful "Elegy," like wine, the sadness of the bygone days grows
stronger with age.

A dispositive answer may never be known, but it was the Munich rhetoric that proved far more relevant five years later in the run-up to Putin's
third presidency in the winter of 2011–12.

"AZBUKA PROTESTA" [THE ABCS OF PROTEST]/POLIT.RU

Protest signs from 2011–12 anti-Putin protests.

* * * *

The Russia that Putin found then was different from the one he had bequeathed to Dmitry Medvedev for place-holding four years earlier. After eight years of unprecedented and seemingly unstoppable growth of incomes in Putin's first two presidential terms, the economy was suddenly vulnerable. In one year of the 2008–09 world financial crisis, Russia lost almost 8 percent of its gross domestic product (GDP), the largest decline among the G20 countries.[37] Oil was back up to $111 a barrel in 2012, yet unlike the previous decade, the economy did not follow: GDP growth lagged behind that of 2011.[38]

It was also a restless, angrier Russia. The protest rallies in over 100 Russian cities and towns were—and still are—the largest of Putin's tenure. Although triggered by the shameless falsifications of the results of the Duma election, their thrust was unmistakably and ad hominem anti-Putin: jeering, taunting, often vulgar, and occasionally cruel.

A poster crossed with a noose was to remind Putin of the end of two dictators. Addressing him by a boy's diminutive, Vova, it asked, "Are you going to be courageous like Saddam [Hussein] or tremble like [Nicolae] Ceauşescu?"[39]

Mocking Putin's assertion that the demonstrators were "supported" by the US State Department[40] headed by Hillary Clinton, another poster asked sarcastically: "Hillary, where is our money?! Putin promised!"[41] Four years later, Putin's belief in Clinton's "signal" to the demonstrators and his conviction that if elected president she would continue her "anti-Russian" policy were key reasons for Russia's anyone-but-Hillary meddling in the US presidential election.

The post-Soviet professionals, those whom Putin thought were forever in his debt for the comforts and opportunities that had sprung up in his first two terms—restaurants, decent clothes and food, cars, foreign travel, and "euro-remodeled" apartments with dishwashers and bidets—were biting the hand that fed them—his hand.

Yet there was more to it than casual ingratitude. Looming over the first crisis of Putin's rule were the twin hobgoblins that had destroyed the Soviet Union: moral rejection of the regime by a significant share of the urban middle class and a sharp economic downturn.

The slowdown looked like a systemic problem, not a one-off fluctuation. The culprit was an increasingly toxic investment climate. The sources of the poison had been identified by economists inside and outside the government since at least the 2008 crisis: the swelling of state control over the economy; violation of property rights; courts for sale or bent by the "telephone law," as Russians called orders from political authorities at every level; rampant *reyderstvo*, or the forced takeover of profitable businesses by local authorities or better connected competitors; use of arrests, kangaroo courts, and lengthy prison terms for business owners who tried to defend their property; and shakedowns of businesses by officials at every level—from the fire and sanitation inspectors to mayors, regional governors, and government ministers.

Likely the most troubling to Putin was the diagnosis of someone he had learned to trust and even counted among his few "friends."[42] A fellow *Leningradets*, Alexei Kudrin had known Putin since the early 1990s when they worked for Mayor Anatoly Sobchak. Kudrin was one of a handful of men responsible for Putin's move to Moscow in 1996 and his first job in the Kremlin.[43] He was Putin's first finance minister and deputy prime minister, serving for 11 years before resigning in 2011 over increased defense spending.

The Russian economy had "hit the wall," Kudrin insisted. It could not develop "effectively" because of structural constraints that choked investments and undercut labor productivity. Corruption was endemic and ubiquitous, he insisted: The traffic policeman, the teacher, the doctor, and the bank manager who issued loans were all open to bribery. Echoing the demonstrators, but of course never mentioning Putin, Kudrin called for institutional reforms in politics as well as the economy: fewer state-owned companies, independent courts, and a state "accountable to society." Russia needed competitive "free elections" with the participation of new political parties, honest counting of votes, equal access to the media by all candidates, and businesses funding opposition parties without the fear of punishment by the Kremlin. Russia, Kudrin declared, had to "take a chance on more democracy!"[44]

Absent such reforms, the country's economy was to be stuck between stagnation and recession: growing or shrinking by 1.5 percent, *regardless* of the price of oil.[45] (Kudrin would be proven right almost instantly: In 2013, with oil still at $110 a barrel, the economy expanded at only 1.8 percent, or half of the previous year's rate.)[46]

The political implications of Kudrin's forecast were as clear as they were dire: Without economic and political liberalization, Putin could forget about the unprecedented growth of incomes that between 2000 and 2008 cemented his popularity, on which the legitimacy of his regime was founded.

Some of the writing was already on the wall. Three in five Russians told pollsters in 2012 that they were tired of waiting for Putin to fulfill his promises to improve the economy and raise living standards.[47] People were upset by the rising prices of food staples and utilities, deteriorating health care and education, and rising rents—problems that, as political sociologist Mikhail Dmitriev put it in the summer of 2013, the Kremlin did not know how to solve.[48] In 2013, over half of respondents in a national poll wanted someone other than Putin to be elected president in 2018.[49] Trust in Putin was plunging, Dmitriev reported, and there was no "bottom" in sight.[50] By November 2013, Putin's 61 percent approval rating was the lowest since he was first elected president, in 2000.[51]

Yet cemented by blood and money, the "vertical of power"[52] that Putin had so assiduously constructed in the previous 12 years was as fragile as it was rigid: Take out just a few bricks, and the entire pillar would list dangerously. More importantly, reforms suggested by Kudrin would go against his vision of the Russian state as an heir to, although not an identical twin of, the Soviet Union.

Navigating masterfully between the loss of control and the loss of support, in the most fateful choice of his political life, between 2012 and 2014 Putin began to shift the base of his popular support from economic progress and the growth of incomes to what Lev Gudkov called "patriotic mobilization."[53] Russia's leading political sociologist Igor Klyamkin labeled Putin's choice "militarized patriotism in peacetime."[54]

Far more than a deft political maneuver, Putin set in motion a transformation of the regime. From a relatively mild authoritarian system in which the government had been largely indifferent to what its subjects thought and believed in so long as they did not seek to challenge it, he began to mold the society to fit into an increasingly rigid framework separating the state-mandated right from the state-deplored wrong.

Russian religious philosopher and historian Nikolai Berdyaev wrote of Ivan the Terrible, whom he called a "remarkable theoretician of absolute monarchy," that he had "taught that a Tsar must not only govern a state, but also save souls."[55] Putin was now in the business of saving souls as well: imparting and enforcing correct mores, telling his compatriots what truths they must accept as absolute, what to aspire to and glorify, what to abhor and whom to hate. Like the Soviet Union's general secretaries before him, president and commander in chief became the highest priest and the enforcer of the creed he prescribed.[56]

* * * *

The guiding encyclical of the new faith was delivered on March 18, 2014, a stem-winder of a speech to a joint session of the Federal Assembly (the parliament) on account of occupied Crimea's "admission" to the Russian Federation.

Putin proclaimed that power in Kyiv had been seized in a coup by neo-Nazis, Russophobes, antisemites, and "Banderovites" (Hitler's Ukrainian henchmen in World War II). The "curators" and "sponsors" of the takeover, those who had organized and directed it, were "our Western partners, led by the United States." Why did they behave so "crudely," so "irresponsibly"?[57]

First off, Putin explained, reprising his Munich oration, because such was "their," the West's, modus operandi in global affairs. They were guided not by international laws but by the "law of the powerful." Having persuaded themselves of their "chosenness" (*izbrannost'*) and "exclusivity" (*isklyuchitel'nost'*), they arrogated for themselves the right to decide the fate of the world, to act as they pleased. Their cynicism was amazing: Unashamed, the West subjugated everything to its interests, calling black white one day and white black the next.

Take the so-called color revolutions. The people's hopelessness and the resentment of poverty and tyranny were cynically exploited as the West forced on them alien standards, traditions, and cultural values. The result: chaos, violence, and coups. This is the script that was realized in Ukraine.

But there was another, more troubling reason for the coup in Kyiv. The Kyiv putschists talked about obtaining NATO membership. Imagine NATO's fleet in Crimea, in Sevastopol, a city of Russian military valor! This would have been a military threat to the entirety of southern Russia—not just some theoretical hazard, but a real, material menace.

Seizing power in Kyiv was not some sort of accident and a sudden opportunity too good to pass by. No, it was part and parcel of an agelong effort to degrade and subjugate Russia. The "infamous" policy of "containment" was not invented "yesterday," Putin avowed. The West had deployed it since at least the 18th century. Throughout the country's history, as soon as Russia became strong, excuses were found to constrain its development—all because Russia would not buckle because it insisted on independence in global affairs.[58]

The fall of the Soviet Union made no difference. Again and again Russia was deceived, confronted with decisions made behind its back, and forced to accept done deals. It was constantly "pushed into the corner"[59]—all this despite Russia's persistent offers of cooperation on all key problems and notwithstanding its efforts to make the relationship with the West "equal, open and honest."[60] It was all in vain: No one even tried to meet Moscow halfway. The West hated Russia for being a country with its own, independent position in the world.

But in Ukraine, "our Western partners" had crossed the line. They pushed Russia to the limit beyond which it could not retreat. "Compressed to the hilt," Putin warned, "a spring is bound to expand with force."[61]

Of course, Russia was being threatened with sanctions for the annexation of Crimea. But this, too, was nothing new. It was already being sanctioned: During the Cold War, the Soviet Union had been banned from buying all sorts of technologies, and although "officially" repealed, many of the so-called CoCom (Coordinating Committee for Multilateral Export Controls) bans were still in place.[62] In addition, Western politicians were already hinting at the worsening of Russia's domestic problems. Did they have in mind something like a fifth column—some sort of "national-traitors"[63]—or did they plan to worsen the economic situation in the country and thus provoke people's discontent?

The coda rose to a crescendo: The fate of Russia was being decided that day! Would it be weak and subservient to the West or a proud and sovereign nation? The enemies would redouble their attacks, of course, but he, the president, had no doubts about the path the Russian people would choose:

> We will certainly encounter opposition from abroad, but we have to decide for ourselves: Are we ready to defend our national interests or forever give them up, retreating indefinitely. . . .
>
> It is in moments like this that the maturity of a nation is tested, the strength of its national spirit. And the people of Russia have demonstrated this maturity and this strength, supporting their [Crimean] compatriots by this consolidation.

Medal of the Ministry of Defense of the Russian Federation "for the Return of Crimea: February 14–March 18, 2014."

> The steadfastness of Russia's foreign policy has been founded on the will of millions of people, on national unity, on the support of the leading political and social forces. I want to thank everyone for this patriotic attitude. Everyone, with no exception. But we must continue to preserve this solidarity in order to take on the problems that are facing Russia![64]

At their feet for the third and final standing ovation in the Georgievskiy Hall of the Kremlin, many in the audience waved the Russian tricolor and Sevastopol's coat of arms. Under the arched ceiling's enormous, elaborate chandeliers, the hall rang with chants of *"Rossiya, Rossiya, Rossiya!"*[65]

Correctly gauging the tenor of the speech, some alert courtiers in the audience were wearing *Georgievskie lentochki* (the black and orange Ribbon of Saint George), which since 2005 had symbolized the triumph of the Great Patriotic War, as World War II is almost always referred to in Russia. As a popular Russian daily would put it a few days later, Putin's "mobilization" rhetoric was akin to the kind used during the Great Patriotic War, with the Nazis having been replaced by the West. It was a call to his compatriots to join him in a "battle with the West and its lackeys."[66]

The country would cheer as well. Later in the month, Putin's approval rating skyrocketed to 80 percent, reached 86 percent in June, and stayed in the 80s for the next four years until early 2018. Along the way, his popularity hit its record peak of 89 percent in June 2015.[67]

Sealed by the Crimea Anschluss and the March 14 speech, the gamble of the transition from the distributor of national wealth to the defender of the motherland, the protector of Russians outside Russia, and the in-gatherer of Russian lands proved a resounding success.

* * * *

"The huge iceberg Russia, frozen by the Putin regime, has cracked," popular novelist Vladimir Sorokin wrote two months later. "It split from the European world, and sailed off into the unknown. No one knows what will happen to the country now, into which seas or swamps it will drift."[68]

The final destination of Putin's Russia may have been unknown even to Putin. Yet some Russian observers were remarkably prescient in gauging the general direction. One of these commentators discerned the regime's attempt "to play on prejudices, myths, and other dark sides" of human nature. The Kremlin was unleashing "nationalism and xenophobia, isolationism, imperial mentality, and Stalinism."[69] Another expert witness summarized the country's new direction as "a Russian crusade," not unlike the *Blut und Boden*, blood and soil, of German imperialism and Hitler's Nazism, founded on a "geopolitical myth."[70]

To a chronicler of post-Soviet Russian politics, the Kremlin's agenda looked like a return to a "corrected and amended USSR": It was like the Soviet Union of the late 1970s, when the dissident movement was steadily strangled and finally crushed by Andropov's KGB. The "European path"—on which the West had been a distant and hazy but nevertheless persistent destination under Gorbachev and Yeltsin and to which, until then, Putin at least paid lip service—had been abandoned; a new "iron curtain" had come down across it.[71]

Albeit not as a dirge but a bravura march, the consensus on the fatefulness of the regime change extended from liberal experts to the "national-patriotic" left on the other end of the political spectrum. "A real revolution!" exulted Aleksandr Dugin, a former leader of the National Bolshevik Party, religious philosopher, historian, and geopolitical strategist, some of whose ideas and texts may have found their ways in Putin's speeches and policies.[72] The annexation of Crimea signified "the end of liberalism" inside the country, Dugin trumpeted. It was Putin's challenge to the America-dominated "unipolar world." There would be no more "resets" with the United States—ever! Russia had passed the point of no return![73]

The longtime editor of the oldest post-Soviet Bolshevik weekly, *Zavtra*, Alexander Prokhanov, too, detected the "strong ideological mutation" of the regime.[74] He began to call his president "Putin Tavricheskiy," or Putin of Tavrida (the old Russian name for Crimea)—the honorary title that Catherine the Great bestowed on her favorite Prince Gregory Potemkin after her travels to Crimea, which he had wrestled from the Ottomans.

* * * *

The observers were right about the tightening of the screws as well. Although nowhere near the height of the Andropov flood, the "reactionary wave" unleashed in 2012 rose to a level not seen since before Gorbachev took over, in 1985: a systematic assault on the most active part of civil society, aimed at intimidating, defunding, marginalizing, stigmatizing, and criminalizing pro-democracy opposition and its ostensibly nonpolitical but nevertheless suspect NGOs. Harsher punishments were meted out for invented "crimes." Punitive psychiatry pioneered by Andropov was back in use, especially in provinces.

Participation in "unauthorized demonstrations"—and, unless pro-Kremlin, they all would be rendered "unauthorized"—now could entail huge fines or lengthy prison sentences. Three members of the feminist band Pussy Riot were sent to jail for two years for "hooliganism motivated by religious hatred" after performing an anti-Putin "punk prayer" in the Christ the Savior Cathedral.[75] Ten participants in a peaceful protest at Putin's inauguration on May 7 were held in pretrial detention for almost two years,[76] and seven were given prison terms of between two and a half and four years. One of the leaders of the December 2011 protest rallies in Moscow, Sergei Udaltsov, was sentenced to four and a half years for "inciting mass disorder"; another, Alexei Navalny, received a five-year suspended sentence for "embezzlement."[77]

As protest rallies were sweeping through Russian cities in December 2011, Putin called for "tougher punishment" for those who, as he saw it, sought to influence Russian politics on the orders of foreign governments.[78] Foreign states spent hundreds of millions of dollars on their "lackeys" inside the country, Putin said, and the government must protect the country's sovereignty.[79]

Follow-up legislation duly sailed through the Duma three months later. Noncommercial organizations that received funding from abroad were to be designated "foreign agents" by the Foreign and Justice Ministries. These NGOs had to submit exhaustive expense reports every three months and financial and business accounts twice a year. They also were audited annually. Every publication by these groups, especially internet posts, had to be identified as coming from a "foreign agent." Failure to comply carried hefty fines and could eventually result in shuttering for noncompliance. Worse yet was the stigma: In national surveys, over half the respondents associated "foreign agents" with "traitors and spies."[80]

The line between "foreign agents" and those whom Putin called "agents,"[81] or Russian citizens recruited by foreigners to spy, grew thinner still after the state treason article of Russia's Criminal Code was amended. If before, betrayal had been defined as threatening only the "external security" of the country, it now covered "financial, material, technical, advisory or any other support given to a foreign country."[82]

In another update, no longer just those with professional access to state secrets could be held liable: Anyone who somehow came about such materials could be brought up on charges of treason and sentenced to up to 20 years in prison. In just the first three years after the adoption of the amendments, the number of cases would quadruple to around 3,000.[83]

Senior government functionaries, deputies of the Federal Assembly, governors, and mayors were put on notice that they were not immune from punishment in the unlikely but possible event that they harbored sympathies for the "terrorists" and "extremists" who planned "color revolutions." Almost always charged with corruption or embezzlement, the number of arrested and jailed officials would double between 2012 and 2018.[84] While hardly a purge—no more than two dozen were affected—it was as gentle a reminder as the Kremlin could muster of the dangers of disloyalty or uncommon rapacity.

* * * *

A month after Putin's speech, a banner seven meters high was unfurled from the top of Moscow's largest bookstore, the Dom Knigi on Novy Arbat. Featured on the poster were the most prominent and vocal critics of the Crimean Anschluss: rock stars Andrei Makarevich and Yuri Shevchuk; Navalny; Duma Deputy Ilya Ponomarev, who alone had voted against the annexation of Crimea; and Boris Nemtsov, an opposition leader and first deputy prime minister in the Yeltsin government.

The portraits were framed by black-suited creatures with pointy heads—extraterrestrials from the 1979 sci-fi film *Alien*.[85] One of them held a briefcase emblazoned with a white ribbon, a symbol of the winter 2011–12 protest rallies.

The work of an alleged NGO, Glavpost.ru, the poster was soon removed. Yet as former First Deputy Prime Minister Nemtsov explained to a Russian reporter, Novy Arbat was a route traveled by top government officials to the Kremlin, so FSB and FSO (Federal Protective Service)[86] agents were posted "every ten meters" there. It would have been impossible to mount a giant poster on the roof without the secret services' complicity.[87]

"Fifth Column. Aliens Among Us" poster on the Dom Knigi attacking critics of the Crimean annexation.

The banner was a signal, Nemtsov added, a symbol of a sharp turn in Russia's direction. Putin had triggered a second cold war. He was erecting a new iron curtain and wanted Russia to be "squeezed out" of Europe. Russia was on its way to enormous social and economic upheavals, Nemtsov said. Crimea was the beginning of Russia's descent into a bottomless crisis. The Kremlin was destroying the country.[88]

What would the regime do to the leaders of the opposition like yourself? the interviewer asked. "Jail," Nemtsov answered. "Concoct criminal charges and jail. Kill, perhaps, but most likely jail." Regardless, he added, "they will never be able to make me stop speaking up, they simply won't."[89]

Ten and a half months later, on February 27, 2015, Nemtsov was assassinated on a bridge a few hundred meters from the Kremlin.

2

The House That Putin Built

"If there is Putin, there is Russia! No Putin, no Russia!"[1] declared Vladimir Putin's first deputy chief of staff, Vyacheslav Volodin. Crude flattery, of course—and quite profitable for Volodin, who two years later became the speaker of the Duma.

But the truth is that much of today's Russia *is* Putin.

Ralph Waldo Emerson's maxim that there is properly no history, only biography, encapsulates Russia's history since 2000.

Much of what has been written on the subject has focused narrowly on the Kremlin, with little, if any, attention to the underpinnings of the Putin regime. The resulting image is that of an autocracy supported solely by propaganda, political manipulation, and repression. This is a dangerous oversimplification because it vastly underestimates Putin's ability to sway and mobilize his compatriots.

He has relentlessly molded national identity: how Russians see themselves, their country, and their history. He has refashioned and reawakened the country's legitimizing mythology—and deployed it in ways that have proved gratifying to tens of millions of Russia's citizens.

Why has he succeeded?

Four years of brilliant moral wisdom of de-Stalinization under Mikhail Gorbachev's glasnost[2] and of earnest but haphazard de-Bolshevization under Boris Yeltsin proved too brief to extirpate the centuries-old identification of national glory with imperial sway. An impeccable Soviet patriot, Putin sensed that which pro-democracy revolutionaries of the late 1980s and early 1990s tended to disregard: the deep-seated and "widely recognized" trauma[3] from the loss of what they believed was their country's exceptional status, from the forfeiture of its exalted place in the world.

Asked in a 2010 national survey whether "Russia must restore its status of a great empire," 78 percent replied "[it] must," "certainly," or "more yes than no."[4] It was not the Soviet Union they wanted back—crabby gray, with food queues, stern enforcers of the party line in books and movies, and impenetrable borders. It was its status as the world's superpower, the moral as well as military counterweight to the United States. Putin tapped into that sentiment by advertising the recovery of this lofty station as the most important part of his foreign policy.

Recalling his native Trinidad, V. S. Naipaul wrote of "the shame of smallness."[5] Geography, of course, was not an issue. Even after the fall of the Soviet Union, Russia remained huge. But in the eyes of millions of Russians, Putin took on Russia's post-Soviet geopolitical "smallness" to restore their country to the center of world politics, where the Soviet Union used to be. In 1999, only one in three Russians thought their country was a "great power" (*velikaya derzhava*). By 2019, after the annexation of Crimea and the sharpening confrontation with the West, seven in 10 were convinced this was the case.[6]

Putin both stoked and exploited the widespread indignity instilled by the Soviet Union's collapse. He sounded sincere because he was. Putin and his closest circle were "overcome with feelings of humiliation and betrayal by the West," contended a Kremlin insider.[7] For Putin, Crimea was not about the territory: It was about the "redemption of one's own humiliation," reported another well-informed Russian commentator.[8]

There is "pleasure" to be derived from "too vivid an awareness of one's humiliation,"[9] mused the hero of Dostoevsky's *Notes from the Underground*. The Russians who, like Putin, felt humiliated by the disappearance of the Soviet Union and America's "victory" in the Cold War may not have wallowed in their disgrace as did Dostoevsky's unhinged protagonist, but humiliation can be both an addiction and a source of dark energy. It may fuel nefarious deeds. Those who "thrive on humiliation" may in turn seek to humiliate others to "avenge" the indignity they believed they suffered.[10] If they gain power and tap into this sentiment among their followers, war and genocide may follow: Such was the case for Hitler, the Somali dictator

Siad Barre, Slobodan Milosevic of the disintegrating Yugoslavia, and the Hutu extremist elite, who instigated the 1994 genocide in Rwanda.[11]

* * * *

Putin both assuaged and used the post-Soviet trauma in yet another way. Thought to have been gone and buried by the Gorbachev-Yeltsin revolution—and taking with it the best years of millions of Russians—the much-mourned Soviet Union was far from dead! he insisted. What was the Soviet Union? Putin asked. Russia, of course, only under a different name![12] No one in the Kremlin had equated the two before. To the Communists, the tsarist empire, which Lenin called "a prison of peoples,"[13] was deplorable and utterly incompatible with the Communist project, while the revolutionaries of the 1980s and 1990s did not want to be tainted by the crimes of the Soviet regime.

Putin had no such qualms. The Soviet Union was reborn in Putin's state, not as a political entity but as a living legacy and an inspiration. There was also a warning there to the post-Soviet states: You were not the Soviet Union's; you were Russia's. And Russia is back.

A street urchin from the slums of postwar Leningrad, Putin also shared with millions of Russians another core element of the Soviet identity: equating respect with fear and self-assertion with aggression. Three months after the Crimea Anschluss, Lev Gudkov, then director of Russia's only independent national polling firm, the Levada Center, noted that Putin was believed by many to have "restored the West's respect for Russia."[14] He made Russia equal to the leading world powers, the other members of what had been the G8, and "the people very much appreciate this."[15] The polls also revealed that almost nine in 10 Russians believed their country was feared, and three in four thought it a good thing.[16]

Putin also drew on a central component of the national tradition: the myth of Russia's exclusivity. Referring to Rome, which fell to the Visigoths early in the fifth century, and Constantinople, conquered by the Ottoman Turks in 1453, the early 16th-century Pskov monk Philotheus declared the Orthodox Christian Moscow the heir to both: the third Rome, the only true Christian kingdom left in the world. "So know, pious king," the monk wrote to Grand Prince Vasily III of Moscow, the father of Ivan the Terrible, "that all the Christian kingdoms came to an end and came together in a single kingdom of yours, two Romes have fallen, the third stands, and there will be no fourth."[17]

Almost five centuries later, Russian sociologists heard respondents in focus groups readily acknowledging Russia's "special path." There was "satisfaction" from her "exclusivity," her being incomparable and unmatched by the "others."[18] In a long article published in the run-up to his third presidency in 2012, Putin pronounced Russia not merely a country or a state but a state-civilization—and a "unique" one at that.[19] Since then, the "thousand-year-old" Russia, distinct from "Europe" and the "West," became one of the most frequent themes in his speeches.

He was effective here as well. In 1992, only slightly more than one in 10 Russians believed they were "a great people with a special destiny in world history"; in 2017, more than six in 10 thought so. The share of those who felt they were just like any other people went down from eight in 10 to one in three.[20] By 2021, 64 percent of Russians considered their country "non-European"—up from fewer than one in four in 2008.[21]

* * * *

The Soviet identity was recovered and promoted through confrontation and defiance. It may seem strange that millions would seek comfort in the reprise of anxiety and fears of the Cold War years. But one does not have to be a Freudian, much less have spent much time on the couch, to know that we often repeat painful or destructive behaviors just because they are familiar.

Putin became a symbol of the resurrection of a besieged but proud and recovering power. By 2021, more than eight in 10 Russians felt that the "enemies are all around."[22] Yet, like their president, the respondents in focus groups felt that the "more they pressure us, the greater we are."[23]

The identification with the alleged "greatness" of the Soviet Union, Russian sociologists suggested, was a "very important mechanism" of

Soviet propaganda poster "Ne balui!" [Don't You Fool Around!].

collective compensation for the powerlessness in the face of the authorities at every level.[24] Such redress for oppression has been a centuries-old legitimation device of Russian rulers. As the great Russian poet Mikhail Lermontov put it almost two centuries ago: *Puskay ya rab/No rab tsarya vselennoy*! "I may be a slave/But a slave to the tsar of the universe!"[25]

There is a classic Soviet Cold War poster from 1948 with a Russian soldier admonishing Uncle Sam.[26] The soldier is handsome, strong, and confident. On his cartoonishly broad chest is the Soviet Union's highest military award, the gold star of the Hero of the Soviet Union, and in his hand is a book of World War II history. Uncle Sam holds a nuclear bomb and a torch, about to set the world on fire. His ugly face is contorted by impotent hatred. The caption, *Ne balui!*, can be loosely translated as "Don't you fool around!" The implication is clear: Although the enemy is different, the outcome of a possible confrontation will be the same.

This is the national sensibility that Putin has resurrected, augmented, and made the cornerstone of his regime: enmity, danger, and fear—and glory and pride.

* * * *

What should the patriot of Putin's Russia remember and be proud of? What should the young, especially, draw on?

The foundation and armature were to be provided by Russian history. But it was no longer merely an ennobling memory. The past was to become a bracing inspiration, a call for action and, if need be, sacrifice.[27] The "bright future" of the Soviet ideology was replaced by the largely mythical bright past.[28] A Russian scholar called it the "state policy of memory."[29]

The work began in June 2007 when teachers of social sciences met in Moscow at a national conference to discuss "the acute problems in the teaching of modern Russian history" and develop "state standards of education." Putin invited the participants to his Novo-Ogaryovo residence outside Moscow.

Their heads and those of all of the teachers of history, Putin told them, were filled with *kasha*, the "mishmash of ideas." "Common standards" were urgently needed.[30]

His guests appeared to agree—at least those who spoke up. In the 1990s, we disarmed ideologically, said one. We adopted an uncertain, abstract ideology of all-human values. "Russia was told by the West: you become democrats and capitalists and we will control you." Putin nodded: "This is a tried-and-true trick. If outsiders get to grade us, they will claim the right to manage us as well."[31]

In the past two decades, our youth have been subjected to "a torrent" of diverse information about our historical past, said another guest to

Novo-Ogaryovo. And this information contains different conceptual approaches, interpretations, and value judgments. You see, Putin replied, some textbooks in schools and colleges are written by those who are paid with foreign grants. "And, naturally, they are dancing the polka ordered by those who paid them."[32]

To provide his own dance music for some of the most dramatic passages of the Soviet narrative, Putin went further than his Soviet predecessors. War veterans all until Gorbachev came along, the Politburo members had seen firsthand the disastrous results of Stalin's trust in Hitler and preferred to be mum about the Molotov-Ribbentrop Pact. The Soviet Union had never acknowledged the existence of the secret protocols to the pact that deeded eastern Poland to the Soviet Union. Romania's Bessarabia was to be occupied the next year, along with Estonia, Latvia, and Lithuania.

Putin ordered the protocols "found" in 2019, in time for the 80th anniversary of the beginning of World War II. In a long essay that same year, he expatiated at length and passionately on the "origins of WWII." He blamed Great Britain and France for abetting Hitler and the US for investing in German industry. He reprised and elaborated on the Soviet excuses: the threats from Hitler in the West and Japan in the East. It was only after it became clear that France and Great Britain would not help Poland and that the Wehrmacht was about to occupy all of Poland and "appeared" to approach Minsk that the Soviet Union decided to send the Red Army into what Putin called Eastern Borderlines (nowadays part of Belarus, Lithuania, and Ukraine).[33]

The Red Army did not "seize" the Polish territory, Putin said at the annual nationally televised press conference in December 2019.[34] The Soviet troops merely "entered" Poland after the German army "vacated" parts of it. "The Soviet Union did not take anything from Poland!" Putin told the leaders of several post-Soviet states at a summit in St. Petersburg the next day.[35] Besides, Stalin did not "stain himself" by "direct contacts with Hitler"—unlike leaders of France and Great Britain who "met with him and signed little papers."[36] Putin's minister of culture, Vladimir Medinsky, called the pact a "diplomatic triumph."[37] Two and a half years later, Putin would appoint Medinsky chief negotiator in the so-called Minsk process peace talks with Ukraine.

Other crimes of Stalinism, while not quite explained away, were allowed to recede safely into a distant and increasingly nebulous past. As in the Soviet Union, mass murders were renamed "repression," with no addresses for mass executions and no names of the perpetrators. "As to some problematic pages in our history—yes, we've had them," Putin told the teachers in Novo-Ogaryovo. But what country did not? he asked.

> And the Soviet Union had fewer of such episodes than certain other countries—and ours were not as horrible as theirs. . . . Let us remember the events beginning in [the Great Purge of] 1937, let us not forget about them. But other countries have had no less, and even more.[38]

Standing next to Alexander Solzhenitsyn's widow, Natalia, at the opening of the Wall of Grief memorial in Moscow, Putin deplored "repressions"—and then cautioned against holding the culprits to account:

> We need to remember the tragedy of the repressions. But this does not mean calling for the settling of scores. Society should not be pushed toward a dangerous confrontation. It is important now to be guided by the values of trust and stability.[39]

Stalin was not mentioned once.

Three weeks later, Putin spoke at the Kremlin reception to celebrate the 100th anniversary of the "state security organs." He called the Cheka-GPU-OGPU-NKVD-MGB-KGB torturers and executioners "real patriots who honorably and honestly carried out their duty, placing above all the service to the fatherland and the people."[40]

Russia's sole Gulag memorial and museum, in the Perm region in the northeast, was redesigned to "focus more on the guards than the inmates," as an independent news outlet put it.[41] "It is now a museum of the camp system, it is not about political prisoners," said the former director of the museum, which had been managed by a nonprofit organization until the state had effectively seized it. "There's nothing about the repressions or about Stalin."[42] Six years later, the authorities shut down Memorial International, founded by Andrei Sakharov in 1989 to research and preserve the memories of Stalinist terror and monitor political imprisonment in the Soviet Union and later Russia.

The Russian historian Yuri Dmitriev, who uncovered graves of at least 9,000 victims[43] of Stalinist terror in Sandarmokh in the Karelia region of northwestern Russia, was sentenced to 13 years in camps on charges of pedophilia. An official in the region had complained that Dmitriev's work created an "unfounded sense of guilt" and was used by "foreign powers as propaganda against Russia."[44]

An article on the "Rehabilitation of Nazism" that was added to the Russian Criminal Code and signed into law by Putin in May 2014 made it a crime to "spread obviously false information about the actions of the USSR during World War II." Another punishable transgression was "spreading information that demonstrated obvious disrespect for the military glory and commemorative dates of Russia." The sentences ranged from a substantial fine of between 3 million and 5 million rubles ($78,000–$124,000 at the 2014 rate of exchange) or three to five years of forced labor in a penal colony.[45]

When Putin amended the constitution in 2020, one of the dozens of amendments postulated "the defense of historical truth" and banned the "diminution of the significance of the people's feat in defense of the Motherland."[46]

Still unsatisfied, the Duma deputies proposed adding more punishable transgressions to the Russian Criminal Code. One such provision would penalize "declaring the USSR responsible for starting the Second World War," "denying the leading role of the USSR in the victory over the Axis countries in the Second World War," and "equating" Communism and Nazism.[47]

By 2020, regular police were apparently deemed inadequate to the task of enforcing "historical truth." The job was entrusted to the Investigative Committee (roughly an equivalent of the FBI), headed by General of Justice Alexander Bastrykin, Putin's classmate at the Law Department of Leningrad State University and reportedly his close friend and adviser. A special department was set up in the committee to "investigate crimes connected to the rehabilitation of Nazism and the falsification of the history of the Motherland."[48]

I wonder if Bastrykin had looked for inspiration to another history-minded Russian policeman—his namesake Count Alexander Benckendorff, a personal friend of Nicholas I and the head of the secret political police, known as the Third Department of His Imperial Majesty's Chancellery. "Russia's past was extraordinary," Benckendorff wrote. "Its present is more than magnificent, and as to its future it exceeds the most daring imagination."[49]

3

Russia Under Siege

On September 1, 2004, the first day of the Russian school year, Islamic militants took over 1,000 children and their parents hostage in a school in the North Ossetian town of Beslan. On the third day of the siege, Russian troops stormed the building with flamethrowers, tank cannons, and grenade launchers. In all, 334 people were killed, 186 of them children: shot, torn apart, burned alive.

The next day, Vladimir Putin addressed the terrified nation. "[It's] hard to speak," he began. "The grief is overwhelming. All of us have been anguished in our hearts these three days."[1]

How did it come to that? How could this tragedy happen? The government was to blame for the inadequacy of law enforcement, corruption, and unguarded borders. Most of all, we appeared weak, and the weak are beaten, Putin quoted almost verbatim from Stalin's 1931 speech.[2]

But who had exploited this weakness? Who put it to use? What we had in Beslan, Putin explained, was not just an isolated attack. It was an instance of a "total, merciless, large-scale" war, an aggression by international terrorism against Russia. And the actual perpetrators were but a front, a screen. Behind them were those who "want to tear from us as fat a chunk as they can" and "others who help them." "Help," he continued, "thinking that Russia, one of the largest nuclear powers of the world, is still a threat to someone. Which is why this threat must be eliminated. And terrorism, of course, is only an instrument in reaching these goals."[3]

Three weeks later, Putin's then top domestic policy adviser, Vladislav Surkov, followed up by asking, "Why us? Why Russia?" Because, he answered, "some consider the collapse of the Soviet Union their achievement and they are trying to build on their success. Their goal was the destruction of Russia." The *Komsomolskaya Pravda* tabloid subtitled the

Surkov interview "The President Declared That Russia Had Been a Sub-ject of Aggression, That the Country Is De-Facto in a State of War."[4] Putin did not have to name the culprits. Everyone understood they were the collective West.

Until his third presidency, the unspoken contract between Putin and the Russians had been: "Stay out of politics, and I'll make you prosper-ous." After 2012, the pact quickly evolved into: "Stay out of politics, and I'll defend you." As in Iran or North Korea, a perennial war with the America-led "West" became integral to the regime's legitimacy. Chime-rical external threats became indispensable to "national consolidation," said a top independent Russian pollster. The shadow of the external enemy muted complaints about growing poverty and abusive authorities.[5] Putin reinvented himself as a wartime president and his country as a besieged fortress by convincing millions of the perennial—and utterly fantastic—danger of war and making war—fought and won, past, present, and future—into the symbol of national glory and national purpose.

Voyna (war) became part of the quotidian discourse. By early 2022, over half of Russians were scared of a world war—a larger proportion than during the last years of the Cold War. Russians were more afraid of war than illness, abuse by the authorities, and poverty. Only the sickness of one's children was scarier. [6]

The confrontation with the West that Putin engineered has been com-pared to the Cold War. One of the problems with this parallel is that the Politburo elders did not need the threat of war to justify their hold on power. They had their ideology. World War II veterans abhorred war as only veterans can. *Lish by ne bylo voyny* (anything but war) was their mantra.

By contrast, Putin's approval ratings had been directly correlated with the perceived conflict with the West: They fluctuated with the rhetoric of confrontation and were "galvanized" when tensions became especially acute.[7] His support skyrocketed after the five-day war with Georgia and the annexation of Crimea six years later.[8] In the words of a focus group participant, "The only man who can definitely defend the country is Putin. If, God forbid, there is some conflict, who [else] would defend [us]?"[9]

* * * *

Everyone is "afraid of our hugeness," Putin told millions of Russians watching his multi-hour annual "Direct Line" press conference. But the motherland has nothing to worry about so long as the army and the navy—Russia's "only allies"—are in place and well cared for.[10]

Both quotes were from Alexander III, who ruled from 1881 to 1894. Enormous and brutish, he was perhaps Russia's most consistently reactionary tsar. Set up in the first year of his reign, the secret police, the Okhrana, was all-powerful. Harsh censorship was reimposed after the limited, but real, freedom of the press under his father Alexander II. A fervent nationalist and virulent antisemite, he pursued forced "Russification" of ethnic minorities and encouraged pogroms: There were over 100 in 1891 alone, with local authorities ordered not to interfere in any way to protect the Jews.

There he was, in the park of Livadia Palace, in annexed Crimea: bronze, 4 meters tall, in his military uniform and soldier's jackboots, leaning on a sword, with a two-headed eagle behind him and the dictum about the army and the navy etched in gold on the pediment.

He was a patriot, Putin said as he unveiled the monument. A man of "unbending will and courage," who started Russia's rearmament and achieved peace not by concessions but by "just and unmovable firmness."[11]

Another giant statue of the emperor went up in Gatchina, outside St. Petersburg. Alexander III "loved Russia," Putin declared, and sought to do everything he could for its "progressive and confident development." He jealously protected Russia's interests and strengthened its state "in Europe and the world."[12]

And Putin's state needed protection, more and more. The threats of which the president had warned his compatriots in the wake of Beslan grew and multiplied. Never wrong but perennially wronged, Russia was under siege: slighted, plotted against, subverted. The enemy fomented instability on Russia's borders, sabotaged the country's development, and used special services to weaken and subjugate Russia.[13] In the 1990s and the early 2000s, Putin avowed, the West "definitely" and "most actively"

Monument to Alexander III in Livadia, Crimea.

Vladimir Putin delivering address at unveiling ceremony for Alexander III statue at Gatchina Palace.

supported Islamic militants in the North Caucasus.[14] The chief of the General Staff weighed in: The US and its allies were training for offensive military operations against Russia.[15] Worse still, the enemy was perfecting the use of nuclear weapons for such an attack.[16]

The reaction to these increasingly stark threats, too, grew more explicit. The organizers of any provocations that threatened Russia's security would regret their deeds as they have not regretted anything for a long time, Putin said.[17] Everyone wanted to bite us or bite something off us, but whoever is planning this ought to know that we will "knock out their teeth."[18]

The 2018 presidential election, too, was surrounded with war reminders. Although by law the poll must be held on the second Sunday of the month,[19] Putin chose the third Sunday, March 18, 2018, the fourth anniversary of occupied Crimea's "admission" to the Russian Federation. The concert that headlined an election victory rally on Manezhnaya Square next to the Kremlin was titled "Russia, Sevastopol, Crimea."

The electoral campaign coincided with the attempted assassination of Sergei Skripal, a former Russian intelligence officer who had spied for Britain. Living in Salisbury, England, openly and without protection, Skripal could have been killed at any time. Poisoning him and his daughter in a leading NATO country two weeks before the election (and mistakenly causing the death of a British civilian) was a symbolic act.

The truculence may have worked. According to the co-chair of Putin's campaign, the results of the election showed that the Skripal affair had produced what she called "a consolidated response to the pressure that is currently exerted on Russia."[20] Even taken with a large grain of salt, the results seem to support her: Despite incomes being down for the fourth year in a row, more people voted for Putin in 2018 than in 2012—and more than for Dmitry Medvedev in March 2008, after GDP had grown on average 8.5 percent over previous years and was not stagnant as in the 2009–19 decade.

Putin's references to the West read increasingly like war rhetoric: crude and raw to a degree that no Soviet leader, neither Stalin nor even occasionally the rough Nikita Khrushchev, allowed himself, at least publicly.

Russia's enemies were card sharps and cynical speechifiers.[21] They spat on other countries and their peoples. They imposed their will and crushed those who disagreed with them. They were insolent, uncultured, and arrogant.[22] When they deal with Russia, they *zabaltyvayut'* (bury in blabber the real issues)[23] and *vrut* (lie).[24] They swindled and shamelessly deceived (*naduli prosto naglo obmanuli*) Moscow.[25] They were disgusting (*protivno*) even to talk about,[26] and the only appropriate answer to their so-called concerns was *idite vy* (go . . . fuck yourselves).[27]

In the 2019 state-of-Russia address, Putin called America's European allies *satellity* or "satellites," the name the Soviets used for the Axis powers during World War II. They just "oinked along"[28] (*podkhryukivayut*) to America. Two years later, these same "satellites 'yapped along'" with Washington.[29]

Russian diplomats, who used to be known for a pedantic adherence to protocol and their often exquisite knowledge of English, followed suit. To Deputy Foreign Minister Sergei Ryabkov, *primitiv i khamstvo* (crude stupidity and boorishness) were part and parcel of the rhetoric from Washington.[30] "Hey, you, yes you, look here, don't avert your eyes!" the Russian ambassador to the UN addressed his British counterpart. He spoke Russian and used the familiar *ty*, instead of the polite *vy*. "Don't you dare offend Russia any more!"[31]

* * * *

The enemy was not just after Russia's land and political system. Something elusive yet perhaps even more important was in the West's crosshairs: the "spiritual-and-moral values" (*dukhovno-nravstennye tsennosti*) at the foundation of the nation. The menace was all the more acute since Russia was not merely a nation but a "state-civilization," and a "unique" one at that.[32]

Putin revealed the existence of this remarkable polity in a long newspaper article in the run-up to his third presidency in January 2012.[33] Russia, he confirmed eight years later, was a "distinct civilization."[34] Its core, its "central rod," its "connecting tissue" were ethnic Russians. They were the "state-forming people"; their "great mission" was to bind this civilization.

The Russians were well equipped for this august mission. A Russian soul was "wider" and "more generous" than that of other peoples, Putin claimed.[35] A Russian is "less pragmatic" and thinks less of himself. He is "oriented toward the outside," not inside; he recognizes a "higher moral principle." This "genetic code" was "one of our key competitive advantages" in today's world.[36]

Though anchored by ethnic Russians, the Russian civilization-state had been a benign sovereign to its ethnic and religious minorities. Every culture, no matter how small in number, was respected. "Bonded by the Russian people, this state-civilization" has always been "flexible," attuned to the ethnic and religious peculiarities of other peoples. It is, Putin asserted, "in our historical code."[37]

Jews and Catholics; the Muslims of the North Caucasus, Middle Volga, Crimea, and Central Asia; the Chechens and other peoples of the North Caucasus; and countless others may disagree, but to Putin, the "peculiar nature of the Russian statehood" was, as Ilyin described it, like a gentle mother to smaller peoples. Far from "suppressing, enslaving, [and] strangling" other peoples, Russia strove to "respect all, to reconcile all, let everyone pray in their own way."[38]

Of course, as the "global rivalry" heated up and the world was growing "rougher," this tender Russia must be strong economically, technologically, and militarily to push back. Yet the key to its survival was "moral and spiritual" health, which is why, Putin told the Russian and foreign experts and glitterati of the Kremlin-funded Valdai Club, preserving this remarkable civilization and strengthening its "national identity" were the "fundamental issue for Russia."[39]

At first blush, this should not have been a difficult task: According to Putin, the yearning for "spiritual and ideological sovereignty" was the "inalienable" part of the Russian "national character."[40] Yet, like Russia's land, the independence of spirit, too, had to be defended from the West, which was out to destroy Russia's "traditional values" and substitute them with its "pseudo-values" to "erode our people from within" and "lead directly to degradation and degeneration."[41]

Following the boss's lead, this campaign against the bacilli of alien cultures was taken up by top government officials. The chairwoman of the Federation Council, the Russian "senate," called it "a real war for the human soul."[42] The assault on the values of the "unique civilization," which the West waged by "informational war," was aimed at "subjugating" Russia and "ruling it from the outside," the minister of defense instructed his subordinates.[43] The minister's deputy elaborated: The West cannot wage a real war against Russia, but the nonmilitary confrontation did not stop "even for a second . . . in language, in religious faith, in culture, in history."[44]

The subversion of Russia's soul went beyond the attack on the country's "cultural sovereignty," contended Nikolai Patrushev: The goal was to undermine the country's political stability.[45] Patrushev wanted to turn the country into a "besieged fortress" to more effectively counter the external enemy and suppress the enemy within, commented a popular and loyal daily newspaper, *Nezavisimaya Gazeta*.[46] This was not a discrete outburst, the newspaper continued, but a policy to be practiced during the regime's lifetime.[47]

This turned out to be an apt prediction. Three months after Patrushev detailed the dangers of the West's assault on Russia's innate hearts and minds, the menace was elevated to the top of the country's defense preoccupations. Among the perils listed in the National Security Strategy of the Russian Federation were the planting of alien ideals and values, the "Westernization of culture," and the weakening of the "state-forming people," the Russians.[48] Putin signed the National Security Strategy in July 2021.

* * * *

No one could accuse Putin of not putting his money where his mouth was: The defense matched the presumed danger!

Running for his third term in 2012, he promised an "unprecedented" modernization of the armed forces and defense industrial complex.[49] It turned out to be unprecedented indeed for post-Soviet Russia. The price tag was going to be 23 trillion rubles, or $759 billion at the February 2012 exchange rate. This money was to buy all manner of expensive hardware, including 2,300 tanks; 20 submarines, eight of them of the "strategic designation" (that is, armed with nuclear missiles); 500 planes; and 28 S-400 surface-to-air missile systems.[50] On January 1, 2012, the salaries of the servicemen and -women were tripled.[51]

In the end, he would spend even more. The first state rearmament program, which cost $700 billion,[52] was to be implemented between 2011 and 2020. Two years before the end date, Putin ordered another 10-year program, to last until 2027, that would cost over $300 billion.[53]

In all, between 2000 and 2019, Russia's military expenditures grew by 175 percent.[54] While dwarfed by the Pentagon's annual budgets in absolute terms, these allocations were enormous in a $1.7 trillion economy, which is less than 10 percent of the United States'.[55] By 2020, Russia spent more on defense as a percentage of gross domestic product (GDP) (4.3 percent) than did any major industrial country.[56]

Esli zavtra voyna, esli zavtra v pokhod, bud' segodnya k pokhodu gotov! ("If a war is tomorrow, if you are to march tomorrow, be prepared for the march today!") exhorted a 1930s Soviet song. In yet another borrowing from the Soviet motherland, it was not just the country's armed forces that needed to be in battle order. According to Chief of the General Staff General Valery Gerasimov, the state as a whole had to be prepared for war.[57]

Putin agreed. In one of the semiannual meetings with Russia's military brass at his Sochi villa in November 2017, Putin announced that all Russian large enterprises, whether state-owned or private, must be able to "rapidly increase defense-related production and services at a time of need"[58]—just as in the Soviet Union, where every plant and factory had to have a wartime "conversion" plan.

The massive rearmament was all the more momentous because it was embarked on when the economy began to sputter. A rich state in a destitute country had been Russia's predicament for centuries. "Upper Volta with nuclear missiles," Chancellor Helmut Schmidt famously, if perhaps apocryphally, called the Soviet Union in the 1970s. The national pattern surfaced again: Defense expenditures swelled as the people grew poorer.

In 2021, the incomes of almost 18 million Russians, or 12 percent of the population, were below the official "subsistence minimum"[59] of 11,788 rubles per person a month, or about $162.[60] Yet poverty was more pervasive than these numbers implied. The Russian state statistical agency, Rosstat, reported in 2019 that 80 percent of families were unable regularly to buy a "minimal assortment of goods"[61] and every third family could not afford two pairs of shoes for each family member.[62] "Poverty has become Russia's disgrace!" fulminated Alexei Kudrin.[63]

Health care was on par with the general penury. In a country where life expectancy at birth was the same as in Bangladesh and lower than in Malaysia, Mauritius, Nicaragua, and Sri Lanka,[64] health care expenditure as a percentage of GDP was half the EU average[65]—and still steadily cut year after year.[66]

* * * *

Patriotism, Putin declared, was Russia's "national idea": "We don't have and cannot have any other unifying idea except patriotism."[67] Yet a mere love of the motherland was not enough. Affection to the motherland was to be active and armed, instilled with devotion to the state, self-sacrifice, and mercilessness toward the state's enemies.

This patriotism was on full display in Putin's last preelection rally of 2012, held at Moscow's Luzhniki Stadium, with between 100,000 and 130,000 people in attendance. The gathering was on February 23, the Defender of the Motherland Day, formerly Soviet Army and Navy Day. Why then? Because, Putin explained in the first minute of his short and inspired speech, "today we are all true defenders of the Motherland."[68]

In a black parka over a white sweater, fit, compact, and exuding confidence and energy, he continued: "We came here to say that we love Russia, to say loudly enough for the entire country to hear. So I am going to ask you a question," he called out to the stadium, "and please answer with a short, simple, unequivocal 'Yes': Do we love Russia?"[69]

"*Daaaaaaaaa!*" the stadium roared back.

But a mere affection for Russia was not sufficient, he continued. We must be ready to defend Russia, at all times, always. We will not allow anyone to interfere in our internal affairs, to foist their will on us. Because we have our will. That will that has always helped us be victorious. We are a people-victor. It is in our genes. And now we will prevail again.

"Will we win?"

"*Daaaaaaaaa!*"

Yet the victory would not be automatic, he warned. The love of the motherland meant rejecting subversive sentiments, repudiating intrusions from outside, and standing up to homegrown sedition. Do not betray the motherland by looking to greener pastures abroad or veering "to the left," slang for actions harmful to the state. Stay with us, work for the motherland, and love it as we do, with all our heart.

"And so I ask you again: Do we love Russia?"

"*Daaaaaaaaa!*"

"Remember the poem by Lermontov we all learned in school?" Putin asked the stadium at the end. "The one about our ancestors battling the Napoleon invaders at Borodino near Moscow in 1812? Remember those heroes' oath? 'Let's die defending Moscow!'" he recited.[70]

"The battle for Russia continues!" Putin concluded. "Victory will be ours!"[71]

* * * *

Faithfulness to the "great values of patriotism" is a "sacred duty" of every Russian, and Putin wanted it to "be spoken about always and at every level."[72]

Yet there were obstacles to overcome. When we rejected Soviet ideological "stereotypes," Putin said, we lost many moral guidelines; we threw the baby out with the bathwater.[73] The people most hurt by this post-Soviet anomie were those who were babies, or not even born, when the Soviet Union was no more—and thus were deprived of the moral fiber instilled by the Soviet state.

For patriotism to become the "key moral guideline" of Russian teens, it must be inculcated in school. This task is the "main mission" of teachers of the humanities, he told the winners of the "Teacher of the Year" national competition.[74]

It was not an easy job: "Spiritual and moral values" of Russia were an object of a "carefully designed propaganda assault." Just like the struggle for mineral resources, the attempts to influence the worldview of entire peoples and subjugate them to the alien purpose never stopped. The result was "national catastrophes" of disintegration and the loss of sovereignty.[75]

With the stakes that high, schools needed help. Since 2000, four four-year programs of "Patriotic Education of Citizens of the Russian Federation" have been adopted and implemented by 29 ministries, state agencies, veterans' groups, and authorities at every level. The most recent, the fourth program (2016–20), cost 1.7 billion rubles, or $23.8 million at the 2020 exchange rate.[76]

After the anti-Putin rallies of the winter of 2011 and 2012, two objectives were added to the programs' goals: "overcoming extremist manifestations among particular groups of citizens" (that is, the political opposition) and the "strengthening of national security."[77] By the time the fourth program was in place, confronting the "external threat" had become the key task of a patriotic upbringing.[78] The aim now was to ensure that the youth of Russia were ready—morally, psychologically, and physically—to defend the motherland and eager for military duty "in peacetime and war."[79] Accordingly, the programs called for the revival of Soviet military sporting events and other "traditional" ways of nurturing patriotic citizens.[80]

Putin, too, looked to the Soviet Union and the Russian Empire for what he called the finest examples of upbringing and education.[81] What was needed were children and teens deeply engaged with the national agenda, like their Soviet counterparts. Oh, those conscientious children of the Soviet motherland: the 7-year-old Oktyabryata, who sported a red star with a photo of baby Lenin in the middle; the 10-year-old Young Pioneers in red neckerchiefs; and 14-year-old Komsomol members, with Lenin's profile against a red banner on the lapel pin.[82]

In 2015, Putin resurrected the Soviet "physical culture and sports complex" GTO (the acronym for "Ready for Labor and Defense") for all citizens between age 6 and 70.[83] Regional and city governments were to oversee the fitness exams, and every year the government was to submit to the president a report about "the level of physical preparedness of the country's citizens."[84] A few years later, he ordered the government to "monitor" young Russians' online behavior and produce "moral and spiritual content" for them.[85]

In 2019, Russia's most popular state television network, Channel One, launched a broadcast division targeted at the young. The outlet's around-the-clock programming was dedicated solely to World War II. The new channel's name was "Pobeda," or "Victory."

* * * *

To further enhance the physical and moral fitness of young patriots, in 2015, Minister of Defense Sergei Shoigu launched the "all-Russian children-and-youth military-patriotic public movement"—"Yunarmia," or "Young Army." The goal, Shoigu explained, was to "popularize military ideology" and foster a special bond between young Russians and the army.[86] Recruits ranged from second graders to high school students. The latter were promised preferential treatment in college admissions, free higher education in the best military colleges, and "social support" from the ministry.[87]

Claiming wondrous enrollment in the first few years—170,000 in 2017 and 590,000 in 2019—the ministry pledged one million members by 2020, the 75th anniversary of the World War II victory.[88] A year later, Shoigu reported to have added almost 200,000 kids between May and December 2021.[89] The millionth member was inducted by the head of the Main Military-Political Directorate of the Armed Forces.[90]

In addition to the inevitable fiddling with the numbers, the phenomenal growth of Yunarmia was frequently secured by adding up all the middle and high school classes. Some school administrations were reported having received money to organize Yunarmia "cells." In one school, the fifth graders' day was prolonged to make room for "militarized subjects" and "marching," while other after-school activities—sports, arts, music, and dance—were canceled.[91]

Yunarmia cadets stand in front of a poster of Vladimir Putin and other senior Russian officials.

Another source of Yunarmia draftees consisted of "deviant" teens and orphans between age 7 and 17. Nikolai Patrushev insisted that the most effective way of dealing with "difficult youth" was to send them to "military-patriotic" camps.[92] Tested in eight regions in 2018, the project was approved for more than 1,600 Russian orphanages.[93]

Putin welcomed Yunarmia troops to Red Square Victory Day Parades. In November 2015, Putin greeted boys and girls from another "military-patriotic" outfit.

Created by veterans of the elite "Vympel" unit of the *Spetsnaz* (special ops troops), the eponymous movement was aimed at "moral health, patriotic and labor education of children and adolescents."[94] As Russia rises from its knees, went the "Address to the Youth" on the organization's website, those bent on world supremacy (that is, the US) looked at it in fear and anger. The enemy's attacks on Russia were aimed at the annihilation of the Russian spirit and unity, the weakening of the army and navy, and the destruction of the financial and economic foundation of our fatherland. "A de-facto war has been declared on us, a war

INFORESIST/TOWN OF LUBERTSY

Weapons training for Yunarmia cadets in the Moscow suburb of Lubertsy.

ILIYA PITALEV VIA REUTERS

Yunarmia cadets marching in Red Square for Victory Day, 2020, Moscow.

MINISTRY OF DEFENSE OF THE RUSSIAN FEDERATION

Yunarmia cadets at the 2019 Victory Day Parade on Red Square.

ALEXEY NIKOLSKY/RIA NOVOSTI

Vladimir Putin with Yunarmia cadets at the Vostok 2018 military exercises in the Transbaikal region of the Russian Far East.

KREMLIN.RU

Vladimir Putin meeting on Red Square with youth members of the Vympel Military-Patriotic Association, 2018.

KREMLIN.RU

Vladimir Putin meeting on Red Square with youth members of the Vympel Military-Patriotic Association, 2015.

merciless and cynical, a war without a front line, and the enemy may already be among us."[95]

The *Spetsnaz* veterans hoped that young Russians would make the "right choice" between the "society of consumption" and the "uncompromising struggle for the freedom and independence of Russia." They were ready to help those who followed the true path—but the teens first needed to realize that the Russian people were in "mortal danger" and that they must be "courageous and strong" in the cause of providing "security and prosperity" for the motherland.

Another addition to Yunarmia was "cadet classes," which started in the fifth grade. The cadets wore uniforms, usually black; their classrooms were decorated with a banner and a code of honor; and upon entering the classroom, the cadets said an oath. The second half of their school day included combat and sports exercises, usually supervised by retired officers. The sponsors were the top law enforcement agencies: the Ministry of Internal Affairs, the Ministry of Emergency Situations, and the Investigative Committee.[96]

The Volgograd cadets became famous for following the Duma Deputy Anna Kovychko in a rendition of the song *Dyadya Vova, my s toboy!* ("Uncle Vova, we are with you!") against the background of the 1967 monument *Motherland Calls* on Mamaev Kurgan, the site of some of the fiercest fights of the Stalingrad battle:

> The samurais will never
> Have the island chain.[97]
> We will defend the capital of amber with our lives.[98]
> Sevastopol is ours and Crimea
> Will be passed on to our descendants.
> We will return Alaska to the harbor of the Motherland.

And the chorus:

> From the northern seas
> To the southern borders,

Volgograd cadets singing, "Uncle Vova, we are with you!" in front of the Motherland Calls *monument.*

> From the Kuril Islands
> To the shores of the Baltic Sea,
> All we want for our land is peace
> But if the chief commander
> Calls on us to fight in the final battle,
> Uncle Vova, we are with you![99]

The song is about our great Russia, explained Deputy Kovychko, who had organized the performance. "And, of course it also about our President and about how we must learn to love our Motherland and be ready to stand up for it!"[100]

The Kremlin did not endorse the song, but neither did it disavow it. As the Kremlin's spokesman put it, "Different strata of society could express their affection for the president in their own ways."[101]

Premiered in November 2017, the song spread across the country. A year later, children were filmed singing it during class and after school in the southern city of Krasnodar.[102] Three years later it was performed in the Pskov region of northwestern Russia and the city of Chita in the Far East.[103]

* * * *

Ivan Ilyin, Putin said, thought that the soldier "represents the Russian people's unity, the Russian national will, its strength and its honor."[104] He persuaded his subjects that it should be so: Between 2012 and 2017, trust in the army went from 39 percent to 69 percent.[105] Three years later, the army was the most trusted national institution.[106] (The president came in second, the Federal Security Service third.)

To start making soldiers early and let them bond with weapons that Yunarmia, Vympel, or the cadets could not supply, Patriot Park was inaugurated by Putin in the summer of 2015 in Kubinka, 60 kilometers west of Moscow, next to Russia's major air force base and one of the world's largest tank museums. In the park, children as young as 10 could shoot blank rounds from semiautomatic rifles, while older boys and girls drove tank simulators.[107] There was also a model of the Reichstag to be stormed.[108]

The park, Putin said at the inauguration, would be "an important element of our military-patriotic work with young people."[109] Speaking in front of a military choir and a balalaika orchestra, Putin also announced the addition of 40 new intercontinental ballistic missiles to the Russian strategic nuclear arsenal—weapons capable of breaking through the most advanced missile defense systems.[110]

At a nearby stand, a park instructor demonstrated missile- and rocket-propelled grenade launchers. Surface-to-air missile launchers might be too heavy for small children, he explained, but smaller grenade systems were perfect for kids of all ages. Men were defenders of the motherland, and they must be ready for war, whether the war came or not.[111]

The facility reportedly cost the Ministry of Defense 20 billion rubles, or $291 million. Since then, five more Patriot Parks have been opened, including by December 2021 one in Severodvinsk on the White Sea, just below the Arctic Circle.[112]

Soon, Kalashnikovs migrated into schools where students in grades six to 10 disassembled the weapons on their desks and ran with them. They also learned to throw hand grenades and shoot pneumatic pistols.[113] A Yunarmia unit was reported visiting a kindergarten to introduce the

PATRIOT PARK

Weapons training for children at Patriot Park, Kubinka, Russia.

PATRIOT PARK

Weapons training for children at Patriot Park.

PATRIOT PARK

Child holding a rifle at Patriot Park.

PATRIOT PARK

Children inspecting weapons at Patriot Park.

children to Kalashnikovs. "It was all very festive and beautiful," the kindergarten's director told a local newspaper. "It was the first time the tots have seen anything like it. Of course they want to be like soldiers—graceful and brave."[114]

In beginning of the 2023 school year, the "Foundation of Military Preparedness" course became a required course in the national curriculum.[115]

* * * *

The inspiration and the guiding light of militarized patriotism was the Great Patriotic War. Severed from the immense tragedy preceding it, in a truncated official version, the victory overshadowed the horrors and sacrifices. The war became something to celebrate—a brilliant culmination of national history, proof of the invariably victorious Russian character and the key to national identity.[116]

After the June 24, 1945, parade, presided over by Stalin and reviewed by Marshal Konstantin Zhukov, there were no May 9 military parades in Red Square, and Victory Day was not a holiday until 1965. Red Square rallies—with no soldiers or weapons—took place only on the "round" anniversaries in 1965, 1970, 1985, and 1990.

Military parades became annual in 1995 but did not include heavy equipment: tanks, artillery, missiles, and armored vehicles. In 2008, Putin added them all. They rumbled through Red Square, along with the 23-meter, 47-ton intercontinental ballistic missile Topol-M.[117] The annual damage to Moscow's downtown streets and the Red Square cobblestones was estimated at one billion rubles, or $44 million at the time.[118]

The war was sacralized and canonized, and deviations from the canon were no longer permitted. Absent were Stalin's monstrous mistakes that cost the lives of millions of Soviet soldiers: killed, taken prisoner, and starved to death in German camps.[119] Forgotten were all the findings of the glasnost truth seekers.[120] ("We simply did not know how to fight," the popular writer Viktor Astafiev, a veteran, said in 1988. "We ended the war not knowing how to fight. We drowned the enemy in our blood; we buried him under our corpses.")[121]

KREMLIN.RU

Msta-S self-propelled artillery drive on Red Square on Victory Day, 2018.

KREMLIN.RU

Pantsir air defense systems pass through Red Square on Victory Day, 2017.

Pantsir air defense system moves through Moscow during Victory Day Parade, 2019.

Aerial demonstration team flies over a statue of Kuzma Minin, a legendary citizen of Novgorod who resisted the Polish invasion of Moscow in 1616.

For the war veterans in the Politburo, Victory Day had been "a holiday with the tears in our eyes," as a song of my childhood went—and a never-again pledge. Now the end of the slaughter and return to peace were all but displaced by a merrymaking, a carnival. Among the older folks, three times as many felt "joy" as felt "grief over the millions who died" in the war; among the younger men and women, the proportion was five to one.[122]

The victory was all the more brilliant since the Soviet Union had now achieved it alone. Stalin used to call the US and Britain "our brave allies"; Putin disposed of them in his 2021 Victory Day speech:

> We will always remember that in the most difficult time of war, in the decisive battles that determined the outcome of the struggle with fascism, our people were alone, alone on the most difficult, heroic and self-sacrificial path to Victory.[123]

In this version, there were no battles in North Africa and Italy, no Coventry and London bombed savagely by the Germans, no D-Day in Normandy, and no lend-lease aid that fed the Soviet army and fueled its tanks and planes.[124] In 2020, nearly half of respondents in a national survey said that World War II began in 1941, with Germany's attack on the Soviet Union; only one in three recalled 1939.[125]

The lesson of the war was no longer that it should never happen again, observed a US expert on the rituals of the Soviet Union and post-Soviet Russia. On the contrary, since the Great Patriotic War was such a success, then another war, should it happen, would end in victory as well.[126] *Na Berlin!* (to Berlin) and *Mozhem povtorit'!* (we can do it again!) were among the most popular Victory Day posters, streamers, and windshield signs. "Here's a new generation of victors!" Putin declared as he welcomed troops to Red Square on May 9, 2018.[127]

The Great Patriotic War was still going on. Russia was still surrounded by enemies, be they the ever perfidious and aggressive West or its clients, the Ukrainian "Nazis." On Victory Day in 2015, some Russian cities displayed posters comparing the defeat of the Ukrainian troops in January of that year to the Soviet victory in the 1943 Battle of Kursk, one of the largest encounters of World War II.[128]

The foes loomed in every one of his Victory Day speeches. The "new threats" were fed by "intolerance" and "claims to exclusivity," code words for the United States,[129] which is why he pledged to do "everything possible" to strengthen Russia's armed forces.[130]

"I'm dying but I won't surrender," Putin said, quoting the graffiti left by the defenders of the Brest Citadel in the first days of the war. That is what he expected from his soldiers and what, to him, was the "main guarantee of the invincibility of Russian arms."[131]

* * * *

Victory Day has been compared to a "quasi-religious cult."[132] Of the many embodiments of this state religion, the largest was the Main Cathedral of the Armed Forces, next to Kubinka Patriot Park.

Another project—in addition to Yunarmia—of Defense Minister Shoigu, a civil engineer who never served in the army, the cathedral is a veritable architectural gospel of the Great Patriotic War. The church's steps are cast from melted-down Nazi weapons.[133] The bell tower is 75 meters high to mark the 75 years since the end of the war. The height of the four small cupolas is 14.18 meters, for the 1,418 days and nights of the war.[134] The stained glass mosaics portray scenes from the Bible and those of the Red Army's victory over the Nazis.

The cathedral is the world's third-tallest Orthodox church, after Christ the Savior in Moscow and St. Isaac in St. Petersburg. The blessing of its cornerstone in September 2018 was attended by Putin, Shoigu, and Patriarch Kirill of Moscow and All Russia. Before its installation in the cathedral, its main icon, a 12th-century "Savior Not Made by Hands" (*Spas Nerukotvorniy*), was to said to have been exhibited in 300 army units and 120 cities, starting in the annexed Sevastopol. The main icon's copy that looks down from the central dome is said to be the largest image of Christ's face ever created in mosaic.[135] Completed in 2020, the cathedral's estimated cost was between $82 and $92 million.[136]

SERGEY SEBELEV/WIKIMEDIA COMMONS

Main Cathedral of the Russian Armed Forces at Patriot Park, Kubinka, Russia.

Victory Day excesses prompted critics to call it *pobedobesie*: literally, "victory run amok" or "victory possessed." ("The devil," *bes*, and "go mad," *besit'sya*, share the same root, *bes*.) On sale were military tunics (*gimnasterkas*) and garrison caps (*pilotkas*) for 2- to 3-year-olds. There were also khaki onesies with "real army buttons" billed as "victory costumes for babies from 0 to 8 months."[137] Kindergartners in Red Army uniforms marched, looked at large-caliber machine guns, and attempted a military salute. Babies, also in uniforms, sat in carriages fashioned into tanks and jets.

A parade in Saratov featured a song-and-dance performance by kindergarten girls. "You became my most precious dream, my dear Army," they sang. "When I grow up I'll become a soldier/I will be brave, strong, and proud." And the chorus said: "Our Army is the bravest, our Army is the strongest, our Army is the proudest."[138] In a Moscow kindergarten, a gift calendar celebrated the 75th anniversary of the victory in 2020 with photos of bloodied children-soldiers.[139]

Children participating in the annual "Immortal Regiment" World War II memorial march in Kaliningrad Oblast, May 2019.

Children ride scooters at a military parade in Rostov-on-Don, Russia.

Kindergartners march in a military parade in Rostov-on-Don, Russia.

Child riding in a mock-up tank carriage in a competition, Pyatigorsk, 2018.

EDUARD KORNIYENKO/REUTERS

Child saluting at military parade in Rostov-on-Don, Russia.

ESTONIAN FOREIGN INTELLIGENCE SERVICE

Children inspecting weapons after a parade in Rostov-on-Don, Russia.

ANDREI BILGIDIN/MASTERHOST

SUSPILNE MEDIA

Images from a World War II–themed children's calendar.

Following the Kremlin's lead, other government-approved interest groups exploited Victory Day. "Defend me today [so that] I'll be able to defend you tomorrow!" a fetus pleaded with an expectant mother on billboards in Moscow,[140] as it morphed from a fuzzy sonogram image to a stern soldier in a helmet.

In a television spot, a distraught pregnant young woman spoke into a cell phone, wondering if she should have an abortion. "Think, my dear," a

Antiabortion social media campaign from 2022 incorporating patriotic imagery.

Great Patriotic War nurse, Lt. Galina Petrova, exhorted the young woman from a portrait on the wall. "Give your son the gift of life!"

"Yes," the woman replied after some contemplation. "I must give birth to a son! My son will live!" she announced as the veteran gazed down on her with approval. The clip ends with the woman accompanied by a partner and her son at an antiabortion rally. The placard read: "We have vanquished the fascists! We shall overcome the abortionists!"[141]

* * * *

The celebration of war propelled Putin's Russia back to Stalin's Soviet Union. "The military-patriotic hysteria brings to mind the USSR of the 1930s, the era of athletes' parades, tank mock-ups and dirigibles, and shaved napes," wrote leading essayist Sergei Medvedev. "Today the people again joyfully dress in Red Army uniforms, take pictures of themselves on tanks and await war." In the endless victory liturgy, Putin has forged a nation of

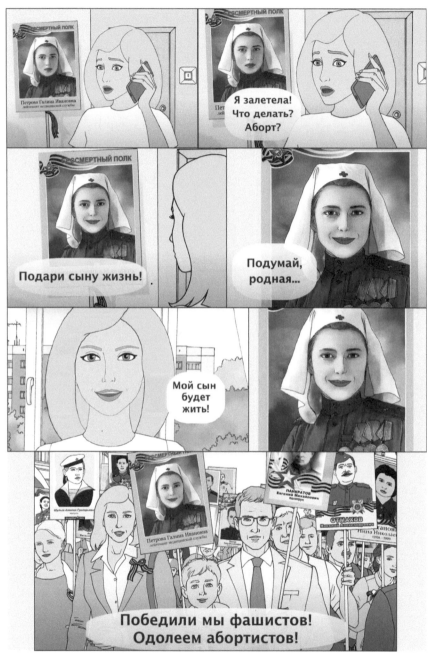

DMITRY SMIRNOV

Images from a patriotic antiabortion video.

war that has "battened the hatches and views the world through the lookout slit of a tank."[142]

On TV—in films, series, and talk shows—Stalin's creation, the Soviet state, was a mighty power and happy place, with the world's best ballet, a great hockey team, wonderful cheap ice cream, low rents, and free sanatoria on the Black Sea. Three in four Russians considered the Soviet period the "best time" in the history of their country.[143]

Stalin's ghost arose from the restored primacy of state over civil society. "Man for state or state for man?" was among the key dilemmas glasnost revolutionaries grappled with in the late 1980s as they searched for the roots of Soviet totalitarianism. Should state serve society, or is society there only to be a pedestal to state?[144] The former arrangement, they eventually agreed, led to authoritarianism and terror; only a state subjugated to civil society could preserve liberty. Again at the mercy of authorities at every level, the Russians' attitudes toward their state were once more confined to fear, awe, and impotent resentment.

Day after day, year after year, the decreed "defense of the historical truth" refashioned Russia's Soviet past. Could the victimization of the Soviet people during the Stalin era be justified by the great aims and the "results achieved in the shortest possible time"? pollsters asked. In 2008, 60 percent said "no"; in 2019, the proportion was down to 44 percent.[145] Among younger adults, four in 10 said they knew "little or nothing" about the mass murders.[146]

In 2015, the Duma passed a law to provide state pensions to secret police informers. Known as *stukachi* (literally "those who knock," the Russian verb *stuchat'* being slang for informing on or denouncing someone), they were a ubiquitous feature of Stalinism. The law called them "volunteer law-enforcement assistants."[147]

In 2005, four in 10 respondents agreed that Stalin's purges in the 1930s that killed tens of thousands of officers—from marshals and generals down to colonels and majors—contributed to the staggering defeats in the first year of war. By 2021, that share went down to 17 percent. Was Stalin's "disregard for casualties" to blame for the Red Army's losses being

Siberian Communists unveil a Stalin monument in Novosibirsk.

so much higher than those of the Germans? In 1991, 33 percent agreed; in 2018, fewer than one in 10 did.[148]

His crimes obscured by the official triumphalism of *pobedobesie*, seven in 10 respondents viewed Stalin's "role" in the history of their country as fully or somewhat "positive."[149] By 2021, Stalin was "admired," "respected," or "liked" by 60 percent of Russians and disliked, feared, or hated by 14 percent. (In 2001, the numbers were 34 percent and 43 percent.)[150] Stalin even elbowed out Alexander Pushkin and Peter the Great among the "most distinguished figures in world history," holding first place since 2012, with a plurality of around 40 percent of the vote.[151]

Slava narodu-pobeditelyu! ("Glory to the people-the-victor!") Stalin declared toward the end of his radio address to the nation on May 8, 1945, announcing the capitulation of Germany.[152] Aware of the phrase's origin, Soviet leaders used it rarely. Putin repeated it at the end of most of his Victory Day speeches.[153] On Putin's 60th birthday, in October 2012, Putin's favorite television talk show host, Dmitry Kiselev, concluded his tribute by telling viewers that of all Russian and Soviet leaders of the 20th century, Putin was comparable only to Stalin.[154]

There were around 150 monuments to Stalin in 2022,[155] all allegedly paid for by private donations, mostly by the Communist Party of the Russian Federation. The one in Novosibirsk, installed on the 2019 Victory Day, looked especially imposing. The mounting of the bust was photographed at precisely the right moment: The builder of Soviet totalitarianism was not quite in place but securely on his way up.

* * * *

"Tell me who your friends are, and I'll tell you who you are," the proverb advises. But one's enemies define one as well, and they are easier to produce than friends: Friendship requires reciprocity; enemies can be nominated. Designating the mightiest and the richest country as your adversary elevates your nation—and you with it.

It was a logical choice. Putin set out to make Russia an heir to the Soviet Union, and confrontation with America was a key aspect of Soviet "superpowership." "Strategic confrontation" with the US was needed to validate Russia's exclusive status in world politics.[156]

Obsession with America is a Russian national tradition. America the foe, the antagonist, the rival, yes—but also an etalon, an ultimate reference, a gold standard. Like Hitler, while reviling American capitalism and imperialism, the Soviet leaders from Lenin and Stalin on admired America as the paragon of industrial might, inventiveness, energy, and *delovitost* (efficiency). It was the only country that ultimately mattered, the only other continental power, the only global equal of seemingly unlimited possibilities.

To be respected by America, or at least to have America's attention, had been paramount for the Kremlin's self-respect. Negative attention was better than none: When Russia is off America's radar, it is off the world scene; it is no longer participating in shaping the world.

To confront and berate America and yet be *like* America in some key respects—rich, mighty, and self-confident—was behind Khrushchev's slogan *Dognat' i peregnat' Ameriku!* (To catch up with and surpass America!) The people among whom I grew up agreed: They loved America's plenty, its cars, jeans, music, and freedom—glimpses of which made it past censors or were conveyed in guarded whispers by the few hugely envied men and women who authorized to enter the lair of the imperialist beast.

America is "our most important country," the Levada Center's principal Alexei Levinson said, summarizing this attitude in the summer of 2021.[157] The "jubilation" over the annexation of Crimea was not merely due to the peninsula's becoming part of Russia: In the minds of millions of Russians, their country finally behaved like they believed only America could. "We ignored the United States's [displeasure] and thus became its equal, like the Soviet Union used to be."[158]

Vicious as its anti-American rhetoric was, Putin's Kremlin exhibited signs of this love-hate ambivalence in matters small and grand. While ostensibly preparing to go to war with America, Defense Minister Shoigu replaced the Soviet officers' high-collared tunic (the *gymnastyorka*), shirt, and tie with that of his American colleagues: a green T-shirt under an open collar and a name tag over the breast pocket.

Telling the Duma to effectively annul his previous three presidential terms so that he could run again in 2024, Putin cited America's example of not having had limits on presidents' terms in office until 1951. Why so late in America's history? Because, Putin explained, only after the turmoil of the Great Depression and World War II was past did America feel confident enough to afford to introduce the "turnover of power."[159]

Of course, occasional nods to America never interfered with denunciations. It often occurred to him, Putin confessed, that somewhere in America someone was conducting an experiment over countries and peoples as if they were rats.[160] To all its weapons, America had added pandemics. One after another, Duma Speaker Vyacheslav Volodin,[161] Deputy Foreign Minister Ryabkov,[162] and of course Patrushev[163] accused the United States of setting up biological warfare labs along Russia's borders and "genetically engineering" COVID-19.

Russia was in a "total confrontation" with the United States, Chief of Staff Gerasimov averred in 2018.[164] So far this global battle was being waged by "non-military means"—political, economic, and informational—and it spread into virtually "all facets of modern society": diplomatic, scientific, athletic, and cultural. Yet, Gerasimov added, it would be "incorrect to conclude that the military struggle has receded into the background."[165]

Standing in front of a large screen with a bright yellow mushroom cloud, Kiselev reminded the viewers of his top-rated program that only Russia could turn the United States into a "heap of radioactive ash."[166] (A few months earlier, Putin had appointed Kiselev general manager of the RT media group, the umbrella company for all Russian external broadcasting.)[167]

No matter where and whom Russia fought, it fought America, the respondents told the pollsters in national surveys.[168] World War III had already started, and behind the warring sides in all local conflicts were America and Russia.[169] The United States was the only country Putin mentioned by name in the predawn address to the nation on the eve of the second invasion of Ukraine. NATO was busy forging an "anti-Russia" out of the "territories" adjacent to Russia, but of course, NATO is only "an instrument" in America's hands.[170]

* * * *

Like in every besieged fortress, enemies outside the walls were aided by turncoats within. Those whom Putin labeled the "fifth column" and, using Hitler's phrase, "national-traitors"[171] provoked domestic instability, undermined the values that united the Russian society, and ultimately helped weaken Russia and "subjugate it to external control."[172]

Of course, Putin mused at a Valdai Club session, he supported civil society playing a key role in the development of Russia: The voice of Russia's citizens must be decisive, and the government should follow their wishes. But the question was: What sort of wishes? Whose voice should the state be listening to? How would the state know the real voice of the people from behind-the-scenes whispers or loud, "sometimes hysterical yells" that have nothing to do with the people? What if people's legitimate concerns were replaced with interests of this or that "small social group" or, "let's be direct about it," were directed from abroad?[173]

The fifth columnists were to play a central role in the enemies' plans. The Pentagon began developing a new strategy of military operations, Gen. Gerasimov told the meeting of the Academy of Military Sciences.[174] The essence of this doctrine was the "active utilization" of domestic protests organized by the "fifth column." The disturbances were to coincide with strikes at Russia's most important targets by highly accurate weapons. Gerasimov even knew the Pentagon's code name for this strategy: "Trojan Horse."[175]

Guarding against those hidden inside "Trojan Horse" commenced shortly after Putin returned to the presidency in 2012. Although the 2012 "foreign agents" law was supposed to apply only to organizations engaged in "political activity," soon others, decidedly apolitical, were swept in. Before it was ordered shut, the Memorial Center—where for over 30 years researchers had sifted through crumbling yellow documents and faded photos to restore the memories of the millions perished in the Gulag—had been declared a foreign agent as well. The Levada Center became one too.[176]

Four years later, the law was amended to vastly broaden the definition of "political activity": It now included the "formation of social and political views and convictions," including public opinion surveys and sociological research.[177] Monitoring elections made one a foreign agent as well. The violators of the multiple government requirements were closed down by courts on charges brought by the Ministry of Justice. (The Memorial Center was shuttered ostensibly for failure to brand all its publications, media posts, and functions as those produced by a "foreign agent.")[178]

To receive funding from abroad was only one of many offenses. It was enough to "disseminate materials" created by foreign media that were themselves defined as "foreign agents" or "participate" in creating such materials. In practice, a scholar, journalist, or blogger talking about his or her research on YouTube[179] or posting or reposting something on an internet platform was liable to be added to the "registry" (*reestr*) of foreign agents. Citing or being cited by a "foreign agent" made one a foreign agent as well.

According to the guidelines by the Ministry of Science and Higher Education, scholars meeting with their foreign contacts were to notify their management at least five days in advance, receive permission, and attend only in the presence of another Russian scholar.[180] Afterward, the head of the scientists' institute was to submit to the ministry an "exhaustive account" of the meeting.[181] Since 2020, four top physicists have been arrested on treason charges.[182] Not surprisingly, the number of scientists who left Russia was five times greater in 2021 than in 2012.[183]

Journalists were another high-risk profession. A meeting with a foreign colleague in Russia could be interpreted as *verbovka* (recruitment) and an exchange of messages as an intelligence assignment.[184] In April 2023, for the first time since the end of the Cold War, a US reporter, Evan Gershkovich, was arrested on spying charges.

Yet the sword of Damocles also hung over Russians who were neither scientists nor journalists. In 2008, the year of the Russo-Georgian "five-day war," a saleswoman in a Sochi market saw a column of military hardware and sent a text to a friend in Georgia. Five years later, she was sentenced to six years in a penal colony. In the same year, another Sochi resident received a text from a Georgian acquaintance asking if there were tanks in the city. She replied that there had been before. She was handed a seven-year sentence for state treason. During a trip to Georgia, an elderly Russian retiree commented on an article in the *Krasnaya Zvezda* (*Red Star*) newspaper published by the Russian Ministry of Defense. According to the prosecutors, his interlocutor worked for Georgian secret services. He was punished with 12 years in jail.[185]

According to the advocacy organization Komanda 29 (Team 29), which provided legal assistance to people accused of state treason, since 2012 the number of convictions increased from an average of two to three a year to 15.[186] In all, since Putin came to power, 378 Russian citizens have been found guilty of state treason, espionage, and disclosure of state secrets.[187] In the summer of 2021, the Team 29 site was blocked by the government, and later the same year, the Federal Security Service brought charges of state treason against the head of the organization, lawyer Ivan Pavlov.[188]

Two years later, in April 2023, the pro-democracy opposition leader
Vladimir Kara-Murza was found guilty of treason, among other charges,
and sentenced to 25 years at a maximum security prison. In the same
month, Putin signed into law an amendment to the Russian criminal code
that meted out a life sentence for treason.

* * * *

Important as they were, legitimacy, solemn dreams of glory, and political
imperatives of his regime's preservation were not the only wellsprings of
wartime presidency. Putin was passionate about all things military: from
rifles to uniforms to intercontinental missiles. He liked to play soldier.

He was aboard a destroyer and inside a submarine.[189] He shot a fancy
sniper rifle at a target 600 meters away and pulled the trigger on a replica
of the legendary Kalashnikov. With the minister of defense on his side, he
checked out yet another gun.

"Putin loves the showy-heroic aspect of military life," wrote a leading
Russian military expert.[190] He seems to enjoy escaping the "hostile and
corrupt" world of politics and finding himself in "a pure, simple and hon-
orable domain of the military."[191]

"Do you know what our advantage was?" Putin asked an interviewer in
a documentary about the invasion of Crimea. "It was that I personally was
in charge."[192] In the early morning of February 23, 2014, it was *he* who followed in real time the cortege of Viktor Yanukovich, the ousted pro-Russian
Ukrainian president. And it was *he* who looked at the map and realized
that Yanukovich would be ambushed and shot at with "large-caliber
machine guns." *He* then ordered Russian military helicopters to pick up the
ex-president.[193]

Once Yanukovich had been flown to a Russian ship in Sevastopol and
then to safety in Rostov, Putin turned to the aides in the situation room
and said, "We have to start the work of returning Crimea to Russia." He
then gave "direct orders" to the Russian Armed Forces to be "ready for any
possible developments," in case the West attempted to interfere. "Does
this mean that we brought our nuclear force to the state of war-fighting

Testing a sniper rifle at Patriot Park in Kubinka, Russia, 2018.

Aiming a Kalashnikov at a Russian Railways exhibition, 2012.

Inspecting military hardware with Sergei Shoigu.

Observing tank maneuvers in the Leningrad region, 2014.

A mural of Vladimir Putin watches over Simferopol, Crimea.

readiness?" the interviewer asked. "We were ready to do so," Putin replied. "We were ready for the most untoward development of the events." And it was he who selected the troops for the Crimea operation: elite units from the Main Intelligence Directorate of the General Staff of the Russian Armed Forces, marines, and paratroopers.[194]

Putin may be exaggerating or even fabricating. But we do not boast of that of which we are not proud. A mural in the center of Simferopol, the capital of the conquered and annexed Crimea, would not be splashed on the wall of an apartment building if Putin were not pleased by the image: a naval officer, hands on the helm, decisive, competent, his eyes focused on the horizon.

Much as Russian wits made sport of Putin's attempt to sidle up to the dead dictator—"to grab onto Stalin's military overcoat and to slip into his battle boots," in the words of a prominent Russian political philosopher[195]—there is little doubt that Putin greatly enjoyed being a

FOTO.META.UA AND PRESSMANIA.PL

With Joseph Stalin.

hands-on supreme commander-in-chief, the title that Stalin gave himself in the first months of the Nazi assault on the Soviet Union.

Although the first and general secretaries were ex officio in charge of the Soviet military,[196] no Soviet leader since Stalin had been so publicly addressed. Putin's defense minister, Sergei Shoigu, was among the first, reporting Russia's successes in Syria.[197] Since then, the title was repeated at every military or paramilitary function Putin attended, whether a meeting at the Ministry of Internal Affairs,[198] the headquarters of the Russian police, or a naval parade.[199] "Comrade Supreme Commander-in-Chief," deputy commander of the "Euphrates" artillery group at a Russian air base in Syria, Gen. Dmitri Klimenko, addressed Putin, "our accomplishments here have reinforced the belief of the soldiers, sergeants and officers in our victory under your guidance."[200]

Although Putin was spared the draft as a full-time college student, the soldier's uniform was his favorite off-duty garb. Whether fishing or riding, his bare or tank top–clad torso is always framed by a regulation army hat and trousers.

He wore the hat and trousers again on the eve of his 67th birthday, in 2019, hiking and mushroom picking in the Altai Mountains. His only companion was his minister of defense.

Веховный Главнокомандующий ВС РФ (Supreme Commander-in-Chief of the Armed Forces of the Russian Federation) was emblazoned on the front of a zip-up jacket, which Putin wore on a hike in the Siberian taiga.

On a hike in the Siberian taiga.

Fishing on a Siberian holiday.

With Shoigu on holiday in Siberia, 2019.

Unlike the Soviet leaders or Yeltsin, Putin not only attended every Victory Day Parade[201] but spoke there as well, his speeches growing longer and fierier every year until, in 2023, both the speech and the parade were abbreviated in the shadow of the Ukraine war.

A pandemic had not been allowed to stand in the way of the array. When in July 2021 St. Petersburg's authorities banned public gatherings because of COVID-19, the parade marking the 325th anniversary of the Russian Navy proceeded as planned with only one spectator.[202] He must have been especially pleased to see the brand-new strategic submarine (that is, carrying nuclear intercontinental ballistic missiles) named after his namesake and hero, Prince Vladimir, the baptizer of Kievan Rus.

In 2006 and again in 2015, two presidential decrees resurrected the Soviet "professional holidays and commemorative days" for branches of the armed forces. The Day of the Navy is on the last Sunday of July,

Air Force Day on August 12, Tank Crews Day on the second Sunday of September, and Rocket Troops and Artillery Day on November 19. Putin also added a few new ones: Military Intelligence Officers Day (November 5), Radio and Electronic Warfare Specialists Day (April 15), and Nuclear Weapons Support Specialists Day (September 4). The Special Operations Forces are celebrated on February 27 to mark their exploits in the invasion of Crimea.

For its part, the military marked Putin's birthdays with presents of its own. On his 63rd birthday, in 2015, 26 cruise missiles[203] were fired over-night into Iraq and Syria from warships in the Caspian Sea. Five years later, Gen. Gerasimov reported by a video link to the Novo-Ogaryovo residence outside Moscow. The general preceded the usual "Comrade Supreme Commander-in-Chief" with *Zdraviya zhelayu!* ("wishing you good health!"), the tsarist and Soviet army address of men or officers to their superiors. The chief of the General Staff then reported a successful test of the Tsirkon hypersonic missile: Launched from a frigate in the White Sea, four and a half minutes later it hit its target in the Barents Sea, 450 kilometers away.[204] It is an important event, Putin replied, not only in the life of the armed forces but of the entire country. Outfitting our military with most modern systems that no one else in the world has ensures the defense of our state for the long term![205]

4

Worshipping the Nukes

The annual Address to the Federal Assembly is the Russian president's main speech of the year. In addition to the deputies from both houses of the assembly—the Duma and the Federal Council—the event is a parade of the Russian elite: ministers and university deans; the patriarch, chief rabbi, and grand mufti; the most loyal of the top businessmen, actors, and editors; Vladimir Putin's favorite talk show hosts; and regional governors currently in the Kremlin's favor.

For all the glitter, by the 19th year of Putin's reign, the affair had become routine and the oration predictable. The West's enmity notwithstanding, Russia's "sovereign democracy" was robust and developing; education and health care were progressing; the country was poised for scientific, technological, and economic breakthroughs; and the world's respect for it was growing. Of course, there were problems, but they were the fault of local authorities and corrupt, callous, and incompetent mid-level bureaucrats who would be dealt with accordingly.

The venue—the Georgievskiy Hall of the Kremlin—had been the same for the previous 10 years. So when less than three weeks before the 2018 presidential election, the imperial opulence of the Georgievskiy—with its massive golden chandeliers on the vaulted roof, Corinthian columns, and parquet floors intricately inlaid and waxed to a mirror-like shine—was traded for the Manezh Exhibition Hall—built in the early 19th century for military cavalry dressage, with austere, even drab, long, and low-slung ceilings with cement floors—intrigue was in the air.

Putin's spokesman, Dmitry Peskov, said only that the change of venue was necessitated by the need for "infographics" and a larger audience: At 705, the number of accredited journalists was unprecedented.[1] Something was afoot.

Yet for almost three-quarters of the speech, both the speaker and the audience had settled into a polite tedium. Putin dutifully droned on, and the public stared ahead listlessly, napped with their eyes open, or chatted with their neighbors in low whispers.[2]

Then Putin asked: "How did we respond to the American global anti-missile defense system?" He paused and answered: "Here's how."[3] He had their attention now.

Russia, he continued, had added 80 new nuclear intercontinental ballistic missiles (ICBMs) to its arsenal and had taken "long and fast" steps toward creating novel kinds of strategic nuclear weapons.[4]

The walls flanking the stage became giant screens on which a missile, which Putin said was the newest ICBM, Sarmat, blasted off from a silo. No missile defense system, present or future, could hinder Sarmat, Putin avowed. Its range was "practically unlimited,"[5] and it could approach targets from either the South or North Pole. On the animation video, the warhead split into a dozen or so "individually targeted vehicles" streaming toward what looked like Florida.[6] The audience broke into hearty applause.

Next up was something that, Putin claimed, "no one else in the world had!" A nuclear-tipped cruise missile outfitted with a nuclear engine, capable of staying aloft "indefinitely."[7] A few seconds after a filmed launch, the missile became a white cylinder in a video game–like animation. It zigged and zagged in wooded canyons, flew over the Atlantic, evaded missile defense sites, rounded Cape Horn at the southernmost tip of South America, and approached the West Coast of the United States.

The third wonder weapon was a giant nuclear-armed and nuclear-powered torpedo. Designed to attack "cities and shore infrastructure," in addition to ships, the "unmanned apparatus" was faster and quieter than submarines and deftly maneuverable. "This is simply fantastic!" Putin exclaimed.[8] The torpedo emerged from a submarine's hull and swam close to the bottom, weaving around underwater ridges. In the animation's coda, the floating bomb surfaced to hit a warship and a port.

All "developed countries" were after hypersonic weapons, Putin continued, after the applause abated. He paused. "Dear friends, Russia has such

Vladimir Putin demonstrates new Russian nuclear weapon systems in an address to the Federal Assembly, 2018.

a weapon! Already has!"[9] An air-launched ballistic missile by the name of "Kinzhal" (Dagger) could fly over 2,000 kilometers at up to 10 times the speed of sound. In a video, a jet took off with a missile under its belly. After separating from the jet, the missile evaded radar and zeroed in on what

Vladimir Putin demonstrates new Russian nuclear weapon systems in an address to the Federal Assembly, 2018.

looked like a warehouse. An explosion, high flames, and flying debris filled the screen. The jet landed to another round of applause.[10]

The final tableau in the apocalyptic gallery was "a winged glider block." A black triangle inside the red-hot cone of a warhead swooped down to earth, evading missile defense sites. It was supposed to fly toward its target at up to 20 times the speed of sound. "Like a meteorite!" Putin exalted. "Like a burning ball, a ball of fire!"[11] The weapon was capable of withstanding temperatures between 1,600 and 2,000 degrees Celsius.

Our Western "partners" would not talk to us, Putin concluded, would not listen to us. "Well, hear us now!"[12] He received a standing ovation.

Of course, some of it was bombast. No evidence could be found of the deployment of 80 "new" ICBMs by 2018.[13] At the time, Sarmat was yet to lift off out of the silo ("silo-tested"),[14] and Russian sources listed the ICBM's maximum range as 18,000 kilometers—impressive, but not "unlimited."[15]

The nuclear-powered cruise missile blew up on the testing ground slightly over a year after Putin's address. The hypersonic Kinzhals would be shut down by Ukrainian air defenses.[16]

Yet a great deal of it was real. At 35 meters long and weighing 208 tons, the Sarmat was almost certainly the largest and heaviest missile ever built. When operational, it was capable of carrying 10–15 warheads. In the 10-warhead version, each warhead yielded 750 kilotons (kt) of the TNT equivalent, or 50 Hiroshima bombs, and in the 15-warhead version, 450 kt.[17]

The nuclear torpedo was successfully tested nine months later.[18] In the 2019 address, Putin would report that the first nuclear-powered submarine capable of launching the torpedo—which by then had a name, Poseidon—was now "in the water."[19] In the same speech, Putin would herald the arrival of another hypersonic missile, "Tsirkon" (Zircon), with a range of over 1,000 kilometers and a speed of nine times that of sound.[20]

The Avangard glider was being deployed in 2021.[21] A "game changer," according to a US expert, the lethal triangle could indeed penetrate whatever defenses the American military had in mind.[22]

* * * *

No Soviet or post-Soviet leader invoked Russia's nuclear weapons as frequently nor extolled them as extravagantly and in such detail as Putin. During his third presidency, between 2012 and 2018, Russia's spending on nuclear weapons more than doubled.[23] While the expenditures on other kinds of weapons and hardware—conventional, planes, and ships—were "modest," as Putin said in early 2012, nuclear weapons had enjoyed "an absolute priority": Whatever the General Staff had asked for, he had given "100 percent."[24]

Putin compared Russia's nuclear "shield" to the Russian Orthodox faith: Both, he said, strengthened the Russian state, and both were necessary for

Vladimir Putin crosses himself during a service with Patriarch Alexiy II at the Cathedral of St. Seraphim of Sarov in Sarov, July 31, 2003.

maintaining security inside and outside its borders.[25] The missile and the icon were joined in Putin's first presidential term when the nuclear arsenal acquired a patron saint: St. Seraphim of Sarov.

A small town about 300 miles southeast of Moscow, where the saint lived in a monastery almost two centuries ago, Sarov had been chosen by the chief of Soviet secret police and the manager of the Soviet nuclear project Lavrenty Beria as the headquarters of Soviet nuclear weapons research and construction. By then, the St. Seraphim monastery and its nine churches had long been desecrated and the monks executed or sent to the Gulag.

Sarov is still Russia's main nuclear weapons research and design center, but the monastery and churches are back. In July 2003, the 100th anniversary of St. Seraphim's canonization, Putin and Patriarch Alexiy II of All

Russia prayed on the town's main square in front of St. Seraphim's relics.[26] Before meeting with the nuclear scientists and engineers, Putin spoke at what the official Kremlin website described as the "ceremony of the blessing of the procession" in the saint's honor.[27] On another visit to Sarov nine years later, he prayed in St. Seraphim Church.[28]

In 2007, the 60th anniversary of the 12th Main Directorate of the Ministry of Defense (GUMO), which was responsible for designing, producing, and storing nuclear weapons, was celebrated with a thanksgiving prayer in Russia's largest church, the Christ the Savior Cathedral. Bishop Amvrosiy of Bronnitsa, the vicar, or deputy, and a top aide to the patriarch, asked the congregation of generals, top government officials, and managers of the military-industrial complex to give their thanks to God for "His kindness and past assistance with the nuclear shield of Russia" and to ask Him to bestow His blessings on St. Seraphim of Sarov, "the guardian of the nuclear weapons specialists."[29]

After the prayer, Amvrosy read a note of greeting from the patriarch. For centuries, Alexiy II wrote, the Russian Orthodox Church had blessed feats of military heroism and prayed for victory over Russia's enemies. And today, like before, it continued and strengthened its fruitful cooperation with the armed forces and supported the efforts to "revive Russian military traditions."[30] Afterward, the best GUMO detachments were presented with pennants imprinted with the image of St. Seraphim.[31]

A decade later, at a session of the Kremlin-funded Valdai Club of Russian and foreign culturati, journalists, and experts, Putin said that in the case of a nuclear war, the Russians, "as victims of aggression and martyrs, would end up in paradise," while their enemies "would just croak (*sdokhnut*) because they wouldn't even have the time to repent."[32] Even in this well-trained audience, the laughter seemed forced.[33]

* * * *

In a break from the central trope of his oratory, Putin did not blame America for forcing Russia to embark on the breakneck expansion and modernization of its now-blessed nuclear arsenal. Russia was not "responding,"

MOSKVA NEWS AGENCY

Russian Orthodox priests bless a Topol-M intercontinental ballistic missile before Moscow's Victory Day Parade, 2015.

ALEXEY KHLEBIN/VOLGODONSKAYA DIOCESE

Priest with the Volgodonskaya Diocese of the Russian Orthodox Church blesses the missiles of an Su-27 fighter jet.

Priests bless an Su-27 fighter jet at an air force base in Belbek, Crimea, 2014.

Nuclear weapons officers and priests pose with a portrait of St. Seraphim.

to use one of his favorite figures of speech, to the upgrading or expansion of the US strategic forces.[34] Instead, in the case of each of the showcased weapons, he stressed again and again the new systems' ability to somehow get through—penetrate, evade, outsmart—US missile defenses in an all-out nuclear war.

Of course, like the Soviet Union before it, Russia had had that ability, many times over, before the Putin modernization started. By the 2022 count, the country's nuclear "shield" contained 1,588 strategic warheads (that is, deliverable at distances of over 5,500 kilometers, or 3,420 miles) deployed on missiles, submarines, and long-distance bombers and 977 more in storage.[35] According to a leading independent Russian military expert, it would take an estimated three to five missiles to intercept one warhead. Even assuming that the US may have as many as 100 interceptors by 2025, its missile defense could neutralize at best 30 Russian ICBMs.[36]

Why, then, this enormous investment of Putin's time and effort, the reverence for the nuclear arsenal, and the money spent on expanding and bettering it?

For Putin, nuclear weapons were the most precious legacy of the Soviet Union as a superpower, the most tangible way in which his Russia resembles his beloved, mighty, and feared Soviet motherland. The missiles are, as a Russian commentator put it, the foundation of his presidential "superpower ambitions."[37] The arsenal is the invaluable bridge between his means and these ambitions, for the supreme commander-in-chief was no longer in possession of the 5,000,000-strong Soviet army and those of its Warsaw Pact allies, yet he was bent on recovering—and perhaps even surpassing—the Soviet Union's glory.

Each of Russia's four largest conventional military exercises, which are held yearly and rotate among four geographic locations—Zapad (West), Vostok (East), Tsentr (Center), and Kavkaz (Caucasus)—involved the live-fire or computer-simulated launches of ICBMs or tactical (shorter-range) missiles. The largest of the four drills, a typical Zapad exercise, was most recently bracketed by the test-firing of Yars ICBMs three days before the drill and on its last day.[38]

SOKOLRUS/WIKIMEDIA COMMONS

A Yars-24 intercontinental ballistic missile driving through Moscow for Victory Day, 2015.

KREMLIN.RU

Vladimir Putin observes the Zapad 2017 military exercises with Chief of the General Staff of the Russian Armed Forces Valery Gerasimov.

Vladimir Putin oversees the Grom-2019 nuclear exercises.

Putin either attended or followed on a screen all four exercises. Scripted to simulate a war with NATO, and thus the most important of the four games, Zapad has been of special interest: Not only did Putin observe it live, but he came down to the test grounds and then summed up the results of the games in a video conference call with his generals.[39]

When it came to nuclear drills outside the conventional exercises, he was no longer just an eager spectator or commentator, but the commanding officer. In official accounts and media comments, he was there *lichno* (personally), and the exercises were conducted *pod ego rukovodstvom* (under his direction). In October 2017, he presided over an unprecedented test of all the components of the Russian strategic triad. Launched from the Arkhangelsk region in northwestern Russia, a silo-based Topol-M strategic missile was said to hit its target in the far-eastern peninsula of Kamchatka, just north of Japan. From the depths of the Sea of Okhotsk in eastern Siberia, two submarine-launched ballistic missiles (SLBMs) headed in the opposite direction, toward Arkhangelsk, and another SLBM flew to Kamchatka from the Barents Sea. Putin was reported to have pushed the "red button" to launch all four ICBMs. Presumably, he also gave the command for three long-range strategic bombers to fire cruise missiles.[40]

The "Grom" (Thunder) drills in October 2019, too, were conducted under Putin's "personal supervision." Again, he handled all the keys on the "supercomputer" in the National Defense Control Center on Znamenka Street, a 10-minute walk from the Kremlin. A year later, he commanded the launches of an ICBM, an SLBM, and long-distance cruise missiles.[41]

* * * *

Like those of other nuclear states, including the United States, the operational details of Russia's "first use" are top secret. Yet official documents, remarks by Putin and his top aides, and the content of Russia's military exercises point to a drift away from the Soviet and early post-Soviet approach, with its abhorrence of nuclear weapons outside a global war.

The mutually assured destruction theory, which dominated both Soviet and US thinking during the Cold War, was based on the assumption that the use of nuclear weapons by either side would inevitably and quickly lead to Armageddon. No matter how many proxy battles they fought all over the world, Moscow and Washington were extremely wary of direct confrontation. The first post-Soviet Military Doctrine of the Russian Federation, too, warned only that a conventional attack on Russian strategic nuclear forces, its early warning systems, and nuclear power or chemical installations "may result" in escalating into a nuclear war.[42]

Yet already in the first year of Putin's presidency, the next version of the doctrine asserted Russia's *right* to use nuclear weapons in the case of "large-scale" aggression in "situations critical to national security."[43] Toward the end of the first Putin decade, Gen. Nikolai Patrushev pushed the threshold further down, suggesting that a "preventive strike" could be ordered in a "regional" and "even in a local" conventional conflict.[44]

Although the doctrine that Putin signed four months later did not repeat Patrushev's specifications, they were implied by the omission of

Vladimir Putin and Belarusian President Alexander Lukashenko oversee nuclear exercises in Moscow, February 2022.

the size of the conflicts in which Russia could first use nuclear weapons. Instead, Russia "reserved the right" to use nuclear weapons to repel a conventional "aggression" when the "very existence of the state" was endangered.[45] Before his paean to the Sarmats, the Poseidons, the Avangards, and the Burevestniks in the 2018 state-of-Russia address to the Federal Assembly, Putin recited the Military Doctrine's Article 27, which listed these conditions. "All is very precise, clear, and concrete," he concluded.[46]

As he proceeded to occupy Crimea, Putin stood the doctrine on its head by warning against the West's interference into Russia's *own* aggression in a *local* war. By a "direct order," mentioned in an earlier chapter, he put the nuclear forces on a higher alert.[47]

He made this threat more explicit in his address to the nation on the eve of the second invasion of Ukraine. The adjective he used to describe the consequences for "any potential aggressor" left no doubts about what sort of retaliation he had in mind: He called them *uzhasnyy* (horrifying).[48] A week after the start of the war, on March 1, Yars ICBMs were mounted on mobile launchers and "dispersed in forests" to practice "secret deployment."[49]

* * * *

The evolution of military doctrines, the brandishing of nuclear weapons before and during the two invasions of Ukraine, the persistent flaunting of Russia's nuclear arsenal, and the insertion of strategic and tactical nuclear weapons in all the largest conventional exercises[50] all point to a growing acceptance of the use of nuclear weapons in conventional conflicts. A limited nuclear war was being domesticated.

Russia's resorting to a nuclear strike to terminate a conventional conflict that was not going its way became known as an "escalate to de-escalate" theory.[51] Intended to scare the enemy and coerce armistice rather than inflict massive damage and precipitate an open-ended strategic nuclear exchange, a "de-escalation" is likely to involve low-yield tactical weapons detonated away from densely populated areas.[52] Russia is estimated to have between 1,850 and 2,000 tactical nuclear weapons, delivered by missiles or gravity bombs, with the yields ranging from 10 kt (5,000 tons of TNT or about one-third of the Hiroshima bomb) to over 100 kt.[53] The 2017 Naval Strategic Doctrine included the "demonstration of [Russia's] readiness and determination" to use nonstrategic nuclear weapons as a means of deterring the adversary.[54]

One of the likeliest tools in the sequence of escalating to de-escalating is the Iskander missile. Based in Kaliningrad, a Russian exclave on the Lithuanian western border, Iskanders are Russia's most modern dual-use systems—that is, capable of carrying either conventional charges or nuclear warheads with yields of between 5 and 50 kt.[55]

The Ukraine blitzkrieg turning into a grinding war of attrition gave rise to fears that Russia might resort to a nuclear strike to force Ukraine to accept the "peace" of dismemberment. "We have been hearing from

MINISTRY OF DEFENSE OF THE RUSSIAN FEDERATION

Iskander ballistic missiles move through Red Square during the 2015 Victory Day Parade.

VITALY V. KUZMIN

Iskander readied for launch.

Russian pop star Anna Semenovich: "Sanctions? Don't make my Iskanders laugh."

our television screens that the nuclear silos should be opened," Nobel Peace Prize laureate and editor of the banned newspaper *Novaya Gazeta* Dmitry Muratov said in July 2022. "And we also hear that these horrible weapons should be used if the supply of weapons [from the US and its NATO allies] to Ukraine continues."[56]

A more plausible scenario, which will be taken up in the next chapter, might be precipitated by a collision of two unyielding realities. One is the sum of the convictions, perceptions, fears, and dreams of revenge and glory that constitute the Putin "story," told in the beginning of this book. The other truth is an enormous technological and numerical gap between Russia's armed forces and those of NATO. Having started a war, Putin would have to end it quickly to keep what he conquered and forestall an imminent defeat. As a Russian expert put it after the 2017 Zapad exercises, "It's all about strategic messaging of coercion directed at the U.S. and NATO."[57]

In the meantime, the domestication of the nuclear arsenal continues apace. "Gradually, [the people] are being housetrained to believe that nuclear weapons are not so bad, that we should think of various ways of using [them]," said Muratov. "Sometimes I think that if we had a television show in Russia, where the winner of the show could press the red button 'live,' there would be a lot of takers."[58]

5

The Next War

In the second year of the war he started in February 2022, Vladimir Putin was stuck in a vast and savage combat he could neither win nor walk away from. Could not because—his utterly fake charges of NATO attacking Russia from Ukraine aside—a West-oriented, free, democratic, and, eventually, stable and prosperous Ukraine was an existential threat to his regime. Sooner or later the Russians were bound to start asking: Why can't we have what our Ukrainian cousins have? He invaded Ukraine not for anything it had done, but for what it was.

This Ukraine proved far more resilient than he had expected. Speaking to his secret police comrades on the Day of the Workers of the Security Agencies, Putin admitted that the situation in the occupied areas of Ukraine was "extremely complicated."[1]

It certainly was. And not just there.

Mired between 2009 and 2019 in the longest stagnation in modern Russian history,[2] the economy was headed for at best an anemic performance as far as the eye could see.[3] As little of quality had been made in Russia, the sanctions on high-tech items were slowly but inexorably degrading entire industries.[4] Machine-building, automotive, and aircraft industries were atrophying the fastest.[5] Labor shortages were deepening as some of Russia's best educated,[6] most skilled,[7] and most entrepreneurial citizens were among the hundreds of thousands, perhaps close to a million, men and women who fled the country after the invasion of Ukraine.[8]

In just the first four months of 2023, the war drove the state's expenditures 26 percent higher than during the same period the previous year, while Western sanctions halved gas and oil export revenues, which accounted for at least half the budget.[9] Caught in these widening budget "scissors," Putin was not yet running out of money, but he was becoming increasingly constrained in his ability to bribe with raises in pensions and salaries for his core constituents: retirees; government employees, including most doctors and teachers; the police; and the army.

Yet the war's greatest damage was in tarnished symbols and the erosion of official mythology. When in his third term Putin began to shift the foundation of his support—and thus his regime's legitimacy—from economic progress and the growth of incomes to militarized patriotism, he reinvented himself as the unyielding and victorious defender of Russia against the perennially plotting West. He became "Vladimir the Vanquisher," like Russia's patron saint, George the Victorious, on the country's coat of arms, spearing the NATO dragon writhing under the hooves of his steed.

Born seven years after the end of the Great Patriotic War, Putin appointed himself heir to and owner of its sanitized and, as we have seen, increasingly vulgar official version. The invasion of Ukraine, too, had been yoked to the 77-year-old win and billed as "de-Nazification."[10] But the similarity ended there. There was no Victory Day in sight.

That was the biggest danger. A history buff, Putin knew only too well about regime changes that happened after military setbacks. The 1853–56 Crimean War precipitated Alexander II's revolution from above, including the liberation of the serfs. Four decades later, the Russo-Japanese war brought about the first Russian Revolution. Nicholas II's abdication and the Bolshevik takeover followed the failures in World War I, and Nikita Khrushchev's retreat in the Cuban missile crisis led to his ousting two years later. The Afghanistan quagmire became a key factor in Mikhail Gorbachev's glasnost revolution.

Even with hundreds of thousands of NKVD and SMERSH[11] agents hunting for "traitors" and "panic-mongers," Stalin seemed genuinely surprised and hugely relieved that the Russians had not rebelled at what he called the "desperate moments" in the first two years of the Great Patriotic War. Another people, Stalin said at the victory celebration in the Kremlin on May 24, 1945, might have told its government to "go away," but the Russians were "patient" and "trusted the government."[12] He raised his glass to them.

Even at its worst, the war in Ukraine would not become a national catastrophe like the disastrous defeats and retreats of 1941–42. But then again, the Russians are not in a fight for their own and their country's existence. Unlike their grandparents, they *could* run out of "patience" and lose "trust" in the Kremlin.

True, propaganda and repression have so far held the line. Merely calling the war a "war," instead of a "special military operation," could send one to a penal colony for 15 years, while "besmirching the armed forces"— that is, telling the truth about the savagery the Russian troops perpetrated on Ukrainians—carried a nine-year sentence. In his customary Day of the Workers of Security Organs speech, Putin called on his former comrades to redouble the efforts of catching "traitors, spies, and saboteurs."[13]

Yet how long would it take for the growing dislocation, scarcity, and grief for the killed and wounded to thin out the rally around the flag? One never knows, of course, when and how the dam might burst, but embarking, at age 72, on a presidency for life—a six-year term until 2030 and then, if still alive, another six—could turn into the first catalytic occasion in a country suffused with the shameful memories of senile paranoia, outright debility, and revoltingly false adulation of past gerontocrats, including Stalin, Khrushchev, Leonid Brezhnev, Yuri Andropov, and Konstantin Chernenko.

Yes, there was the National Guard of Russia: a 340,000-strong militarized police force set up in 2016 under Putin's ex-bodyguard Viktor Zolotov. But the Guards had yet to be truly tested. Would they be as brave and enthusiastic shooting at soldiers' mothers as they had been clubbing boys and girls on Moscow streets?

* * * *

Putin and his generals have neither the skill nor the wherewithal nor yet the manpower and morale for anything but a defensive crouch. While sending tens of thousands of Russian men to die and raining destruction and terror on Ukrainian cities by missiles and drones, the supreme commander-in-chief would hope to avoid a rout in one Ukrainian offensive, then survive another, then perhaps one more until "Ukraine fatigue" sets in in the West and Kyiv is pushed by the West toward a "settlement."

Yet two can play the waiting game. If the West does not blink, how long will it be before the largely conformist and indifferent Russians grow first anxious and then angry? When would emboldened populist warmongers begin training their Telegram outbursts at the Kremlin instead of denouncing the minister of defense and the chief of the General Staff? And, most perilously for the regime, at what point—exasperated by the callousness, corruption, and inaptitude of the high command, with no hope of victory and no end to the relentless slaughter in sight—would one unit after another follow in the footsteps of their great-grandfathers, who in the fourth year of World War I refused to fight, deserted en masse, or engaged in open mutiny. The revolt of the Wagner "private military company" in June 2023 might have been a preview of this unraveling.[14]

Putin's other option is to force a direct confrontation with NATO—if need be, all the way to the precipice of an all-out strategic nuclear exchange with the United States—and then step back, calling on a scared West to forge an "overall negotiated settlement," which would include a "neutral" (disarmed) Ukraine and Russia's holding on to Crimea and Donbas.

While far more perilous than the waiting game, the latter choice promises a quick resolution and would be in accord with the national tradition of solving complicated problems by opting for shortcuts and ignoring risks. *Klin klinom vyshybayut!* ("To push out a stuck wedge, hit it with another wedge!") says a Russian proverb. Putin followed the dictum, a rough equivalent of cutting the Gordian knot, by successfully doubling down in Chechnya in 1999–2009, Crimea and Donbas in 2014, and Syria in 2015. In the case of frightening the West into "peace" negotiations in Ukraine, the desired outcome would look to him all the more plausible because of the built-in advantage that every authoritarian aggressor enjoys over a bourgeois democracy: The West wants peace, while Putin needs victory.

Extricating himself from Ukraine without a defeat would be the most urgent and proximate objective of the manufactured confrontation, but far from the only one. Several powerful motives would coalesce to propel Putin toward the face-off.

Avenging the failed blitzkrieg would swell millions of Russian hearts, and it certainly would Putin's! Was it not NATO's fault that the "special military operation" so brilliantly designed by Putin and his Federal Security Service (FSB) advisers had turned into a bloody slog? Did not this perennially aggressive anti-Russian coalition give the Ukrainian "Nazis" thousands of American Javelins and British NLAWs (Next-Generation Light Anti-Tank Weapons) that burned his tanks and the Stingers that downed his planes and choppers? Didn't it hand Ukrainian sharpshooters the British sniper rifles that picked off his colonels and generals and deliver the HIMARS (High Mobility Artillery Rocket System) launchers that sent GPS-guided missiles as far as 80 kilometers behind Russian lines to hit ammunition depots, communication hubs, and HQs?

Like Saddam Hussein, who invaded Kuwait after the eight-year stalemated war with Iran and the deaths of an estimated quarter-million Iraqi soldiers, Putin badly needs a vivid and shiny triumph that would obscure harder lives and drown the shame of the Ukraine campaign in a reprise of the "patriotic euphoria" that followed the annexation of Crimea.[15] With nary a protest from the jubilant or the scared, in one fell swoop, Russia would be where he wanted it: a military dictatorship with presidency for life, elections be damned!

Yet the key allure for such a feat might have lain deeper still. For many years, rumors from the Kremlin had conjured up a man increasingly isolated and immured in solemn dreams. Some of Russia's most knowledgeable Kremlin watchers found these reports plausible. Putin views himself as an actor on "a grand historic scale," and he is running for "history textbooks," wrote one of these analysts.[16] He sinks deeper into self-absorption and wraps himself into delusional (*bredovye*) "fantasies," said Alexander Nevzorov.[17] A fellow Leningradets and the host of Russia's most popular television show, *600 Seconds*, in the late 1980s, Nevzorov had known Putin for 30 years and worked on his 2012 reelection campaign. "Putin is a man of ideas," Nevzorov contended. And this "pathological commitment to ideas" was progressing. Others thought that the Russian president had reinvented himself as a missionary,[18] or even a messiah[19] sent by God to save Russia. Little doubt that he also thinks the motherland lost without him—like Nicholas I in Tolstoy's *Hadji Murad* ("What would Russia be without me?") or Stalin in a Politburo meeting ("You are blind like young kittens. What will happen without me?").[20]

A quick winning blow to the enemy that even the mighty USSR would not confront on the battlefield would align closely with Nevzorov's "ideas." Could there be a more condign retribution for the West's defeat of the Soviet Union in the Cold War, for the arrogance and humiliation that Putin believed it visited on his vanquished motherland? This could be a moment he had anticipated and longed for.

Of course, even a limited poke at NATO would be irrationally risky in conventional military-strategic terms. But we *know* that Putin is no longer "rational" in the common sense of the word. If he had been, he would not have invaded Ukraine.

A different kind of "rationality" takes over: "a triumph of will," to recall Leni Riefenstahl's paean to Nazism, of determination over reality.[21] Was it "rational" of Hitler to declare war on the US? Was Hussein "rational" when he started a war with Iran or taunted the UN with the specter of chemical weapons that he did not have? Such wars are less about what Soviet political strategists used to call the "correlation of forces" and much more about the magical thinking of maniacal leaders high on hubris, anger, revenge, visions of grandeur, and an addiction to unlimited power.*

With the war on Ukraine, Putin may have joined the most exclusive club of political leaders: the utopians, who are constrained solely by the limits of their imagination[22] and are among modern history's worst murderers: Robespierre, Lenin, Stalin, Hitler, Mao Zedong, Pol Pot, and Saddam.

---

* One of the most astute students of the Kremlin's inner workings, Tatiana Stanovaya supplied a plausible explanation for this "different" rationality. Vladimir Putin, she wrote, was quite "rational" within his "very narrow ideological framework," but he was becoming "less and less receptive" to information that did not "fit into his understanding." See Tatiana Stanovaya, "K diskussii o ratsional'nosti Putina" [On the Discussion of Putin's Rationality], Telegram, November 3, 2022, https://t.me/stanovaya/1546.

* * * *

Did the Ukrainian calamity shake Putin's faith in his infallibility or erode his confidence in the brilliance of his plans? Did it make him more cautious, less trusting of his intuition, and more likely to seek truthful information? Not likely. True to type, he wouldn't have blamed himself. Instead, in his motherland's rich tradition, perfected by Stalin, he would have put the botched offensive at the door of "wreckers," "saboteurs," and "traitors." (Two weeks after invading Ukraine, Putin ordered the arrest of the head of the FSB's Fifth Intelligence Directorate responsible for Ukraine.)[23]

The *klin klinom* recklessness long preceded the war and would almost certainly survive the initial debacle. In 2018, the government announced a raise in the pension age for men to 65 years—in a country where, on average, men died at age 67 and four in 10 men were projected to die before age 65.[24] That summer, tens of thousands rallied throughout the country. In the ABCs of politics, appeals by the head of state are a tactic of last resort: If they fail, the drawdown from a leader's political capital could be huge, which is why even in totalitarian countries such pleas are rare. Putin, too, had refrained from such entreaties in the past. It was hard to imagine a Putin of 15, 10, or even five years before going to the pulpit when 70 percent of the Russians were "sharply negative" toward the reform and 19 percent were "rather negative."[25]

Besides, there was no need to go out on a limb: The government was going to implement the measure anyway, and, as had happened many times before, the prime minister, not the president, would have been blamed. Yet Putin went on national television anyway.

It was purely magical thinking: the faith in his imperviousness to the laws of politics, his supernatural "gut feeling," and his God-given ability to bend millions to his will. In this case, Putin's appeal barely made a dent in people's views; the "againsts" shrank by only 4 percent, and the "fors" were up by 3 percent—while Putin's ratings went down sharply to start a long downslide.[26]

Two years later, on March 6, 2020, Russia ended its agreement with the Saudi-led OPEC+ coalition on price-supporting production cuts. Predicting "serious losses," top Russian oil producers advised Putin against unleashing a price war.[27] Instead, as a Russian commentator put it, the Russian president chose to become the "arbiter of the world oil industry's destiny."[28]

The Saudis retaliated immediately by unleashing cheap oil on the world. The Russian Urals brand dropped from an average $64 a barrel in 2019 to $29,[29] and the ruble fell 30 percent against the dollar.[30] About to lose tens of billions of dollars—Russia needed at least $42 a barrel to balance its budget—Moscow capitulated a month later. The cuts Russia agreed on—2.5 million barrels, or about one-fifth of its daily production at the time—were four times the decrease Putin had rejected before.[31]

Two days after he threw down the gauntlet to the Saudis, Putin went to the Duma to deliver an unscheduled 16-minute speech.[32] Until then, Moscow had been abuzz in speculations about the ways in which Putin could arrange to stay in the Kremlin after 2024 without violating the constitution's limit on two consecutive terms in office.

Would he leave the presidency but become chairman of the Security Council, like Kazakhstan's Nursultan Nazarbayev did on his "retirement" in 2019? Or would he follow Deng Xiaoping, who had given up party and state titles but kept the chairmanship of the Central Military Commission until he was 85 years old? Or would he turn Russia into a parliamentary, rather than presidential, republic; replace Dmitry Medvedev as the head of the ruling United Russia party; and become prime minister? Or perhaps he'd make the obscure State Council, of which he was already chairman, a top decision-making body. Or, finally, maybe he would create a new state by enacting the "Union State of Russia and Belarus" (on paper for 20 years) and become its president.

Instead, discarding all subterfuges, dodges, and ploys, Putin did away with the elaborate choreography and delivered an in-your-face squat-dance kick: constitutional amendments to allow himself two more six-year terms in office. The change was to be made by neither a Constituent Assembly nor an elaborately scripted constitutional referendum, as prescribed by the constitution, but by the rubber-stamping Duma and the Constitutional Court and then validated by extra-constitutional "national voting."[33]

Two weeks later, over a third of the respondents said they were "perplexed" or "indignant," and 42 percent did not want to see him in the Kremlin after 2024.[34] Still, he proceeded with the vote—in a country that at the time had the world's fourth-largest number of confirmed cases of COVID-19 and an average of 7,500 new cases and 135 deaths a day.

All stops were pulled in the effort to increase turnout. Ballot boxes were placed on park benches, stood up in apartment building courtyards, and set in open car trunks.[35] The official result—79 percent in favor, with a turnout of 65 percent—was widely decried as the greatest falsification of Putin's rule.[36] Up to 22 million votes were estimated to have been "thrown in" or added to the "for" tally.[36] (Copies of a new constitution had already gone on sale in Moscow bookstores before the vote.)[38]

* * * *

A professional illness of long-reigning authoritarians, hubris is almost always buttressed by the conviction of the moral faultlessness of one's choices. Like most long-ruling autocrats, Putin was possessed of the belief in his unerring knowledge of what was best for his people and of the trust in their ultimate approval and gratitude.

The longer Putin ruled, Russian researcher Olesya Zakharova found, the more he had invoked the "people" to justify his policies: The people "supported," "expected," "wanted," or even "demanded" them.[39] "When in your mind you are confident that your actions are aimed at the defense of the people of Russia, if you have that internal conviction, then everything works out," Putin said of his decision to occupy Crimea.[40]

Skewed data validated the choices. It would have been strange if after over two decades in power, papers reaching Putin's desk had not been tailored to please rather than inform, to give him what he wanted to see rather than what he needed to know. "This group seeks to satisfy the president's work-related needs and—just as importantly—his psychological comfort," Tatiana Stanovaya wrote of Putin's entourage. "This creates incentives to provide Putin with information that conforms to his existing worldview and outlook and will not spoil his mood." The distorted evidence abets and furthers seemingly irrational decisions, causing what Stalin famously diagnosed as "dizziness from success" (*golovokruzhenie ot uspekhov*). Hence the obviously fantastic hopes of the Ukrainians meeting the Russian "liberators" with flowers and kisses, the Ukrainian army melting away, and President Volodymyr Zelenskyy running off to Warsaw or perhaps Berlin.

The West, too, had been weighed in balance and found wanting. All the more so since the pleasing evidence was not hard to find: Barack Obama's retreat from the redline he had drawn in Syria after Bashar Assad had killed or injured thousands of his citizens with sarin and chlorine gas. Donald Trump's cancellation of a retaliatory strike against Iran after learning that it might kill 150 people. Joe Biden's flight from Afghanistan, after almost 2,500 American soldiers were killed and nearly 21,000 wounded in two decades of war, leaving behind thousands of US citizens and Afghans who had worked for the United States.

Further evidence of the West's fecklessness was undoubtedly served up in the red briefing folders[41] that Putin's foreign policy aide and former ambassador to the United States, Yuri Ushakov, put on his desk every morning. There was French President Emmanuel Macron contending that NATO was "brain-dead" and doubting America's capability to come to Europe's assistance "if something happens at our borders."[42] Or the report of the Munich Security Conference titled "Westlessness" lamenting the "decay of the 'Western project'" and, for the first time in NATO's 71 years, broaching the possibility of the alliance "disbanding."[43]

Did Ushakov also slip in the results of a 2020 public opinion survey in NATO member states? Asked if their country should come to the assistance of a NATO ally if Russia "got into a serious military conflict"[44] with it, majorities in half of the NATO member states, including France, Germany, Italy, and Spain, said no. In the last three, the "nos" led by more than a two-to-one margin.

Did NATO's support for Ukraine change Putin's view of the alliance or shift the flow of information closer to the truth? Not likely. The West's lack of resolve and the inability to endure sacrifices in defense of its principles had been fed to him for too long, and he was not a man to tolerate cognitive dissonance.

True, the West suddenly showed more spine—and, *pace* President Macron, a still-functioning brain. Yet the solidarity with Kyiv could have been easily written off in the Kremlin or Novo-Ogaryovo as a spasmodic one-off, an effort destined to be exhausted sooner or later. The notion of policies sustained in democracies by public opinion is alien to Putin. To this KGB lieutenant colonel, nothing is spontaneous, people are a mere tool of the elites, and, in both his convictions and the information that invariably supported them, these elites are hardly impressive in their resolve and steadfastness.

As for the possibility of NATO for the first time confronting Russia on the battlefield, well, it was one thing to "fight to the last Ukrainian,"[45] as Putin put it, and quite another to send its own sons and daughters to die in some obscure country in Eastern Europe.

Extolling the feats of Russian troops, Putin told the story of a Russian pilot shot down over Syria, who kept firing his gun at the closing-in enemies and blew himself up to avoid capture. "What matters," Putin concluded in his tribute, "is that they [the West] will never have people or officers like Russian pilot Guards Major Roman Filipov."[46]

* * * *

Of the 15 former republics of the Soviet Union, only Estonia, Latvia, and Lithuania had joined NATO. But even that was an inexpiable sin. "We have done so much for them and they, ungrateful, have 'gone to the West'"[47] was the prevailing attitude among Russians. Among the most vocal critics of Russia's human rights abuses, in public opinion polls the three Baltic countries were always among the "unfriendly nations."[48]

In the eyes of millions of Russians, Estonia, Latvia, and Lithuania were traitors. And traitors, Putin had explained, were worse than enemies.

> You are at war with your enemies, then you negotiate an armistice with them, then peace and then they become your allies in

another war. And then you may be at war with them again. But it is always face-to-face. A traitor, on the other hand, was some-one who pretended to be with you but would stab you in the back or below the belt when you weaken or he thought you had weakened. For someone like that, there should be no mercy.[49]

A traitor must be crushed, Putin added.[50]

To this historian-in-chief, the Baltic nations' transgressions had been magnified by their lack of appreciation for the beneficence that the Soviet Union had shown them after the conquest. As Putin put it in a long essay on the "lessons of World War II,"

> In the autumn of 1939, the Soviet Union, pursuing its strategic military and defensive goals, started the process of the incorpora-tion of Latvia, Lithuania and Estonia. Their accession to the USSR was implemented on a contractual basis, with the consent of the elected authorities. This was in line with international and state law of that time. Besides, in October 1939, the city of Vilna and the surrounding area, which had previously been part of Poland, were returned to Lithuania. The Baltic republics within the USSR preserved their government bodies, language, and had represen-tation in the higher state structures of the Soviet Union.[51]

Some of Putin's ire may have been personal as well. In a cable made public by WikiLeaks, an Estonian diplomat complained that relations with Russia were "difficult at the political level" because Putin, who "alone" determined his country's policy toward Estonia, had "a personal gripe with Estonia."[52] The "gripe," which Putin described in a book of interviews, was about Estonians betraying Putin's father and his comrades to the Germans after they had parachuted behind enemy lines with a detachment of an NKVD "sabotage battalion."[53]

Reconquered by the Soviet Union in 1944, Tallinn is the closest Bal-tic capital to St. Petersburg: only 291 kilometers, or 181 miles, away. As a student at Leningrad State University, Putin must have driven there many times in a tiny, boxy, two-door Zaporozhets,[54] a knockoff of the Fiat 500, which his mother had won in the national lottery. Did that make it harder to see Estonia go when the Soviet Union fell—and more urgent to claw at least some of it back?

Fresh from an exhibition titled "Peter I. The Birth of the Empire" on the tsar's 350th birthday, in June 2022, Putin declared the accepted version of history wrong. Peter did not "detach anything" from Sweden during the 21-year Great Northern War.[55] Instead of conquering Swedish lands, the tsar merely "returned and strengthened" ancient Russian domains. "It looks like fate decreed that we too must return and strengthen," Putin told a gathering of young entrepreneurs, engineers, and scientists. "These are basic values, the foundation of our life."[56] Among the territories "returned and strengthened" by Peter I was Livonia, a region on the eastern shore of the Baltic Sea, covering most of today's Estonia and Latvia.

* * * *

A more recent history could look encouraging to Putin as well.

In April 2007, the Estonian government ordered the relocation of a Soviet World War II memorial from the center of Tallinn to a military cemetery. Known as the Bronze Soldier, the statue in a Soviet army uniform had been the place of the Victory Day pilgrimage by ethnic Russians, a symbol of their connection with the motherland.

After milling around all day, on the night of April 26, protesters surrounded the fence around the monument and then charged the police guarding the perimeter. The police responded with water cannons and tear gas. An estimated 1,500 mostly young men then rampaged through the city, smashing windows, vandalizing cars, and looting stores. The rioting continued the next night. At least 1,000 people were arrested.[57]

Of the over two dozen men and women I talked to in Estonia, Latvia, and Lithuania—journalists, defense and foreign policy officials, and experts inside and outside the government—not one suggested that a majority of

AP PHOTO/NIPA/TIMUR NISAMETDINOV

Police confront rioters during the Bronze Soldier riots in Tallinn, Estonia.

RAIGO PAJULA/AFP PHOTO

A man walks past a looted store in the aftermath of riots in Tallinn, 2007.

STRINGER/AFP/GETTY IMAGES

Police confront rioters in Tallinn during the 2007 Bronze Soldier riots.

NIPA/AP PHOTO

Aftermath of riots in Tallinn, 2007.

about a million ethnic Russians in the Baltics (roughly a quarter of the population in Latvia and Estonia and about 5 percent in Lithuania) would side with Russia in an armed clash.*

The second invasion of Ukraine made such instances of mass unrest much less likely. As early as a month after the aggression, the number of those who said they "liked" Putin fell by almost half in Latvia and Lithuania and a third in Estonia.[58] The ban on major Russian TV channels in all three Baltic countries almost certainly had a great deal to do with the change.[59]

The reaction to the aggression was far from uniform condemnation. In Latvia, one in five ethnic Russians—or close to 97,000 men and women—supported war on Ukraine,[60] while between a quarter million and almost 300,000 ethnic Russians in Latvia and Estonia felt "positively" about Putin three months after the invasion.[61] How difficult would it be to find among them a few hundred people—or pay them—to start a riot and provoke violence to unleash a propaganda frenzy at home (Russians are being shot again!) to thicken the fog of war?

* * * *

Yet perhaps the time for elaborate stratagems—complete with provocations, fake news, and covert infiltration—has passed and fig leaves should be disposed of in favor of a quicker, leaner, and cruder version of an assault.[62]

---

* Professor Alexander Clarkson of King's College London put such support at between 15 and 20 percent of all ethnic Russians in Latvia and Estonia, or between 117,272 and 156,363 people. See Daniel Boffey, "'I'm Always Looking over My Shoulder': Anxiety Among Estonia's Russians," *Guardian*, August 22, 2022, https://www.theguardian.com/world/2022/aug/22/always-looking-shoulder-anxiety-estonia-russians-tallinn. Dmitri Tsepernik of the Estonian International Center for Defense and Security thought just 12 percent of Estonian Russians (just under 40,000) were a "potential threat." See Belsat, "Rossiyane v Estonii: vmeste, no po otdel'nosti" [Russians in Estonia: Together, but at a Distance], February 24, 2018, https://naviny.belsat.eu/ru/news/rossiyane-v-estonii-vmeste-no-po-otdelnosti. Unlike Estonia and Latvia, which share a 224-mile border with Russia, Lithuania is not contiguous, and the country's ethnic Russians are too few to be profitably "saved" and "liberated." See TASS, "Lithuania's Russian-Speaking Population Shrinks to 5% in Past Decade," January 3, 2022, https://tass.com/world/1383623.

In 2016, RAND Corporation wargamers assessed that Russian troops could be in Riga or Tallinn in 36–60 hours after the beginning of hostilities.[63] The beating that the Russian armed forces took in Ukraine rendered this forecast moot. The Western Military District (WMD), which faces the Baltic states and is the best equipped of Russia's four military districts, was no more than a husk of its pre-Ukraine self, depleted and mangled. Its 6th Combined Arms Army was overrun in Ukraine's Kharkiv offensive in August 2022. A month later, the WMD's top-drawer unit, the First Guards Tank Army, lost at least half its machines. The elite 16th Spetsnaz Brigade, which would have almost certainly spearheaded an assault on the Baltics, was pulled to Ukraine as well, and the 76th Airborne Division was wrecked almost completely.[64] Early in 2023, a large chunk of the WMD was parceled out to the newly created Leningrad and Moscow Military Districts.

The devastation visited on Russia's armies in Ukraine deepened the already enormous qualitative and quantitative gap between Russia's and NATO's armies. A conventional war of any significant length would be suicidal for Moscow. But Putin would not be looking for such a war. Instead, he was likely to opt for a smash-and-grab occupation of narrow slivers of land with large ethnic Russian populations, the better to claim their "liberation" and then "reunification with the motherland."

In Estonia, the target would be Ida-Viru County, where three-quarters of the inhabitants are ethnically Russian and its largest city, Narva, on the Estonian-Russian border, is 80 percent Russian. Alternatively, in Latvia, the attack would aim at the Latgale province, which is one-third Russian and whose capital, Daugavpils, is almost half Russian. Both counties are small: Ida-Viru is around 1,150 square miles and Latgale 5,600 miles. The former's farthest point from the Russian border is 43 miles, and the latter's is 95 miles.

Even in the military's current disarray, Russia's supreme commander-in-chief should have no difficulty assembling enough troops for the initial assault. As of this writing, Estonia and Latvia hosted between 3,300 and 6,000 NATO troops, at most two dozen tanks, two artillery batteries,[65]

20 Apache helicopters,[66] one air defense platoon, and undefined "air defense assets."[67] Estonia fielded 10,500 soldiers of its own and Latvia 7,500.[68]

Emergency reinforcements could be rushed in, but they are likely to be too little, too late. NATO's Very High Readiness Joint Task Force (VJTF) is a light infantry brigade of 5,000 soldiers that could deploy its "lead elements" of unspecified strength within 48 hours, with the rest of the force to follow within a week.[69] There is no public record of the VJTF exercising in the Baltic states, and NATO officials have acknowledged that the force is "too small" to prevent a "Russian attack on Estonia."[70]

The US "rapid-response" 82nd Airborne Division could dispatch between 200 and 750 light infantry within 18 hours of notification.[71] With the flight time from Fort Bragg, North Carolina, to the Baltic states, they could arrive in about 36 hours. It would take another 72 hours for a brigade of 3,000–5,000 troops from the same division to join their comrades.[72]

The Estonian Prime Minister Kaja Kallas did not think these troops would be enough to push back the aggressor. "Our people, our nation would all be wiped off the map" by a Russian invasion, she said in the summer of 2022.[73] She asked NATO for a division of troops—between 10,000 and 20,000 soldiers—to be stationed in the three Baltic countries.[72]

No reinforcements were sent to Estonia in response to the prime minister's plea, but in November 2022 the US deployed 10,000 soldiers in Poland, of whom only 4,000 servicemen and women were from the rapid-response 101st Airborne Division.[75]

Regardless of where they are stationed, the emergency deployment of US or NATO troops would be severely handicapped by Russia taking advantage of the absence of NATO air defense systems in the area to pulverize the Baltic countries' airfields with missiles in the first hours of the aggression and thus deny the delivery of heavy equipment: tanks, artillery, and armored personnel carriers. It is far from certain that under these circumstances a NATO or US general would send in lightly armed paratroopers.

Since even a relatively small troop concentration would be visible from satellites and planes, the invasion's most likely cover would be a military exercise, like those that preceded the five-day war with Georgia in August 2008 and the invasions of Ukraine in 2014 and 2022. The WMD's last wargame before the war, in September 2021, featured 200,000 troops, 250 aircraft, and 290 tanks.[76] The drill's script had the Russian troops repulse an invasion by a "coalition of NATO states" and counterattack after depleting the "aggressor's" force. A quadrennial exercise, Zapad was not due till 2025. Yet in December 2022, Defense Minister Shoigu suddenly announced that it would be held again in 2023.[77]

A drill of a smaller scale could materialize as a "snap" or "surprise combat readiness inspection." Since 2012, dozens of these exercises had been conducted in all of Russia's four military districts.[78] At least seven of them were held in the WMD, including the one in February 2022.

* * * *

Once Ida-Viru or Latgale were declared part of the motherland, whether following fake "referendums" on joining Russia—supervised, like those in Kherson and Zaporizhzhia, by Russian soldiers in black balaclavas with their fingers on the triggers of Kalashnikovs—or discarding propaganda niceties altogether, recovering them would be tantamount to a war with Russia. Russia's military doctrine,[79] mentioned in the previous chapter, gives the president the right to use nuclear weapons when the state's existence is threatened. Of course, Putin, alone would determine the degree of threat to the state.*

How effective would his ultimatum be?

Putin's army may be a Potemkin mess, but his 306 strategic ballistic missiles, with names like Poplar, Sky Blue, and Mace, still blast from underground silos and nuclear submarines, delivering single or multiple warheads—each carrying between seven and 53 Hiroshima bombs' worth of payload.[80]

The most immediate threat in Russia's nuclear blackmail would be a tactical Iskander missile, mentioned and shown in the previous chapter.

---

* Putin chose not to invoke the doctrine when the Russians were pushed out of Kherson in November 2022—but then it was not NATO he was against.

Armed with a nuclear payload of between half to almost seven Hiroshima-size bombs[81] and a range of 500 km (311 miles), it covers all of Lithuania and Latvia and most of Estonia and Poland and could reach Vilnius or Riga in about two minutes.[82] Iskanders were live fired in three Zapad exercises and in the computer-simulated "electronic launches" from Kaliningrad in May 2022. On that occasion, the missiles targeted "airfields, defended infrastructure, military equipment, and command posts."[83]

Yet it is the depth and intensity of Putin's personal investment in his nukes that instilled his nuclear blackmail with chilling authenticity. We have seen him pray over the relics of St. Seraphim of Sarov.[84] He claimed to have put the Russian nuclear force on a higher alert when he sent soldiers to Crimea in 2014.[85] He held "snap" strategic nuclear exercises five days before the second invasion of Ukraine.[86] Three days after the start of the war, live on camera in a conversation with his minister of defense and chief of the General Staff, Putin ordered Russia's forces of nuclear deterrence to be put on "a special regime of a war-fighting alert."[87]

We watched him showcasing his nuclear weapons on giant screens during his state-of-the-nation address.[88] As missiles took off from silos or planes, releasing their apocalyptic payloads in videos and animations, Putin's comments were suffused with superlatives: the largest, the fastest.[89] His refrain was the same: No missile defense was going to stop these wonder weapons from reaching their destinations.

In what might be a rehearsal of a future ultimatum, he vowed that Russia would strike not just the territories from which it was "directly threatened" but also places where the decisions are made to deploy missiles against Russia.[90] "They can count, can't they?" Putin asked about Western leaders. Well then, they can calculate the speed of the systems that Russia was developing and then "make decisions that threaten our country."[91] (Yes, he was aware that Russia's nuclear response would lead to "a global catastrophe." But why would he want a world in which "there is no Russia"?)[92]

Eight months into the war on Ukraine, he reminded the West that "some" of Russia's "means of mass destruction" were "more advanced" than those of NATO and pledged to defend the "territorial integrity and sovereignty" of Russia with "all the means" in his possession.[93]

After initial alarm, Moscow's hints of using tactical nuclear weapons in Ukraine were roundly deplored—reportedly also by China, Russia's main economic and geopolitical political pillar of support—and eventually dismissed. Not so when it came to a strategic confrontation with the United States. Putin was "not joking" about the use of nuclear weapons, President Biden said in October 2022.[94] Which is why, Biden explained, the White House sought to "put up guardrails in the conflict"—that is, Russia's war on Ukraine, to "avoid World War III."[95] And surely Putin saw the same anxiety in the White House exacting the promise from Ukraine not to use HIMARS mobile rocket launchers to hit targets inside Russia—and then, just in case, secretly modifying the systems to prevent the deployment of longer-range missiles.

In the end, what mattered was not how credible the *West* considered Putin's rants and fulminations, but what *Putin* thought of their impact. "If people believe things to be real, they are real in their consequences," the great American sociologist Robert Merton told his students at Columbia, myself among them. If Putin believed that his nukes could freeze his enemies in dread, like the head of Medusa on Athena's shield, he would tread over one redline after another.

"We have not faced the prospect of Armageddon since Kennedy and the Cuban missile crisis," Biden said of Putin's nuclear warmongering.[96] At the time, JFK reportedly considered "plausible" a "scenario" in which "a leader is forced to choose between a catastrophic humiliation and a roll of the dice that might yield success."[97]

Let's hope that Putin does not face such a choice, but the depths of the Ukraine war's quagmire may yet release demons that neither he nor we can imagine.

Epilogue

Vladimir Putin and I grew up separated by 700 kilometers, the distance between Moscow and Leningrad. After reading nearly everything he has said publicly about himself, or that others have said or written about him, I suspect that, as children, we read some of the same books, watched the same spy dramas on TV, and listened to the same songs. When I look at photos of Putin as a young man, I recognize my own ill-fitting clothes.

Whether such proximity has made this book more persuasive is for the reader to judge. But long after I left the Soviet Union, we coincided, always at a remove, in unexpected ways. The same week that Putin became acting president and began his mission to reassert the state's Soviet-style dominance over civil society, I published a biography of Boris Yeltsin, the man who presided over the freest Russia there has ever been and, in a tragic error, made Putin his successor. Twelve years later, when Putin inaugurated his third presidency with a sharp turn toward repression and militarized patriotism as his regime's main source of legitimacy, I chronicled in another book the brilliance of Mikhail Gorbachev's glasnost oeuvre, its affirmation of liberty as the supreme value and the essence of human dignity.

By the time Putin invaded Ukraine, I'd learned that the "small victorious war," which I had made this book's working title three years before, was not a mad leader's caprice or an accident, but a plausible and enduring threat bound up in the nature of his regime.

With this book, my oblique travels with Putin are coming to an end.

I'll watch from afar while the gods of Russian history deal with him as they see fit.

Acknowledgments

My thanks to the Smith Richardson Foundation for a grant that allowed me to concentrate on this book.

I'm grateful to Ian Bell, Jonathan Chew, Yevgeniya Gilmore, Emily Hester, Svetlana Houle, David Pasmanik, Micah Pickus, Julian Poirier, Evan Sierra, Kate Spencer, Kateryna Stepanenko, AJ Ulwelling, and Alexei Zemnitca.

More than research assistants, Will Baumgardner, Lance Kokonos, and Joe Sailor were coconspirators, and Wes Culp, Max Frost, and Eileen Welsh terrific pinch hitters. All strove for excellence and persevered under incessant requests for more.

Rachel Hershberger was relentless in ferreting out verbal infelicities, typos, and bibliographical transgressions, and Joe Sailor helped hugely with the endnotes and proofing. Joe and Ben Lefkowitz persisted in securing the images vital to the narrative. Melissa Pranger, Brady Africk, and Ben devised ingenious ways to promote the book, and Claude Aubert toiled to make it beautiful.

For their generous welcome and advice, many thanks to Alexander Clarkson, Ruth Deyermond, and Keir Giles in London; Janis Berzins, Maris Cepuritis, Andis Kudris, Sergei Kuznetsov, Renate Lazdina, Vladimir Mensikovs, Toms Rostoks, and Henrihs Soms in Riga and Daugavpils; Veikko Kala, Mihhail Komaško, Anton Ossipovski, Ivo Posti, Rainer Saks, Ivan Sergejev, James Sherr, and Sergei Stepanov in Tallinn and Narva; Karolis Aleksa, Eitvydas Bajarūnas, Linas Idzelis, Tomas Jermalavičius, Ingrida Laurinavičienė, Giedrius Sakalauskas, Janina Sleivyte, Nortautas Statkus, Živilė Marija Vaicekauskaitė, and Liudas Zdanvicius in Vilnius; and Jan Marian, Michael Romancov, Karel Svoboda, Jonáš Syrovátka, Luboš Veselý, and Veronika Víchová in Prague.

I'm indebted to Cristina Odone and Edward Lucas for a delightful and stimulating evening in London and to Ambassador Jaroslav Kurfürst for a long and enjoyable conversation in the opulence of the Czech foreign ministry.

Derek Leebaert's cheer and close reading of the book's segments were invaluable.

Many thanks to Mark Galeotti for suggesting excellent interlocutors in London and Prague; Fred Kagan for imparting his incomparable knowledge of the Russian military, before and after the second invasion of Ukraine; Michael Kofman for elucidating Russian nuclear strategy; and Paul Goble, whose 50 Windows on Eurasia is the single most valuable chronicle on the political culture of Putin's Russia.

This book could not have been written without the support and encouragement of Danielle Pletka, Kori Schake, and Robert Doar.

Laure Berger read, reread, and read again—clarifying, simplifying, and sharpening the text. Her luminous presence sustained me in myriad vital ways.

About the Author

Leon Aron was born in Moscow and came to the United States as a refugee from the Soviet Union. He is the author of *Roads to the Temple: Truth, Memory, Ideas, and Ideals in the Making of the Russian Revolution, 1987–1991* (Yale University Press, 2012); *Russia's Revolution: Essays, 1989–2006* (AEI Press, 2007); and *Yeltsin: A Revolutionary Life* (St. Martin's Press, 2000). From 2014 to 2020, he served on the board of trustees of the US Agency for Global Media. He holds a PhD from Columbia University and is a senior fellow at the American Enterprise Institute.

Notes

Unless otherwise indicated, all translations from Russian are by the author.

Introduction

1. As is generally attributed to Talleyrand, "It is worse than a crime, it is a mistake" (*C'est pire qu'un crime, c'est une faute*).

2. Sergei Vitte, *Vospominaniya* [*Memoirs*] (Moscow, Soviet Union: Socio-Economic Literature, 1960), 2:291.

Chapter 1. The Vladimir Putin Story

1. Vladimir Putin, "Obrashchenie Presidenta Rossiyskoy Federatsii" [An Address by the President of the Russian Federation], Kremlin.ru, February 24, 2022, http://kremlin.ru/events/president/news/67843.

2. Putin, "Obrashchenie Presidenta Rossiyskoy Federatsii" [An Address by the President of the Russian Federation].

3. Michael Lewis, "How Two Trailblazing Psychologists Turned the World of Decision Science Upside Down," *Vanity Fair*, November 14, 2016, www.vanityfair.com/news/2016/11/decision-science-daniel-kahneman-amos-tversky.

4. Daniel Kahneman, *Thinking, Fast and Slow* (New York: Farrar, Straus and Giroux, 2013).

5. Natalya Gevorkyan, Natalya Timakova, and Andrei Kolesnikov, *Ot pervogo litsa: Razgovory s Vladimiom Putinym* [*From the First Person. Conversations with Vladimir Putin*] (Moscow, Russia: Vagrius, 2000), 39, http://www.lib.ru/MEMUARY/PUTIN/razgowor.txt.

6. Samotsety, "Moy adres—Sovetskiy Soyuz" [My Address Is the Soviet Union], YouTube, May 5, 2011, https://www.youtube.com/watch?v=J9s7Zel1sm4.

7. Gevorkyan, Timakova, and Kolesnikov, *Ot pervogo litsa: Razgovory s Vladimiom Putinym* [*From the First Person. Conversations with Vladimir Putin*].

8. Vladimir Putin, "S'yezd partii 'Yedinaya Rossiya'" [Speech at the 19th Congress of the United Russia Party], Kremlin.ru, November 23, 2019, http://kremlin.ru/events/president/news/62105.

9. Vladimir Putin, "Stenogramma programmy 'Razgovor s Vladimirom Putinym. Prodolzheniye'" [Transcript of "A Conversation with Vladimir Putin. Continued"], *Rossiyskaya Gazeta*, December 15, 2011, https://rg.ru/2011/12/15/stenogramma.html.

10. Vladimir Putin, "Zasedaniye Mezhdunarodnogo diskussionnogo kluba 'Valday'"

[Speech at the Concluding Session of the Valdai Club], Kremlin.ru, October 22, 2015, http://kremlin.ru/events/president/news/50548.

11. Vladimir Putin, "Rasshirennoye zasedaniye kollegii Minoborony" [Remarks at the Meeting of the Collegium of the Ministry of Defense], Kremlin.ru, December 21, 2021, http://kremlin.ru/events/president/news/67402.

12. *Kommersant*, "Tridsat' tri putinksikh bogatyrya" [Putin's Thirty-Three Knights], November 13, 2001, https://www.kommersant.ru/doc/290986.

13. Nikolai Patrushev and Ivan Yegorov, "Nikolai Patrushev: Otrezvlenie ukraint-sev budet zhestkim i boleznenym" [Nikolai Patrushev: The "Morning After" Will Be Tough and Painful for Ukrainians], *Rossiyskaya Gazeta*, October 15, 2014, https://rg.ru/2014/10/15/patrushev.html.

14. Patrushev and Yegorov, "Nikolai Patrushev: 'Otrezvlenie ukraintsev budet zhestkim i boleznenym" [Nikolai Patrushev: The "Morning After" Will Be Tough and Painful for Ukrainians].

15. Patrushev and Yegorov, "Nikolai Patrushev: 'Otrezvlenie ukraintsev budet zhestkim i boleznenym" [Nikolai Patrushev: The "Morning After" Will Be Tough and Painful for Ukrainians].

16. Patrushev and Yegorov, "Nikolai Patrushev: 'Otrezvlenie ukraintsev budet zhestkim i boleznenym" [Nikolai Patrushev: The "Morning After" Will Be Tough and Painful for Ukrainians].

17. Vladimir Putin, "Poslaniye Federal'nomu Sobraniyu Rossiyskoy Federatsii" [Address to the Federal Assembly], Kremlin.ru, April 25, 2005, http://kremlin.ru/events/president/transcripts/22931.

18. Reuters, "Putin, Before Vote, Says He'd Reverse Soviet Collapse If He Could," March 2, 2018, https://www.reuters.com/article/us-russia-election-putin/putin-before-vote-says-hed-reverse-soviet-collapse-if-he-could-agencies-idUSKCN1GE2TF.

19. Fyodor Dostoevsky, *Humiliated and Insulted* (1861; Richmond, London: Alma Books, 2012).

20. Vladimir Putin, "Poslaniye Prezidenta Federal'nomu Sobraniyu" [Presidential Address to the Federal Assembly], Kremlin.ru, March 1, 2018, http://kremlin.ru/events/president/news/56957/work.

21. Geoff Brumfiel, "Megatons to Megawatts: Russian Warheads Fuel U.S. Power Plants," National Public Radio, December 11, 2013, https://www.npr.org/2013/12/11/250007526/megatons-to-megawatts-russian-warheads-fuel-u-s-power-plants.

22. National News Service, "Putin soobshchil, chto v pravitel'stve RF rabotali kadrovie sotrudniki TsRU" [Putin Said That CIA Personnel Worked in the Russian Government], December 9, 2021, https://nsn.fm/policy/putin-soobscil-chto-v-pravitelstve-rf-rabotali-kadrovye-sotrudniki-tsru. He repeated the charge in an interview for the documentary *Rossiya. Noveyshaya istoriya (Russia. Modern History)* and at the meeting of the Collegium of the Ministry of Defense. See National News Service, "Putin raskryl chislo agentov TSRU sredi sovetnikov pravitel'stva v nachale 90-kh" [Putin Revealed the Number of CIA Agents Among Government Advisers in the Early '90s], December 11, 2011, https://nsn.fm/policy/putin-raskryl-chislo-agentov-tsru-sredi-sovetnikov-pravitelstva-v-nachale-90-h; and Putin, "Rasshirennoye zasedaniye kollegii Minoborony" [Remarks at the Meeting of the Collegium of the Ministry of Defense].

23. RIA Novosti, "Putin schitayet, chto raspad SSSR stal tragediyey dlya millionov" [Putin Believes That the Collapse of the USSR Was a Tragedy for Millions], May 5, 2005, https://ria.ru/20050505/39937603.html.

24. Vladimir Putin, "Rossiya sosredotatchivaetsya—vyzovy, na kotorye my dolzhny otvetit'" [Russia Is Getting Ready for Action: The Challenges That We Have to Meet], *Izvestia*, January 16, 2012, https://iz.ru/news/511884; and Vladimir Putin, "Interv'yu Pervomu kanalu i agentstvu Assoshieyted Press" [Interview to Channel One and the Associated Press], Kremlin.ru, September 4, 2013, http://www.kremlin.ru/events/president/transcripts/interviews/19143/photos. Vladimir Putin quoted Alexander Pushkin: "There are many people who are in opposition not to the government but to Russia." And then he added: "Unfortunately, this is our intelligentsia's tradition." In my collected works of Pushkin, I could not find the original quote.

25. Elizaveta Bazanova, "Pochemu za 20 let Rossiya tak i ne pereshla ot stagnatsii k razvitiyu" [Why for 20 Years Russia Never Moved from Stagnation to Development], *Vedomosti*, October 8, 2019, https://www.vedomosti.ru/economics/articles/2019/10/08/813068-20-let-stagnatsii; and Sophie Pinkham, "A Hotter Russia," *New York Review of Books*, June 23, 2022, https://www.nybooks.com/articles/2022/06/23/a-hotter-russia-klimat-thane-gustafson.

26. For Alexei Makarkin's remarks in a discussion at the Liberal Mission Foundation, see Politcom.ru, "Politicheskaya situatsiya i obshchestvennye nastroeniya v Rossii: God posle vyborov; nachalo zastoya ili vremennoe zatishe?" [Political Situation and Societal Attitudes in Russia: One Year After the Elections; the Beginning of a Stagnation or a Temporary Lull?], June 24, 2013, http://politcom.ru/15953.html.

27. Andrei Gromyko, *XXIV S'yezd Kommunisticheskoy Partii Sovetskogo Soyuza. Stenographicheskiy Otchet* [*24th Congress of the Communist Party of the Soviet Union*] (Moscow, Soviet Union: Politicheskaya Literatura, 1971), https://istmat.org/files/uploads/52749/24_sezd._chast_1._1971.pdf.

28. Vladimir Putin, "Vystuplenie i discussiya na Myunkhenskoy konferentsii po voprosam politiki bezopasnosti" [Speech and Discussion at the Munich Conference on International Security Policy], Kremlin.ru, February 10, 2007, http://kremlin.ru/events/president/transcripts/24034.

29. Putin, "Vystuplenie i discussiya na Myunkhenskoy konferentsii po voprosam politiki bezopasnosti" [Speech and Discussion at the Munich Conference on International Security Policy].

30. Putin, "Vystuplenie i discussiya na Myunkhenskoy konferentsii po voprosam politiki bezopasnosti" [Speech and Discussion at the Munich Conference on International Security Policy].

31. Angelika Beer was quoted in Helena Spongenberg, "Putin Speech Raises Alarm on EU-Russia Relations," EUobserver, February 12, 2007, https://euobserver.com/news/23471.

32. Karel Schwarzenberg spoke to Reuters. See Reuters, "Putin's Speech Showed Why NATO Must Enlarge," February 11, 2007, https://www.reuters.com/article/uk-russia-usa-czech/putins-speech-showed-why-nato-must-enlarge-idUSL1126843820070211.

33. Carl Bildt was quoted in Spongenberg, "Putin Speech Raises Alarm on EU-Russia Relations."

34. Daniel Fried and Kurt Volker, "The Speech in Which Putin Told Us Who He Was," *Politico*, February 18, 2022, https://www.politico.com/news/magazine/2022/02/18/putin-speech-wake-up-call-post-cold-war-order-liberal-2007-00009918.

35. Fried and Volker, "The Speech in Which Putin Told Us Who He Was."

36. Vladimir Putin, "Vystuplenie v Bundestage FRG" [Speech in the Bundestag of the Federal Republic of Germany], September 25, 2001, http://kremlin.ru/events/president/transcripts/21340. "Putin captured us," recalled Norbert Rottgen, the then head of the Bundestag's Foreign Affairs Committee. "The voice was quite soft, in German, a voice that tempts you to believe what is said to you. We had some reason to think there was a viable perspective of togetherness." See Roger Cohen, "The Making of Vladimir Putin," *New York Times*, March 26, 2022, https://www.nytimes.com/2022/03/26/world/europe/vladimir-putin-russia.html. According to a story that may well be apocryphal, as the deputies marveled at Putin's German, the future Chancellor Angela Merkel leaned to the person next to her and whispered, "Well, I suppose this is something we should be grateful to the KGB for."

37. World Bank, "GDP Growth (Annual %)—Russian Federation," https://data.worldbank.org/indicator/NY.GDP.MKTP.KD.ZG?locations=RU; and Sergei Guriev and Aleh Tsyvinsky, "Challenges Facing the Russian Economy After the Crisis," Peterson Institute of International Economics, https://www.piie.com/publications/chapters_preview/4976/01iie4976.pdf.

38. US Energy Information Administration, "Europe Brent Spot Price," https://www.eia.gov/dnav/pet/hist/LeafHandler.ashx?n=PET&s=RBRTE&f=A; and World Bank, "GDP Growth (Annual %)—Russian Federation."

39. Vadim Lurie, "Azbuka protesta" [The ABCs of the Protest], Polit.ru, 2012, https://polit.ru/media/files/2012/04/27/Azbuka_Blok_Internet.pdf.

40. Hillary Clinton, Putin said, had "set the tone for some [opposition] activists inside the country, she sent a signal. They heard the signal and set to work, supported by the US State Department." *Novye Izvestiya*, "Putin predlozhil zhestche nakazyvat' prispeshnikov Zapada" [Putin Suggested Tougher Punishments for the Lackeys of the West], December 8, 2011, https://newizv.ru/news/politics/08-12-2011/155943-putin-predlozhil-zhestche-nakazyvat-prispeshnikov-zapada.

41. Lurie, "Azbuka protesta" [The ABCs of the Protest]. Putin's initial retort to all this mockery was likening the white ribbons worn by the demonstrators to condoms and asserting that students among them were paid to participate. See Putin, "Razgovor s Vladimirom Putinym. Prodolzhenie" [A Conversation with Vladimir Putin. Continued].

42. Putin, "Razgovor s Vladimirom Putinym. Prodolzhenie" [A Conversation with Vladimir Putin. Continued].

43. *Kommersant*, "Tridsat' tri putinksikh bogatyrya" [Putin's Thirty-Three Knights].

44. I drew on these sources for Alexei Kudrin's statements. See Andrey Kolesnikov and Alexey Polukhin, "Alexei Kudrin: 'My uperlis' v stenu effiktivnosti'" [Alexei Kudrin: "We Hit the Wall of Effectiveness"], *Novaya Gazeta*, October 10, 2013, https://novayagazeta.ru/articles/2013/10/10/56683-aleksey-kudrin-171-my-uperlis-v-stenu-

effektivnosti-187; Spiegel International, "Former Russian Finance Minister Alexei Kudrin: 'We Have to Take a Chance with More Democracy,'" January 23, 2013, https://www.spiegel.de/international/world/interview-with-putin-ally-alexei-kudrin-on-democracy-in-russia-a-878873.html; and Civil Initiatives Committee, "Vystuplenie Alexeya Kudrina na zasedanii Komiteta Grazhdanskikh Initsiatives" [Remarks by Alexei Kudrin at the Meeting of the Committee for Civil Initiatives], Facebook, September 23, 2013, https://www.facebook.com/watch/?v=413413462097038.

45. Kolesnikov and Polukhin, "Alexei Kudrin: 'My uperlis' v stenu effiktivnosti'" [Alexei Kudrin: "We Hit the Wall of Effectiveness"].

46. Kudrin's forecast was correct in the long run as well. In what turned out to be the longest economic stagnation in modern Russian history, between 2009 and 2019 the annual economic growth averaged 1 percent. Brian Taylor, "Putin's Fourth Term: The Phantom Breakthrough," PONARS Eurasia, July 18, 2019, https://www.ponarseurasia.org/putin-s-fourth-term-the-phantom-breakthrough. In 2020, gross national income (GNI) per capita was 30 percent lower than in 2013. See Macrotrends, website, https://www.macrotrends.net. While some diminution of GNI was due to COVID-19, the pandemic was not a decisive factor: Of other major industrial countries and Russia's peer nations (Brazil, India, and China), only Brazil saw a larger decline, 39 percent, between 2013 and 2020. In 1991, Russia's per capita income was 32 percent larger than that of Malaysia. In 2020, Malaysia was ahead by $286. World Bank, "GDP Per Capita (Current US$)," https://data.worldbank.org/indicator/NY.GDP.PCAP.CD?end=1991&most_recent_value_desc=true&start=1990.

47. Lola Tagaeva, "Lev Gudkov: 'Yesli za vse otvechayet odin chelovek v strane, cherez kakoye-to vremya illyuzii v otnoshenii yego sposobnosti prevrashchayutsya v razdrazheniye'" [Lev Gudkov: "If Only One Man Is Responsible for Everything in the Country, After Some Time the Illusions About His Abilities Start to Irritate"], Republic.ru, June 2, 2014, https://republic.ru/posts/41566.

48. For Mikhail Dmitriev's remarks in a discussion at the Liberal Mission Foundation, see Politcom.ru, "Politicheskaya situatsiya i obshchestvennye nastroeniya v Rossii: God posle vyborov; nachalo zastoya ili vremennoe zatishe?" [Political Situation and Societal Attitudes in Russia: One Year After the Elections; the Beginning of a Stagnation or a Temporary Lull?].

49. Fifty-five percent of the respondents did not want Putin in the Kremlin after 2018; 22 percent did. Levada Center, "Russian Public Opinion: 2012–13," 2013, https://www.levada.ru/sites/default/files/2012_eng.pdf.

50. See Dmitriev's remarks in Politcom.ru, "Politicheskaya situatsiya i obshchestvennye nastroeniya v Rossii: God posle vyborov; nachalo zastoya ili vremennoe zatishe?" [Political Situation and Societal Attitudes in Russia: One Year After the Elections; the Beginning of a Stagnation or a Temporary Lull?].

51. Levada Center, "Dekabr'skie reytingi odobreniya i doveriya" [The December Ratings of Approval and Trust], December 25, 2013, https://www.levada.ru/2013/12/25/dekabrskie-rejtingi-odobreniya-i-doveriya-3. The dominance of the Kremlin propaganda and the absence of functioning democratic institutions and free media competition create an "organized consensus," explained Lev Gudkov, then director of the Levada Center, the country's only independent polling firm. As a result, Putin's approval

cannot go below 60–63 percent. Lev Gudkov, "Tyaga k stalinu—moral'nya tupost' obsh-chestva" [The Appeal of Stalin Is the Moral Torpor of Society], Fontanka.ru, January 8, 2020, https://www.fontanka.ru/2020/01/08/020.

52. See Dmitriev's remarks in Politcom.ru, "Politicheskaya situatsiya i obshchestven-nye nastroeniya v Rossii: God posle vyborov; nachalo zastoya ili vremennoe zatishe?" [Political Situation and Societal Attitudes in Russia: One Year After the Elections; the Beginning of a Stagnation or a Temporary Lull?].

53. Tagaeva, "Lev Gudkov: 'Esli za vsyo otvechaet odin chelovek v strane, cherez kakoye-to vremya illyuzii v otnoshenii yego sposobnosti prevrashchayutsya v razdra-zheniye'" [Lev Gudkov: "If Only One Man Is Responsible for Everything in the Country, After Some Time the Illusions About His Abilities Start to Irritate"].

54. For Igor Klyamkin's remarks in a discussion at the Liberal Mission Foundation, see Politcom.ru, "Politicheskaya situatsiya i obshchestvennye nastroeniya v Rossii: God posle vyborov; nachalo zastoya ili vremennoe zatishe?" [Political Situation and Soci-etal Attitudes in Russia: One Year After the Elections; the Beginning of a Stagnation or a Temporary Lull?]. The original hyperlink no longer works. In a repost, Klyamkin is listed as a speaker, but his remarks are mysteriously omitted. I quote him from the printout of the original post in my possession.

55. Nicolas Berdyaev, *The Origins of Russian Communism* (Ann Arbor, MI: University of Michigan Press, 1976), 10–11.

56. In what seems like a pattern of suggesting Putin's direction before Putin articu-lated it himself, Nikolai Patrushev surprised the members of the Academic Council of the Security Council by calling on them to help strengthen the country's defense in the "spiritual and moral sphere." Taisiya Bekbulatova, Maksim Ivanov, and Ivan Safronov, "Na strazhe dukhovnoy bezopasnosti" [Guarding Spiritual Security], *Kommersant*, April 25, 2013, https://www.kommersant.ru/doc/2178141#id863667. Two years later, the "pres-ervation of traditional values" would be listed among the most important strategic goals in the National Security Strategy of the Russian Federation.

57. Vladimir Putin, "Obrashchenie Prezidenta Rossiyaskoy Federatsii" [Address by the President of the Russian Federation], Kremlin.ru, March 18, 2014, http://kremlin.ru/events/president/news/20603.

58. Putin echoed Russian émigré nationalist philosopher Ivan Ilyin, who had become one of Putin's favorite authors in the mid-2000s. Putin quoted him in speeches, assigned his works to provincial governors to read over Christmas break, and moved the remains of Ilyin and his wife from Switzerland to Moscow's Donskoy Cemetery. He did not quote Ilyin, but the sensibility is unmistakably Ilyin's. The West, Ilyin wrote, is instilled with the "ridiculous fear of a united Russia, with the encrusted enmity toward Russian monarchy and Eastern Orthodoxy." "We know," Ilyin continued,

> that Western peoples do not comprehend and do not tolerate Russia's unique-ness. The united Russian state is like a dam on the path of their trade, their linguistic and military expansion, and they test it again and again. They intend to divide the Russian "broom" into twigs, break those twigs one by one, and rekindle with them the fading light of their civilization. They need to ply Rus-sia apart in order to drag it through West-style levelling and loose mores and thus kill it: a plan of hatred and lust for power.

Ivan Ilyin, *Nashi zadachi: Istoricheskaya sud'ba i budushchee rossii. Stat'I 1948–1954* [*Our Tasks: Historic Fate and Future of Russia. Essays 1948–1954*] (Moscow, Russia: Russkaya Kniga, 1993), 1: 327–28, https://imwerden.de/publ-11960.html. For more on Ilyin, see Anton Barbashin and Hannah Thoburn, "Putin's Philosopher: Ivan Ilyin and the Ideology of Moscow's Rule," *Foreign Affairs*, September 20, 2015; Timothy Snyder, "Ivan Ilyin, Putin's Philosopher of Russian Fascism," *New York Review of Books*, March 16, 2018, https://www.nybooks.com/online/2018/03/16/ivan-ilyin-putins-philosopher-of-russian-fascism; Paula Chan, "I za belykx, i za krasnykh" [For Both the Whites and the Reds] (unpublished paper, December 17, 2014); and CIA Office of Russian and European Analysis, "Ivan Ilyin: National Philosopher of Putin's Russia," November 24, 2014.

59. Putin, "Obrashchenie Prezidenta Rossiyaskoy Federatsii" [Address by the President of the Russian Federation].

60. Putin, "Obrashchenie Prezidenta Rossiyaskoy Federatsii" [Address by the President of the Russian Federation].

61. Putin, "Obrashchenie Prezidenta Rossiyaskoy Federatsii" [Address by the President of the Russian Federation].

62. The Coordinating Committee for Multilateral Export Controls (CoCom) was a Western trade organization established in 1949 to restrict the export of militarily relevant technologies to the Soviet bloc. I found no evidence of limits on exports to post-Soviet Russia before the first invasion of Ukraine in 2014.

63. Attributed to Francisco Franco's Gen. Emilio Mola Vidal, the "fifth column" became a cliché denoting traitors helping the enemy from within. "National-traitor" is a rarer moniker and even more hateful. Enclosed in the quotation marks by Kremlin transcribers, the label was applied by the German right to Matthias Erzberger, Philipp Scheidemann, and other leaders of the early Weimar Republic who allegedly "stabbed Germany in the back" by signing the 1918 armistice and then the 1919 Treaty of Versailles. Hitler used *Nationalverräter* in his speeches and in *Mein Kampf*. At least one Kremlin staffer of the presidential administration was troubled by the Hitler connection enough to suggest that the government propagandists use social media to "dispute/refute/deny the fact that this expression is associated only with Nazism." See Insider, "Anatomiya propagandy: chto podtverdila pochta rabotayushchey na AP Kristiny Potupchik" [The Anatomy of Propaganda: What Confirmed the Email of Kristina Potupchik Who Works for the Presidential Administration], December 26, 2014, https://theins.ru/politika/2320. Although Putin had referred to the pro-democracy opposition as "jackals hanging around foreign embassies, in search of foreign funds, instead of the support of their own people," until the March 18 speech, he had not branded them fifth columnists or national-traitors. *Rossiyskaya Gazeta*, "Vladimir Putin: U tekh, kto khochet vernut' oligarkhicheskiy rezhim, nichego ne poluchitsya" [Vladimir Putin: Those Who Want to Return the Oligarchic Regime Will Utterly Fail], November 22, 2007, https://rg.ru/2007/11/22/putin-forum.html.

64. Putin, "Obrashchenie Prezidenta Rossiyaskoy Federatsii" [Address by the President of the Russian Federation].

65. The images are to be found at Stas Romanoffsky, "Vystupleniye Putina 18 marta 2014 goda Federal'nym sobraniyem po krymskomu voprosu (polnaya versiya)" [The

March 18th 2014 Address of Putin to the Federal Assembly on the Crimean Question (Full Version)], YouTube, March 18, 2014, https://youtu.be/dEXPXj3xvWY?t=2665.

66. Alexandra Samarina, "Fultonskaya rech Putina" [Putin's Fulton Speech], *Nezavi-simaya Gazeta*, March 19, 2014, https://www.ng.ru/politics/2014-03-19/1_speech.html.

67. Levada Center, "Prezidentskie reitingi i polozhenie del v strane" [The President's Ratings and the State of the Country], February 4, 2021, https://www.levada.ru/2021/02/04/prezidentskie-rejtingi-i-polozhenie-del-v-strane.

68. Vladimir Sorokin, "Let the Past Collapse on Time," *New York Review of Books*, May 8, 2014, https://www.nybooks.com/articles/2014/05/08/let-the-past-collapse-on-time.

69. Evgeny Gontmakher, "Esli ne sdelaesh vybor ty, ego sdelaet dzhin" [If You Don't Make a Choice, the Genie Will Make It for You], *Vedomosti*, February 18, 2013. A leading political economist, Evgeny Gontmakher is a professor in the National Research University Higher School of Economics and deputy director of the Institute of World Economy and International Relations of the Russian Academy of Sciences.

70. Sergei Medvedev, *Park Krymskogo perioda. Khroniki tretego sroka* [*The Crimean Era Park. Chronicles of (Putin's) Third Term*] (Moscow, Russia: Individuum, 2017), 27. At the time a professor at Moscow's Higher School of Economics, Sergei Medvedev is a popular opposition blogger and columnist.

71. For Alexei Makarkin's remarks in a discussion at the Liberal Mission Foundation, see Politkom.ru, "Politicheskayasituatsiya i obshchestvennye nastroeniya v Rossii. God posle vyborov: Nachalo zastoya ili vremennoe zatish'e?" [The Political Situation and Societal Mood in Russia. One Year After the Elections: The Beginning of a Stagnation, or a Temporary Lull?]. A prominent historian and political scientist, Alexei Makarkin is deputy director of the Center for Political Technology in Moscow.

72. See, for example, Tara Isabella Burton, "The Far-Right Mystical Writer Who Helped Shape Putin's View of Russia," *Washington Post*, May 12, 2022, https://www.washingtonpost.com/outlook/2022/05/12/dugin-russia-ukraine-putin.

73. Aleksander Dugin, "Konets liberalizma i nachalo patriotizma v Rossii" [The End of Liberalism and the Beginning of Patriotism in Russia], VKontakte.com, March 22, 2014, http://vk.com/wall-2789767_9761.

74. Ellen Barry, "Foes of America in Russia Crave Rupture in Ties," *New York Times*, March 15, 2014, https://www.nytimes.com/2014/03/16/world/europe/foes-of-america-in-russia-crave-rupture-in-ties.html.

75. BBC News, "Pussy Riot Members Jailed for Two Years for Hooliganism," August 17, 2012, https://www.bbc.com/news/world-europe-19297373.

76. The detention often amounted to torture. One of the accused, a partially blind Vladimir Akimenkov, his vision worsening, told the judge he had been able to take a shower for the first time in nearly three weeks. Detention conditions, the judge replied, were "irrelevant to the case." See Kathy Lally, "Trial of Bolotnaya 12 Seen as a Warning Against Challenging the Kremlin," *Washington Post*, October 30, 2013, https://www.washingtonpost.com/world/trial-of-bolotnaya-12-seen-as-a-warning-against-challenging-the-kremlin/2013/10/29/5e1dec92-381f-11e3-89db-8002ba99b894_story.html.

77. BBC Russian Service, "Udal'tsov i Razvozzhayev prigovoreny k 4,5 godam kol-nii" [Udaltsov and Razvozzhayev Were Sentenced to 4.5 Years of Labor Camp], July 24, 2014, https://www.bbc.com/russian/russia/2014/07/140724_udaltsov_sentence_ver-dict; and *Moscow Times*, "Russian Activist Navalny Given 5-Year Suspended Sentence in Kirovles Retrial," February 8, 2017, https://www.themoscowtimes.com/2017/02/08/russian-activist-navalny-sentenced-in-kirovles-case-a57038.

78. *Novye Izvestiya*, "Putin predlozhil zhestche nakazyvat' prispeshnikov Zapada" [Putin Suggested Tougher Punishments for the Lackeys of the West].

79. *Novye Izvestiya*, "Putin predlozhil zhestche nakazyvat' prispeshnikov Zapada" [Putin Suggested Tougher Punishments for the Lackeys of the West].

80. Daria Skibo, "Inostrannykh agentov stanet bol'she" [There Will Be More Foreign Agents], Eurasianet, February 25, 2020, https://russian.eurasianet.org/иностранных-агентов-статет-больше.

81. Vladimir Putin, "Zasedaniye kollegii FSB Rossii" [Speech at the Meeting of the Collegium of the FSB], Kremlin.ru, February 24, 2021, http://www.kremlin.ru/events/president/news/65068.

82. Library of Congress, "Russia Espionage and State Treason Concepts Revisited," November 28, 2012, https://www.loc.gov/item/global-legal-monitor/2012-11-28/russia-espionage-and-state-treason-concepts-revised.

83. Kirill Rogov, ed., *Krepost' vrastaet v zemlyu* [*The Fortress Grows down into the Soil*], Liberal Mission Foundation, 2019, https://liberal.ru/wp-content/uploads/legacy/files/articles/7335/krepost.pdf.

84. Rogov, ed., *Krepost' vrastaet v zemlyu* [*The Fortress Grows down into the Soil*].

85. Ridley Scott, dir., *Alien* (Los Angeles: 20th Century Fox, 1979).

86. The *Fedaral'naya Sluzhba Okhrany* (Federal Protective Service) is an equivalent of the US Secret Service.

87. Elena Masyuk, "Boris Nemtsov: 'Oni ne smogut zastavit menya zamolchat', prosto ne smogut" [Boris Nemtsov: They Will Not Force Me to Be Silent, They Simply Will Not], *Novaya Gazeta*, March 2, 2015, https://novayagazeta.ru/articles/2015/02/28/63231-boris-nemtsov-171-oni-ne-smogut-zastavit-menya-zamolchat-prosto-ne-smogut-187. Boris Nemtsov was interviewed a few days after the installation of the poster in April 2014; the text was published on February 28, 2015.

88. Masyuk, "Boris Nemtsov: 'Oni ne smogut zastavit menya zamolchat', prosto ne smogut" [Boris Nemtsov: They Will Not Force Me to Be Silent, They Simply Will Not].

89. Masyuk, "Boris Nemtsov: 'Oni ne smogut zastavit menya zamolchat', prosto ne smogut" [Boris Nemtsov: They Will Not Force Me to Be Silent, They Simply Will Not].

Chapter 2. The House That Putin Built

1. Ekaterina Galochka, "Volodin:' Est' Putin, est' Rossya, net Putina, net Rossii" [If There Is Putin, There Is Russia, No Putin, No Russia], *Moskovskiy Komsomolets*, October 23, 2014, https://www.mk.ru/politics/2014/10/23/volodin-est-putin-est-rossiya-net-putina-net-rossii.html.

2. I chronicled some of it. Leon Aron, *Roads to the Temple: Truth, Memory, Ideas, and Ideals in the Making of the Russian Revolution, 1987–1991* (New Haven, CT: Yale University Press, 2012).

3. Alexei Levinson and Stepan Goncharov, "Voyna vmesto budyshchego—vykhod iz anomicheskogo soznaniya" [War Instead of the Future—an Exit from the Anomie-Affected Consciousness], *Vestnik obshchestvennogo mneniya* 121, no. 3–4 (July–December 2015), https://cyberleninka.ru/article/n/voyna-vmesto-buduschego-vyhod-dlya-anomicheskogo-soznaniya/viewer.

4. Alexei Levinson, "Nevelikaya imperiya?" [A Not So Great Empire?], Russia in Global Affairs, June 11, 2011, https://globalaffairs.ru/articles/nevelikaya-imperiya.

5. V. S. Naipaul, *The Enigma of Arrival* (New York: Vintage, 1988).

6. Levada Center, "Velikaya derzhava" [A Great Power], January 28, 2020, https://www.levada.ru/2020/01/28/velikaya-derzhava. The *Krymnash!* (Crimea is ours!) victory, wrote leading political sociologists Alexei Levinson and Stepan Goncharov, played the role of "symbolic restitution": It removed the pressure on the consciousness of Russians from the trauma of the Soviet Union's demise. Levinson and Goncharov, "Voyna vmesto budyshchego—vykhod iz anomicheskogo soznaniya" [War Instead of the Future—an Exit from the Anomie-Affected Consciousness].

7. Igor Yurgens, "Razvernut' stranu nazad nevozmozhno" [Turning the Country Back Is Impossible], *Novaya Gazeta*, November 14, 2014, https://novayagazeta.ru/articles/2014/11/14/61943-igor-yurgens-171-razvernut-stranu-nazad-nevozmozhno-hod-istorii-somnet-takoy-algoritm-187. Igor Yurgens was a top adviser to Dmitry Medvedev, first prime minister, then president, and then prime minister again. "It would not be easy to find in Russia today anyone whose knowledge of the psychology and the motives of the top Russian authorities would be as authentic," the opposition *Novaya Gazeta* wrote in the introduction to the interview.

8. Stanislav Belkovsky, "'Ya uberu vsekh, kto posmeyet posyagnut' na russkiy yazyk'" ["I Will Wipe Out All Who Dare Imperil the Russian Language"], *Afisha Daily*, April 23, 2015, https://daily.afisha.ru/archive/vozduh/books/ya-uberu-vseh-kto-posmeet-posyagnut-na-russkiy-yazyk-belkovskiy-o-slovesnosti.

9. Fyodor Dostoevsky, *Notes from Underground* (1864; New York: Vintage, 1994).

10. Evelin Gerda Lindner, *Making Enemies Unwittingly: Humiliation and International Conflict*, Human Dignity and Humiliation Studies, 2005, https://www.humiliationstudies.org/documents/evelin/MakingEnemiesUnwittinglyLong2005.pdf. A hardcover edition was published later. Evelin Gerda Lindner, *Making Enemies: Humiliation and International Conflict* (Westport, CT: Praeger, 2006).

11. Lindner, *Making Enemies Unwittingly*, 146–49, 153, 159.

12. Vladimir Putin, "Polnyy tekst interv'yu Putina rossiyskim telekanalam" [A Complete Transcript of the Interview with Russia's Major TV Channels], RIA Novosti, October 17, 2011, https://ria.ru/20111017/462204254.html. Vladimir Putin was quoted as saying, "In the Soviet days Russia was called the Soviet Union." See Vladimir Putin, "Poslaniye Prezidenta Federal'nomu Sobraniyu" [Presidential Address to the Federal Assembly], March 1, 2018, http://kremlin.ru/events/president/news/56957. In another speech, he said the Soviet Union was "a thousand-year historical Russia." See Vladimir Putin, "Parad Pobedy na Krasnoy ploshchadi" [Speech Delivered at the Victory Parade

on Red Square], May 9, 2019, http://kremlin.ru/events/president/news/60490. Alexander Solzhenitsyn, at whose dacha Putin drank tea in the summer of 2007, wrote: "Russia is to the Soviet Union as a man is to the disease afflicting him. We do not confuse a man with his illness: we do not refer to him by the name of that illness or curse him for it." John Bayley, *The Power of Delight: A Lifetime in Literature: Essays 1962–2002* (New York: W. W. Norton & Co., 2005), 320; and Luke Harding, "Signs of Dispute on Moscow's Solzhenitsyn Street," *Guardian*, December 12, 2008, https://www.theguardian.com/world/2008/dec/12/russia.

13. Vladimir Lenin, *O natsional'noy gordosti velikorossov* [*On the National Pride of the Great Russians*] (Moscow, Soviet Union: OGIZ, 1944), https://www.booksite.ru/fulltext/179758/text.pdf.

14. Lola Tagaeva, "Lev Gudkov: 'Yesli za vse otvechayet odin chelovek v strane, cherez kakoye-to vremya illyuzii v otnoshenii yego sposobnosti prevrashchayutsya v razdrazheniye'" [Lev Gudkov: "If Only One Man Is Responsible for Everything in the Country, After Some Time the Illusions About His Abilities Start to Irritate"], Republic.ru, June 2, 2014, https://republic.ru/posts/41566.

15. Tagaeva, "Lev Gudkov: 'Yesli za vse otvechayet odin chelovek v strane, cherez kakoye-to vremya illyuzii v otnoshenii yego sposobnosti prevrashchayutsya v razdrazheniye'" [Lev Gudkov: "If Only One Man Is Responsible for Everything in the Country, After Some Time the Illusions About His Abilities Start to Irritate"].

16. BBC Russian Service, "Opros: bol'shinstvo rossiyan rady tomu, chto Rossiyu v mire boyatsya" [Poll: The Majority of Russians Are Glad That Russia Is Feared in the World], January 14, 2017, https://www.bbc.com/russian/news-38621441.

17. Philotheus, "Poslaniye velikomu knyazu Vasiliyu, v kotorom ob ispravlenii krestnogo znameniya I o sodomskom blude" [Address to Grand Prince Vasily on the Improvement of the Sign of the Cross and the Sodom Lust], Museum of Historical Russian Reforms Named After P. A. Stolypin, http://museumreforms.ru/node/13626.

18. Levinson and Goncharov, "Voyna vmesto budyshchego—vykhod iz anomicheskogo soznaniya" [War Instead of the Future—an Exit from the Anomie-Affected Consciousness]. In the 2000s, an average of 60 percent of Russians surveyed expressed support for the "unique path for Russia," distinct from the European one, while 20 percent were in favor of the latter. Andrei Kolesnikov, "Russian Ideology After Crimea," Carnegie Moscow Center, September 15, 2015, https://carnegieendowment.org/files/CP_Kolesnikov_Ideology2015_web_Eng.pdf. This notion was embodied as Russia's "unique mission to support the global balance of power" and "to create conditions for peaceful and progressive development of mankind," in Kremlin.ru, "Ukaz ob utverzhdenii Konstsepsii vneshney politiki Rossiyskoy Federatsii" [Concept of the Foreign Policy of the Russian Federation], March 31, 2023, http://kremlin.ru/events/president/news/70811.

19. *Nezavisimaya Gazeta*, "Rossiya: natsional'nyy vopros" [Russia: The National Question], January 23, 2012, https://www.ng.ru/politics/2012-01-23/1_national.html.

20. Lev Gudkov, "Epokha razvitogo militarizma" [The Era of Developed Militarism], *Novaya Gazeta*, May 8, 2019, https://novayagazeta.ru/articles/2019/05/09/80447-epoha-razvitogo-militarizma.

21. Levada Center, "Rossiya i Evropa" [Russia and Europe], March 18, 2021, https://www.levada.ru/2021/03/18/rossiya-i-evropa-2.

22. Gleb Yarovoy, "'Narastayushchaya agressivnost'. Sotsiolog Lev Gudkov o nastroeniyakh rossiyan" ["Increasing Aggressiveness." Sociologist Lev Gudkov About the Attitudes of Russians], Sever.Realii, July 7, 2021, https://www.severreal.org/a/sotsiologlev-gudkov-o-nastroeniyah-rossiyan/31343336.html.

23. Alexei Levinson, "Mental'naya yama" [Mental Abyss], *Novaya Gazeta*, June 3, 2014, https://novayagazeta.ru/articles/2014/06/04/59831-mentalnaya-yama.

24. Tagaeva, "Lev Gudkov: 'Yesli za vse otvechayet odin chelovek v strane, cherez kakoye-to vremya illyuzii v otnoshenii yego sposobnosti prevrashchayutsya v razdrazheniye'" [Lev Gudkov: "If Only One Man Is Responsible for Everything in the Country, After Some Time the Illusions About His Abilities Start to Irritate"].

25. Mikhail Lermontov, "Izmail-Bey," *Sobranie sochineniy v chetyryokh tomakh. Tom vtoroy, Poemy I povesti v stikhakh [Collected Works in Four Volumes. Volume II, Poems and Novellas in Verse]* (Moscow, Soviet Union: Khudozhestvennaya literatura, 1964), 288.

26. Viktor Govorkov, "Ne balui!" [Don't You Fool Around!], 1948, https://calisphere.org/item/4c976b48277958c2e6c8c5975523090a.

27. Vladimir Putin, "Poslaniye Prezidenta Federal'nomu Sobraniyu" [Speech to the Federal Assembly in Moscow], Kremlin.ru, December 12, 2012, http://kremlin.ru/events/president/news/17118.

28. Davis Center for Russian and Eurasian Studies, "The Use and Abuse of Soviet History in Putin's Russia," YouTube, April 6, 2021, https://www.youtube.com/watch?v=AhVxzHTFJsI.

29. Denis Volkov and Sergei Medvedev, "Vozvrashchenie generalissimusa" [The Return of the Generalissimo], Radio Svoboda, September 12, 2021, https://www.svoboda.org/a/vozvraschenie-generalissimusa/31456588.html.

30. Leon Aron, "The Problematic Pages," *New Republic*, September 24, 2008, https://newrepublic.com/article/62070/the-problematic-pages.

31. Intelros, "Minutes of the Meeting with the Delegates of an All-Russian Conference of the Teachers of Social Sciences in Novo-Ogaryovo on June 21, 2007," 2007, http://www.intelros.ru/2007/06/21/stenograficheskijj_otchet_o_vstreche_s_delegatami_vserossijjskojj_konferencii_prepodavatelejj_gumanitarnykh_i_obshhestvennykh_nauk_novoogarevo_21_ijunja_2007_g.html.

32. Aron, "The Problematic Pages."

33. Vladimir Putin, "The Real Lessons of the 75th Anniversary of World War II," National Interest, June 18, 2020, https://nationalinterest.org/feature/vladimir-putinreal-lessons-75th-anniversary-world-war-ii-162982. Great Britain and France declared war on Germany on September 3, 1939. The Soviet Union occupied over half of Poland's territory, with over one-third of the country's population, and incorporated the seized lands into the Belarussian Soviet Socialist Republic (SSR) and the Ukrainian SSR. Less than a year later, the Soviet Union occupied and annexed Estonia, Latvia, Lithuania, and Romania's Bessarabia, which became the Moldavian SSR.

34. Vladimir Putin, "Bol'shaya press-konferentsia Vladimira Putina" [Vladimir Putin's Big Press Conference], Kremlin.ru, December 19, 2019, http://kremlin.ru/events/president/news/62366.

35. Vladimir Putin, "Neformal'nyy sammit SNG" [Informal CIS Summit], Kremlin.ru, December 20, 2019, http://kremlin.ru/events/president/news/62376.

36. Putin, "Bol'shaya press-konferentsia Vladimira Putina" [Vladimir Putin's Big Press Conference].

37. Vladimir Medinsky, "Diplomaticheskiy triumf SSSR" [The Diplomatic Triumph of the USSR], RIA Novosti, August 23, 2019, https://ria.ru/20190823/1557826932.html.

38. Intelros, "Minutes of the Meeting with the Delegates of an All-Russian Conference of the Teachers of Social Sciences in Novo-Ogaryovo on June 21, 2007." Again, as in the Soviet Union, the "repressions" were confined to the Great Purge of 1937, in which the most prominent victims were the party and military elite. Left out were the millions who perished in the decades of relentless terror before and after; in the murderous "collectivization," accompanied by deaths from starvation; and during the 30 years of the exterminations in Gulag camps. These multiple horrors were almost daily brought to light during the apogee of Mikhail Gorbachev's glasnost. I have chronicled some of these revelations in Aron, *Roads to the Temple*.

39. Vladimir Putin, "Otkrytiye memoriala pamyati zhertv politicheskikh repressiy 'Stena skorbi'" [Speech Delivered at the Opening Ceremony of the Wall of Sorrow Memorial to Victims of Political Repression in Moscow], Kremlin.ru, October 30, 2017, http://kremlin.ru/events/president/news/55948.

40. Vladimir Putin, "Torzhestvennyy vecher, posvyashchonnyy Dnyu rabotnika organov bezopasnosti" [Speech Delivered at the Gala Evening to Mark the Day of the Worker of State Security Organs in Moscow], Kremlin.ru, December 20, 2017, http://kremlin.ru/events/president/news/56452.

41. Meduza, "Russia's Only Gulag Memorial Is Redesigned to Celebrate the Gulag," Meduza, March 4, 2015, https://meduza.io/en/news/2015/03/05/russia-s-only-gulag-memorial-is-redesigned-to-celebrate-the-gulag. "Perm-36 now is a museum that tells a story of a hard and noble labor of the brave workers of the Gulag," wrote the replaced museum's supporter. "A story of the technologies they used to shield the great people from the fifth column and assorted Nazis from Ukraine. Imagine: this is not a joke! The first exhibit in the 'new' Perm-36 is about the means of detention, the technical ways of keeping the villainous nationalists, fascists, traitors." Aleksandr Kalikh, "'Perm-36': Unichtozkenie Pamyati" ["Perm-36": The Destruction of Memory], Grani.ru, March 4, 2015, https://graniru.org/blogs/free/entries/238693.html.

42. Grani.ru, "Russia's Only Gulag Memorial Is Redesigned to Celebrate the Gulag."

43. Valerie Hopkins, "Putin Tries to Erase History of Gulag Atrocities," *New York Times*, November 23, 2021, https://www.nytimes.com/2021/11/22/todayspaper/quotation-of-the-day-putin-tries-to-erase-history-of-gulag-atrocities.html.

44. Andrew Higgins, "He Found One of Stalin's Mass Graves. Now He's in Jail.," *New York Times*, April 27, 2020, https://www.nytimes.com/2020/04/27/world/europe/russia-historian-stalin-mass-graves.html.

45. Kodeks Zakony, "Stat'ya 354.1 UK RF Reabilitatsiya Natsizma" [Article 354.1 of the Legal Code of the Russian Federation "On the Rehabilitation of Nazism"], https://www.zakonrf.info/uk/354.1.

46. Gosudarstvennaya Duma, "Noviy tekst Konstitutsii RF s popravkami 2020" [The New Text of the Constitution of the Russian Federation with the 2020 Amendments], March 2020, http://duma.gov.ru/news/48953.

47. International Federation for Human Rights, "Russia: 'Crimes Against History,'" June 2021, https://www.fidh.org/IMG/pdf/russie-_pad-uk-web.pdf.

48. Investigative Committee of the Russian Federation, "Alexandr Bastrykin prinyal uchastie v meropriyatii posvyashchyonnom pamyati zhertv fashizma" [Alexandr Bastrykin Participated in an Event Devoted to the Memory of the Victims of Fascism], September 10, 2020, https://sledcom.ru/news/item/1498218.

49. Ru.citaty, "Proshedsheye Rossii bylo udivitel'no, yeye nastoyashcheye boleye chem velikolepno, chto zhe kasayetsya do budushchego, to ono vyshe vsego, chto mozhet narisovat' sebe samoye smeloye voobrazheniye" [Russia's Past Was Extraordinary, Its Present Is Better Than Magnificent, and as to Its Future It Exceeds the Most Daring Imagination], July 2, 2022, http://ru.citaty.net/tsitaty/653223-aleksandr-khristo-forovich-benkendorf-proshedshee-rossii-bylo-udivitelno-ee-nastoiashchee-bo.

Chapter 3. Russia Under Siege

1. Vladimir Putin, "Obrashcheniye Prezidenta Rossii Vladimira Putina" [Speech Delivered in Moscow in the Wake of the Beslan Hostage Crisis], September 4, 2004, http://kremlin.ru/events/president/transcripts/22589.

2. Joseph Stalin, "O zadachakh khozaistvennikov" [On the Tasks of the Managers of the Economy], 1931, https://fishki.net/anti/2754381-otstalyh-byjut-vyskazyvanie-ivstalina-v1931g-aktualyno-segodnja-kak-nikogda.html. At a speech at the first national conference of the workers of socialist industry in Moscow, Stalin said, "The weak are beaten; if you are weak you can be beaten and enslaved."

3. Putin, "Obrashcheniye Prezidenta Rossii Vladimira Putina" [Speech Delivered in Moscow in the Wake of the Beslan Hostage Crisis].

4. Larisa Kaftan, "Putin ukreplyaet gosudarstvo, a ne sebya" [Putin Is Strengthening the State, Not Himself], *Komsomolskaya Pravda*, September 28, 2004, https://www.kp.ru/daily/23370/32473.

5. Alexander Yankovskiy and Inna Annitova, "Ot global'nikh pretenzii k samoreal-izatsii" [From Global Pretensions to Self-Realization], Krym.Realii, July 6, 2021, https://ru.krymr.com/a/rossiya-putin-kreml-natsionalnaya-strategiya/31343919.html; and Lev Gudkov, Nina Khrushcheva, and Sergei Medvedev, "Zuby proch ot Rossii" [Teeth off from Russia], Radio Svoboda, June 2, 2021, https://www.svoboda.org/a/31272653.html.

6. Levada Center, "Strakhi" [Fears], January 12, 2022, https://www.levada.ru/2022/01/12/strahi-5. The precise numbers are 37 percent and 56 percent.

7. Denis Volkov, "The Popularity Paradox," Chatham House, June 8, 2018, https://www.chathamhouse.org/publications/the-world-today/2018-06/popularity-paradox.

8. Levada Center, Approval Rating, December 16, 2019, https://www.levada.ru/en/2019/12/16/approval-ratings-10.

9. Levinson, "Voyna vmesto budushchego" [War Instead of the Future].

10. TASS, "Putin Agrees with Emperor That Russia's Only Allies Are Army and Navy," April 16, 2015, https://tass.com/russia/789866.

11. Vladimir Putin, "Otkrytiye pamyatnika Aleksandru III" [Opening of the Monument to Alexander III], November 18, 2017, http://special.kremlin.ru/catalog/regions/CR/events/56125.

12. Teller Report, "Putin Unveiled a Monument to Emperor Alexander III in Gatchina," May 6, 2021, https://www.tellerreport.com/news/2021-06-05-putin-unveiled-a-monument-to-emperor-alexander-iii-in-gatchina.Hy9T6YFq_.html.

13. Vladimir Putin, "Zasedaniye kollegii FSB Rossii" [Speech Delivered in Moscow at a Meeting of the Collegium of the FSB], February 24, 2021, http://kremlin.ru/events/president/news/65068.

14. Vladimir Putin, "Obrashcheniye Prezidenta Rossiyskoy Federatsii" [Speech Delivered in Moscow Announcing the Beginning of Russia's Invasion of Ukraine], February 24, 2022, http://kremlin.ru/events/president/news/67843; and Vladimir Putin, "Rasshirennoye zasedaniye kollegii Minoborony" [Speech Delivered at an Expanded Meeting of the Collegium of the Ministry of Defense], December 21, 2021, http://kremlin.ru/events/president/news/67402.

15. Lenta, "Genshtab Rossii obyasnil sut' amerikanskogo 'Troyanskogo konya'" [The General Staff Explained the Meaning of the American "Trojan Horse"], March 2, 2019, https://lenta.ru/news/2019/03/02/kon.

16. Kremlin.ru, "Strategiya natsional'noy bezopasnosti Rossiyskoy Federatsii" [The National Security Strategy of the Russian Federation], July 2, 2021, http://static.kremlin.ru/media/acts/files/0001201512310038.pdf.

17. Vladimir Putin, "Poslaniye Prezidenta Federal'nomu Sobraniyu" [Speech Delivered to the Federal Assembly in Moscow], April 21, 2021, http://kremlin.ru/events/president/news/65418.

18. Vladimir Putin, "Zasedaniye Rossiyskogo organizatsionnogo komiteta 'Pobeda'" [Speech Delivered at a Meeting of the Russian Organizational Committee "Victory" in Moscow], May 20, 2021, http://kremlin.ru/events/president/news/65618.

19. Pravo, "Federal'niy Zakon o Vyborakh Prezidenta Rossiskoi Federatsii" [Federal Law on Russian Federal Presidential Elections], December 27, 2002, https://web.archive.org/web/20220122162250/http://pravo.gov.ru/proxy/ips/?docbody=&nd=102079674.

20. Anton Troianovski and Matthew Bodner, "With Putin's Reelection, Expect Rising Tensions with the West," Washington Post, March 18, 2018, https://www.washingtonpost.com/world/europe/with-putins-re-election-expect-rising-tensions-with-the-west/2018/03/18/8430f69e-2abf-11e8-8dc9-3b51e028b845_story.html.

21. Putin, "Obrashcheniye Prezidenta Rossiyskoy Federatsii" [Speech Delivered in Moscow Announcing the Beginning of Russia's Invasion of Ukraine].

22. Putin, "Obrashcheniye Prezidenta Rossiyskoy Federatsii" [Speech Delivered in Moscow Announcing the Beginning of Russia's Invasion of Ukraine].

23. Vladimir Unanyants, "Ul'timatim Putina: razgnevanniy Kiev, zataivshiisya Tbilisi" [Putin's Ultimatum: An Angry Kiev, and a Lurking Tbilisi], Ekho Kavkaza, December 24, 2021, https://www.ekhokavkaza.com/a/31624923.html.

24. Kremlin.ru, "Bol'shaya Press-Konferentsiya Vladimira Putina" [Vladimir Putin's Big Press Conference], December 23, 2021, http://kremlin.ru/events/president/news/67438.

25. Unanyants, "U'ltimatum Putina: razgnevanniy Kiev, zataivshiisya Tbilisi" [Putin's Ultimatum: An Angry Kiev, and a Lurking Tbilisi].

26. Kremlin.ru, "Bol'shaya Press-Konferentsiya Vladimira Putina" [Vladimir Putin's Big Press Conference].

27. Radio Svoboda, "Putin na vstreche so SMI: 'Idite vy so svoimi ozabochenostyami'" [Putin at a Meeting with Mass Media: "Go to Hell with Your Preoccupations"], December 23, 2021, https://www.svoboda.org/a/idite-vy-so-svoimi-ozabochennostyami-o-chyom-govoril-putin-na-vstreche-so-smi/31623010.html.

28. Vladimir Putin, "Poslaniye Prezidenta Federal'nomu Sobraniyu" [Speech Delivered to the Federal Assembly in Moscow], February 20, 2021, http://kremlin.ru/events/president/news/59863.

29. Putin, "Rasshirennoye zasedaniye kollegii Minoborony" [Speech Delivered at an Expanded Meeting of the Collegium of the Ministry of Defense].

30. RIA Novosti, "Ryabkov: nyneshnei ritorike SShA svoistvenny primitive i khamstvo" [Ryabkov: The Current Rhetoric of the USA Is Typically Primitive and Boorish], April 12, 2017, https://ria.ru/20170412/1492057665.html.

31. RIA Novosti, "'Chto ty glaza otvodish?' Safronov otvetil predstavitelyu Britanii v OON" ["Why Are You Looking Away?" Safronov Answered the British Representative in the UN], April 12, 2017, https://ria.ru/20170412/1492116042.html.

32. *Nezavisimaya Gazeta*, "Rossiya: natsional'nyy vopros" [Russia: The National Question], January 23, 2012, https://www.ng.ru/politics/2012-01-23/1_national.html.

33. *Nezavisimaya Gazeta*, "Rossiya: natsional'nyy vopros" [Russia: The National Question].

34. *Moscow Times*, "Russia Is a 'Distinct Civilization,' Putin Says," May 18, 2020, https://www.themoscowtimes.com/2020/05/18/russia-is-a-distinct-civilization-putin-says-a70295.

35. Vladimir Putin, "'Na Miru i Smert Krasna'" [With One's Own Around You, Death Itself Is Good], Obshchestvenni Kontrol, April 18, 2014, https://ok-inform.ru/tribuna/12084-vladimir-putin-na-miru-i-smert-krasna.html.

36. Vladimir Putin, "Putin: Russkii narod shire dushoi, chem predstaviteli drugikh narodov" [Putin: The Russian People Have Bigger Hearts Than Members of Other Nations], RIA Novosti, April 17, 2014, https://ria.ru/20140417/1004339422.html.

37. Vladimir Putin, "Zasedaniye mezhdunarodnogo diskussionnogo kluba 'Valday'" [Speech Delivered at the Valdai Club], November 19, 2013, http://kremlin.ru/events/president/news/19243.

38. *Nezavisimaya Gazeta*, "Rossiya: natsional'nyy vopros" [Russia: The National Question].

39. Putin, "Zasedaniye mezhdunarodnogo diskussionnogo kluba 'Valday'" [Speech Delivered at the Valdai Club].

40. Putin, "Zasedaniye mezhdunarodnogo diskussionnogo kluba 'Valday'" [Speech Delivered at the Valdai Club].

41. Putin, "Zasedaniye mezhdunarodnogo diskussionnogo kluba 'Valday'" [Speech Delivered at the Valdai Club].

42. Sergei Ryabkov and Evgeny Minibaev, "Voprosy raznye, rezul'tat resheniya odin" [The Questions Are Different but the Decision's Result Is the Same], Topwar.ru, March

13, 2012, https://topwar.ru/12371-voprosy-raznye-rezultat-resheniya-odin.html.

43. Sergei Shoigu, "Shoigu nazval tsel' informatsionnoi voiny Zapada protiv Rossii" [Shoigu Identified the Goal of the West's Informational War Against Russia], June 26, 2019, https://tass.ru/armiya-i-opk/6596144.

44. Shoigu, "Shoigu nazval tsel' informatsionnoi voiny Zapada protiv Rossii" [Shoigu Identified the Goal of the West's Informational War Against Russia].

45. Nikolai Patrushev, "Patrushev znayet o planakh Zapada po razlozheniyu Rossii" [Patrushev Knows About the West's Plans for Russia. Speech at a Conference on the National Security, Khanty-Mansiysk], *Nezavisimaya Gazeta*, March 23, 2021, https://www.ng.ru/politics/2021-03-23/3_8109_west.html.

46. Nikolai Patrushev, "Patrushev znayet o planakh Zapada po razlozheniyu Rossii" [Patrushev Knows About the West's Plans for Russia. Speech at a Conference on the National Security, Khanty-Mansiysk].

47. Nikolai Patrushev, "Patrushev znayet o planakh Zapada po razlozheniyu Rossii" [Patrushev Knows About the West's Plans for Russia. Speech at a Conference on the National Security, Khanty-Mansiysk].

48. Kremlin.ru, "Strategiya natsional'noy bezopasnosti Rossiyskoy Federatsii" [The National Security Strategy of the Russian Federation], July 2, 2021, http://static.kremlin.ru/media/acts/files/0001201512310038.pdf.

49. Vladimir Putin, "Byt sil'nymi—garantii natsionalnoy bezopasnosti dlya Rossii" [To Be Strong Is a Guarantee of the National Security of Russia], *Rossiyskaya Gazeta*, February 20, 2012, https://rg.ru/2012/02/20/putin-armiya.html.

50. Putin, "Byt sil'nymi—garantii natsionalnoy bezopasnosti dlya Rossii" [To Be Strong Is a Guarantee of the National Security of Russia].

51. Putin, "Byt sil'nymi—garantii natsionalnoy bezopasnosti dlya Rossii" [To Be Strong Is a Guarantee of the National Security of Russia].

52. Richard Connolly and Mathieu Boulègue, *Russia's New State Armament Programme: Implications for the Russian Armed Forces and Military Capabilities to 2027*, Chatham House, May 2018, https://www.chathamhouse.org/sites/default/files/publications/research/2018-05-10-russia-state-armament-programme-connolly-boulegue-final.pdf.

53. Connolly and Boulègue, *Russia's New State Armament Programme*.

54. Siemon Wezeman, "Russia's Military Spending: Frequently Asked Questions," Sipri, April 27, 2020, https://www.sipri.org/commentary/topical-backgrounder/2020/russias-military-spending-frequently-asked-questions.

55. World Bank, "GDP—Russian Federation: 1988–2020," https://data.worldbank.org/indicator/NY.GDP.MKTP.CD?locations=RU.

56. Wezeman, "Russia's Military Spending." Of the G20 nations, only Saudi Arabia spends a larger share of gross domestic product (GDP) on defense, and of the smaller countries, Algeria, Israel, Kuwait, and Oman. See World Bank, "Military Expenditure (% of GDP)—Russian Federation, United Kingdom, China, United States, France, Germany, India, Japan, Korea, Rep., Brazil," 2021, https://data.worldbank.org/indicator/MS.MIL.XPND.GD.ZS?end=2020&locations=RU-GB-CN-US-FR-DE-IN-JP-KR-BR&most_recent_value_desc=true&start=2010.

57. Lenta, "Genshtab Rossii obyasnil sut' amerikanskogo 'Troyanskogo konya'" [The General Staff Explained the Meaning of the American "Trojan Horse"].

58. Vladislav Inozemtsev, "Zachem v Kremle Govoryat o Voennoy Ekonomike" [Why Does the Kremlin Talk About the War Economy], *RBK*, November 28, 2017. They meet in Sochi, Putin explained, not because the weather there is good, but because he and his generals were able to "unplug" themselves from the routine and tear themselves away from everything else and concentrate on only the *oboronka* (defense). Kremlin. ru, "Zasedaniye kollegii FSB Rossii" [Speech Delivered in Moscow at a Meeting of the Collegium of the FSB].

59. Interfax, "Rosstat otmetil sokrashchenie urovnya bednosti v yanvare-sentyabre 2021 goda" [Rosstat Noted the Lowering of the Poverty Level from January–September of 2021], December 3, 2021, https://www.interfax.ru/business/806527.

60. Rosstat, "O Znachenii Granits Bednosti i Chislennosti Naseleniya s Denezhnymi Dokhodami Nizhe Granitsi Bednosti za 1-3 kvartaly 2021 Goda v Tselom Po Rossiiskoi Federatsii" [The Significance of the Limits of Poverty and the Number of People with Incomes Lower Than the Poverty Level in the First Through Third Quarters of 2021 in the Russian Federation], 2021, https://rosstat.gov.ru/storage/mediabank/218_03-12-2021. htm.

61. *Gazeta*, "Ne umeret' s golodu: skol'ko deneg nuzhno rossiyanam" [Not to Starve to Death: How Much Money Russians Need], April 3, 2019, https://www.gazeta.ru/ business/2019/04/03/12281539.shtml.

62. *Moskovskiy Komsomolets*, "Kreml' ne poveril, chto u rossiyan nyet deneg na obuv" [The Kremlin Did Not Believe That Russians Have No Money for Shoes], April 3, 2019, https://www.mk.ru/politics/2019/04/03/kreml-ne-poveril-chto-u-rossiyan-net-deneg-na-obuv.html.

63. *Gazeta*, "Eto pozor: Kudrin nazval sverkhostruyu problemu Rossii" [It Is a Shame: Kudrin Named the Most Acute Problem for Russia], June 19, 2019, https://www.gazeta. ru/business/2019/06/19/12425227.shtml.

64. World Bank, "Life Expectancy at Birth, Total (Years)," 2021, https://data. worldbank.org/indicator/SP.DYN.LE00.IN?most_recent_value_desc=false.

65. In 2019, the latest year for which data are available, the EU countries' average was 9.92 percent of GDP; Russia's was 5.65 percent. World Bank, "Current Health Expenditure (% of GDP)—Russian Federation, European Union," October 24, 2022, https://data.worldbank.org/indicator/SH.XPD.CHEX.GD.ZS?locations=RU-EU.

66. Ministry of Finance of the Russian Federation, "Osnovnye napravleniya byudzhetnoi nalogovoi i tamozhenno tarifnoi politiki na 2022 god i na planovyi period 2023 i 2024 godov" [The Main Directions of the Budget, Tax and Customs Tariff Policy for 2022 and for the Planning Period of 2023 and 2024], September 30, 2021,   https://minfin.gov.ru/ru/document/?id_4=134362-osnovnye_napravleniya_ byudzhetnoi_nalogovoi_i_tamozhenno-tarifnoi_politiki_na_2022_god_i_na_planovyi_ period_2023_i_2024_godov.

67. Vladimir Putin, "Putin nazval yedinstvenno vozmozhnuyu dlya Rossii natsional' nuyu ideyu" [Putin Named the Only Possible National Idea for Russia], *RBK*, February 3, 2016, https://www.rbc.ru/politics/03/02/2016/56b1f8a79a7947060162a5a7.

68. Vladimir Putin, "Vystupleniye Vladimira Putina na mitinge v Luzhnikakh" [Speech Delivered at a Rally in Luzhniki Stadium in Moscow], RIA Novosti, February 23, 2012, https://ria.ru/20120223/572995366.html.

69. Putin, "Vystupleniye Vladimira Putina na mitinge v Luzhnikakh" [Speech Delivered at a Rally in Luzhniki Stadium in Moscow].

70. Putin went on to recite the last quatrain of Mikhail Lervmontov's classic poem "Borodino": "Let's die defending Moscow!/Like our brothers died./And to die we promised/And we faithful to our oath/In the battle of Borodino!" Mikhail Lervmontov, "Borodino," 1837.

71. Putin, "Vystupleniye Vladimira Putina na mitinge v Luzhnikakh" [Speech Delivered at a Rally in Luzhniki Stadium in Moscow].

72. RT, "Vladimir Putin: Svyashchenny dolg Rossiyan: Byt' vernym tsennostyam patriorizma" [Vladimir Putin: A Sacred Duty of Russians: To Be Faithful to the Values of Patriotism], June 22, 2015, https://russian.rt.com/article/98867.

73. Vladimir Putin, "Poslaniye Prezidenta Federal'nomu Sobraniyu" [Speech to the Federal Assembly in Moscow], Kremlin.ru, December 12, 2012, http://kremlin.ru/events/president/news/17118.

74. TASS, "Nravstennym orientirom dlya podrostkov dolzhna stat' lyubov k rodine" [Love of the Motherland Must Become the Moral Guideline for Teenagers], October 8, 2012, https://tass.ru/obschestvo/2329167.

75. Vladimir Putin, "Putin o patrioticheskom vospitanii" [Putin on Patriotic Upbringing], Odnako.ru, September 3, 2016, https://web.archive.org/web/20160903084517/http:/www.odnako.org/blogs/putin-o-patrioticheskom-vospitanii-dopolneno-goszakaz-i-kontrol-v-kulture-obrazovanie.

76. Igor Nikolaev, "Chto ne tak s vospitaniem rossiyskogo patriotizma" [What Is Wrong with the Rearing of Russian Patriotism], Moskovskiy Komsomolets, January 23, 2020, https://www.mk.ru/politics/2020/01/23/chto-ne-tak-s-vospitaniem-rossiyskogo-patriotizma.html.

77. Anna Sanina, "Patriotizm i patrioticheskoye vospitanie v covremennoi Rossii" [Patriotism and Patriotic Upbringing in Modern Russia], Sotsiologicheskie Issledovaniya, no. 5 (2016), https://elibrary.ru/item.asp?id=26125604.

78. Iskander Yasaveev, "Militarization of the 'National Idea': The New Interpretation of Patriotism by the Russian Authorities," Russian Analytical Digest, no. 207 (September 26, 2017), https://css.ethz.ch/content/dam/ethz/special-interest/gess/cis/center-for-securities-studies/pdfs/RAD_207.pdf.

79. Ekaterina Khodzhaeva and Irina Meyer, "Mobilizing Patriotism in Russia: Federal Programs of Patriotic Education," Russian Analytical Digest, no. 207 (September 2017): 2–7, https://css.ethz.ch/content/dam/ethz/special-interest/gess/cis/center-for-securities-studies/pdfs/RAD_207.pdf.

80. Dumitru Cazac, "Patriotic Mobilization in Russia," International Crisis Group, July 4, 2018, https://www.scribd.com/document/538962923/251-Patriotic-Mobilisation-in-Russia.

81. Vladimir Putin, "Vstrecha s predstavitelyami obshchestvennosti po voprosam patrioticheskogo vospitaniya molodozhi" [Remarks Delivered to Representatives of the Public at a Meeting on the Patriotic Upbringing of Russian Youth], September 12, 2012, http://kremlin.ru/events/president/news/16470.

82. Vladimir Putin, "Vladimir Putin vyskazalsya za patrioticheskoye vospitanie molodyozhi bez ideologizatsii takoi roboty" [Putin Supported Patriotic Upbringing of

the Young Without Ideologization of This Process], TASS, March 18, 2019, https://tass.ru/politika/6230692.

83. GTO.ru, "Vserossiyskiy fizkul'turno-sportivniy compleks GTO" [The National Physical Fitness and Sports Complex GTO], https://www.gto.ru. Though officially "voluntary," the "complex" had been obligatory between 1931 and 1991. Every place of employment or education was required to report on the testing and results to their bureaucratic superiors. The latter, in turn, had to account to ministries or committees above them.

84. Milena Kostereva, "Putin podpisal zakon o realizatsii kompleksa GTO" [Putin Signed a Law on the Implementation of the GTO Complex], *Kommersant*, October 6, 2015, https://www.kommersant.ru/doc/2825951.

85. *Moscow Times*, "Putin Orders Monitoring Youth Behavior Online," October 17, 2019, https://www.themoscowtimes.com/2019/10/17/putin-orders-monitoring-youth-behavior-online-a67776.

86. Sergei Sukhankin, "Russia's 'Youth Army': Sovietization, Militarization, or Radicalization?," *Eurasia Daily Monitory* 13, no. 180 (November 9, 2016), https://jamestown.org/program/russias-youth-army-sovietization-militarization-radicalization.

87. TASS, "Yunarmeytsam dobavyat bally k EGE" [Yunarmeytsy Will Receive Additional Points in the Unified State Examination], March 29, 2019, https://tass.ru/obschestvo/6273668.

88. The membership numbers are from the December 2017, November 2019, and March 2021 issues of the *Yunarmia* magazine.

89. Yuri Gavrilov, "Minoborony: Chislennost' 'Yunarmii' Do Kontsa Goda Dolzhna Uvelichit'sya Do 1 Mln" [Ministry of Defense: The Number of "Yunarmia" Members Will Increase to 1 Million by the End of the Year], *Rossiiskaya Gazeta*, July 5, 2021, https://rg.ru/2021/07/05/minoborony-chislennost-iunarmii-do-konca-goda-dolzhna-uvelichitsia-do-1-mln.html.

90. RIA Novosti, "V 'Yunarmiyu' vstupil millionnyi uchastnik" [The Millionth Participant Joined Yunarmia], December 5, 2021, https://ria.ru/20211205/yunarmiya-1762239903.html.

91. Vesti Obrazovanie, "Million detey v Yunarmiyu, po yacheike—v kazhduyu shkolu" [One Million Children in Yunarmiya, a Cell—in Every School], September 16, 2019, https://vogazeta.ru/articles/2019/9/16/upbringing/9398-million_detey_v_yunarmiyu_po_yacheyke__v_kazhduyu_shkolu.

92. Alla Hurska, "Putin Seeks to Garner Support of Russian Youth Through Military-Patriotic Upbringing (Part One)," *Eurasia Daily Monitor* 16, no. 51 (April 10, 2019), https://jamestown.org/program/putin-seeks-to-garner-support-of-russian-youth-through-military-patriotic-upbringing-part-one.

93. Aleksei Tarasov, "Detstvo—pod ruzhyo" [Childhood [Shoved] Under the Gun], *Novaya Gazeta*, March 13, 2019.

94. Military Patriotic Center, "O VPTs 'Vympel'" [About the Military-Patriotic Center "Vympel"], https://xn--b1aajydqc7c5b.xn--p1ai/o-nas.

95. Vympel Group Association, "Obrashchenie veteranov Gruppy 'Vympel' k molodyozhi" [Address to the Youth by the Veterans of the "Vympel" Group],

http://group-vympel.ru/index.php/press-sluzhba/stati/110-stati-v-press-byuro/511-obrashchenie-veteranov-gruppy-vympel-k-molodjozhi.

96. Ekaterina Khodzhaeva et al., "Mobilizing Patriotism in Russia: Federal Programs of Patriotic Education," *Russian Analytical Digest*, no. 207 (September 26, 2017), https://css.ethz.ch/en/publications/rad/rad-all-issues/details.html?id=/n/0/2/0/no_207_mobilizing_patriotism_in_russianr.

97. The "island chain" is the Kuril Islands, which were seized from Japan in 1945.

98. The "capital of amber" is Kalingrad, formerly Königsberg in East Prussia, which the Soviet Union received as spoils after World War II.

99. Teksty Pesen, "Kadety—Dyadya Vova my s tobou" [Uncle Vova, We're with You], November 27, 2018, http://teksti-pesenok.ru/en/10/kadety/tekst-pesni-Dyadya-Vova-my-s-toboy.

100. V1.ru, "V Kremle prokommentirovali pesnyu Anny Kuvychko 'Dyadya Vova, my s toboy'" [The Kremlin Commented on Anna Kovychko's Song "Uncle Vova, We Are with You"], November 15, 2017, https://v1.ru/text/gorod/2017/11/15/51500131.

101. V1.ru, "V Kremle prokommentirovali pesnyu Anny Kuvychko 'Dyadya Vova, my s toboy'" [The Kremlin Commented on Anna Kovychko's Song "Uncle Vova, We Are with You"].

102. Golos Kubani, "V krasnodarskoy shkole detey zastavlyayut pet' pesnyu "Dyadya Vova, my s toboy'" [Children Are Forced to Sing the Song "Uncle Vova, We Are with You" in a Krasnodar School], January 26, 2018, https://golos-kubani.ru/v-krasnodarskoj-shkole-detej-zastavlyayut-pet-pesnyu-dyadya-vova-my-s-toboj-video.

103. Kevin Rothrock (@KevinRothrock), "Apparently, this happened in the Pskov region, too. One parent shared the permission request slip sent home with his daughter from school with local journalists," Twitter, May 9, 2022, 10:57 a.m., https://twitter.com/KevinRothrock/status/1523678454977228800; and Kevin Rothrock (@KevinRothrock), "Children in Chita perform the 2017 propaganda hit 'Uncle Vova, We're With You,' where they vow to take up arms in 'the final battle,' if Putin sends Russia to war. (The song also calls for reconquering Alaska, by the way.)," Twitter, May 9, 2022, 9:36 a.m., https://twitter.com/KevinRothrock/status/1523658175525785601.

104. Vladimir Putin, "Annual Address to the Federal Assembly" [Annual Address to the Federal Assembly], May 10, 2006, http://en.kremlin.ru/events/president/transcripts/23577.

105. Levada Center, "Institutional Trust," October 22, 2018, https://www.levada.ru/en/2018/10/22/institutional-trust-4.

106. Levada Center, "Doverie institutam" [Trust in Institutions], September 21, 2020, https://www.levada.ru/2020/09/21/doverie-institutam.

107. Patriot Park, "Trenezhurniy Kompleks Parka Patriot" [Training Complex of Park Patriot], https://patriotp.ru/uslugi/igrovoy-tsentr-parka-patriot.

108. Patriot Park, "Trenezhurniy Kompleks Parka Patriot" [Training Complex of Park Patriot].

109. Vladimir Putin, "Vystupleniye na tseremonii otkrytiya Mezhdunarodnogo voyenno-tekhnicheskogo foruma 'Armiya-2015'" [Speech Delivered at the Opening of the International Military-Technological Forum "Army-2015" in Moscow], June 16, 2015, http://kremlin.ru/events/president/transcripts/49712.

110. Shaun Walker, "Vladimir Putin Opens Russian 'Military Disneyland' Patriot Park," *Guardian*, June 16, 2015, https://www.theguardian.com/world/2015/jun/16/vladimir-putin-opens-russian-military-disneyland-patriot-park.

111. Walker, "Vladimir Putin Opens Russian 'Military Disneyland' Patriot Park."

112. Severodvinsk.info, "V Severodvinske otkryli filial Parka Patriot" [A Branch of Patriot Park Was Opened in Severodvinsk], December 3, 2021, https://www.severodvinsk.info/pr/24602.

113. Milan Cherny, "Ekzamen s avtomatom. Kak 'voyenno-patrioticheskoye' obucheniye zakhvatyvayet shkoly, detsady i tvorcheskiye kruzhki" [The Exam with Machine Guns. How "Military-Patriotic" Education Captures Schools, Kindergartens and After-School Programs], Theins.ru, March 25, 2023, https://theins.ru/politika/260134.

114. Cherny, "Ekzamen s avtomatom. Kak 'voyenno-patrioticheskoye' obucheniye zakhvatyvayet shkoly, detsady i tvorcheskiye kruzhki" [The Exam with Machine Guns. How "Military-Patriotic" Education Captures Schools, Kindergartens and After-School Programs].

115. Cherny, "Ekzamen s avtomatom. Kak 'voyenno-patrioticheskoye' obucheniye zakhvatyvayet shkoly, detsady i tvorcheskiye kruzhki" [The Exam with Machine Guns. How "Military-Patriotic" Education Captures Schools, Kindergartens and After-School Programs].

116. Ol'ga Malinovna, *Aktual'noe Proshloe: Simvolicheskaya Politika Vlastvuyushchei Eliti i Dilemmy Rossiiskoi Identichnosti* [*The Urgent Past: Symbolic Politics of the Ruling Elite and the Dilemmas of Russian Identity*] (Moscow, Russia: Politicheskaya entsiklopedia, 2015), 104–5.

117. Sergei Medvedev, *Park Krymskogo perioda. Khroniki tretego sroka* [*The Crimean Era Park. Chronicles of (Putin's) Third Term*] (Moscow, Russia: Individuum, 2017), 104.

118. *Economist*, "A Parade of Power in Russia," May 9, 2008, https://www.economist.com/europe/2008/05/09/a-parade-of-power-in-russia.

119. "It is as if there had been no horror of the battles around Rzhev and the Kharkov [1942] encirclement," wrote a leading Russian military expert, "no stupid decisions and the losses so enormous that they continue to affect the demographic situation even three quarters of the century later. Instead, there were only endless victories under the wise leadership of comrade Stalin I.V." Alexander Golts, "Istoki 'pobedobesiya'" [The Sources of "Victory Run Amok"], *Ezhednevniy Zhurnal*, May 7, 2019, https://www.ej2020.ru/?a=note&id=33726.

120. See, for example, Leon Aron, "The Unraveling of the Legitimizing Myths, III: The Great Patriotic War," in *Roads to the Temple: Truth, Memory, Ideas, and Ideals in the Making of the Russian Revolution, 1987–1991* (New Haven, CT: Yale University Press, 2012).

121. Aron, "The Unraveling of the Legitimizing Myths, III."

122. Levinson, "Voyna kak proshloe i kak budushchee" [War as the Past and as the Future].

123. Putin, "Parad Pobedy na Krasnoy ploshchadi" [Speech Delivered at the Victory Day Parade on Red Square], May 9, 2021, http://kremlin.ru/events/president/news/65544.

124. According to the State Department, the US provided the Soviet Union with $11.3 billion of lend-lease assistance ($180 billion in 2020). The transfers included

400,000 Jeeps and trucks, 13,000 tanks, 2.7 million tons of petrol products, and 4.5 million tons of food. US Embassy and Consulates in Russia, "World War II Allies: U.S. Lend-Lease to the Soviet Union, 1941–1945," https://ru.usembassy.gov/world-war-ii-allies-u-s-lend-lease-to-the-soviet-union-1941-1945. Derek Leebaert, a prominent political and military historian of the United States, pointed out to me in an email that the Allies, including the US, used some seven billion barrels of oil to defeat the Axis. The US supplied six billion of those. The Soviets had oil, Dr. Leebaert adds, but not the "cracking machinery" to refine aviation fuel. So that, too, was supplied by the US, fueling the Soviet bombers and jet fighters. Derek Leebaert, email to Leon Aron, June 15, 2021.

125. Elena Novoselova, "Pochti polovina Rossiyan schitayut, chto Vtoraya mirovaya voyna nachalas' v 1941-m" [Nearly Half of Russians Think That World War II Began in 1941], *Rossiyskaya Gazeta*, September 2, 2021, https://rg.ru/2020/09/02/pochti-polovina-rossiian-schitaiut-chto-vtoraia-mirovaia-vojna-nachalas-v-1941-m.html.

126. Davis Center for Russian and Eurasian Studies, "The Use and Abuse of Soviet History in Putin's Russia," YouTube, April 6, 2021, https://www.youtube.com/watch?v=Ah-VxzHTFJsI.

127. Vladimir Putin, "Voyennyy parad na Krasnoy ploshchadi" [Speech Delivered at the Victory Day Parade on Red Square], Kremlin.ru, May 9, 2018, http://kremlin.ru/events/president/news/57436.

128. Alexander Golts, "Kak den' pobedy prevrashchayut v voenno-patrioticheskiy maskarad" [How Victory Day Is Being Made into a Military-Patriotic Masquerade], Otkrytye Media, May 8, 2019, https://openmedia.io/news/kak-den-pobedy-prevrashhayut-v-voenno-patrioticheskij-maskarad.

129. Putin, "Voyennyy parad na Krasnoy ploshchadi" [Speech Delivered at the Victory Day Parade on Red Square], May 9, 2018.

130. Putin, "Voyennyy parad na Krasnoy ploshchadi" [Speech Delivered at the Victory Day Parade on Red Square], May 9, 2018.

131. Putin, "Voyennyy parad na Krasnoy ploshchadi" [Victory Parade on Red Square], May 9, 2018.

132. Sergei Medvedev, "Nas zhdyot strashnaya i smeshnaya diktatura" [A Scary and Ridiculous Dictatorship Is Awaiting Us], Grani.ru, July 23, 2021, https://graniru.org/Society/m.282183.html.

133. Medvedev, "Nas zhdyot strashnaya i smeshnaya diktatura" [A Scary and Ridiculous Dictatorship Is Awaiting Us]; and Pat Finn, "The Power of Tradition: Russia's Massive Cathedral Is Dedicated to the Military," Architizer, https://architizer.com/blog/inspiration/stories/russia-military-cathedral.

134. Finn, "The Power of Tradition"; and Will Baumgardner, "Guns and God: Russian Orthodox Conservatism and the Militarization of Masculinity in Contemporary Russia" (bachelor's thesis, Pennsylvania State University, April 6, 2022), https://honors.libraries.psu.edu/files/final_submissions/7946. In addition, the diameter of the drum under the main dome is 19.45 meters for the year (1945) in which the war ended, and the diameter of the dome itself is 22.43 meters for the official time of the signing of the treaty that ended the war—22:43 (10:43 p.m.) Moscow time on May 8, 1945.

135. Finn, "The Power of Tradition."

136. Finn, "The Power of Tradition"; and Stroitel'stvo, "Vo skol'ko oboshlos' stroitel'stvo khrama vooruzhenny sil?" [How Much Did the Construction of the Cathedral of the Armed Forces Cost?], June 23, 2020, https://rcmm.ru/novosti/49570-vo-skolko-oboshlos-stroitelstvo-hrama-vooruzhennyh-sil.html.

137. Alexander Golts, "Istoki 'pobedobesiya'" [The Sources of "Victory Run Amuck"], *Ezhednevniy Zhurnal*, May 7, 2019, https://www.ej2020.ru/?a=note&id=33726.

138. Il'ya Reznik, "Nasha armiya" [Our Army], http://www.ilya-reznik.ru/txt/102_nasha_armiya.html.

139. Vesti, "V Detskom Sadu Poyavilis' Kaleendari s Okrovavlennymi Det'mi v Obraze Frontovikov" [Calendars with Bloodstained Children Dressed as Front-Line Soldiers Appeared in a Kindergarten], February 12, 2020, https://www.vesti.ru/doc.html?id=3239206#. According to the calendar's publisher, children of the firm's employees had posed for the montage, which had been intended solely for individual Victory Day presents. Only 500 copies had been printed, and the publisher had no idea how the calendars ended up in a kindergarten.

140. Irina Tumakova, "Strana sushchestvuet v regime upoitelnogo samoistrebleniay" [The Country Is in a State of Intoxicating Self-Destruction], *Novaya Gazeta*, May 18, 2023, https://novayagazeta.eu/articles/2023/05/18/strana-sushchestvuet-v-rezhime-upoitelnogo-samoistrebleniia.

141. Dmitry Smirnov, "Bessmertnyy Polk Srazhayetsya" [The Immortal Regiment Is Fighting], YouTube, 2017, https://www.youtube.com/watch?app=desktop&v=v7g6FdM2pgs. The video was created by the Saints Peter and Fevronia Foundation for the support of the family and demography.

142. Medvedev, *Park Krymskogo perioda. Khroniki tretego sroka* [*The Crimean Era Park. Chronicles of (Putin's) Third Term*], 108–9.

143. Levada Center, "Struktura i vosproizvodstvo pamyati o Sovetskom Soyuze" [The Structure and the Reproduction of Memory of the Soviet Union], March 24, 2020, https://www.levada.ru/2020/03/24/struktura-i-vosproizvodstvo-pamyati-o-sovetskom-soyuze.

144. Chapters 17 and 18 of *Roads to the Temple* are devoted to this debate. See Leon Aron, "In Man's Image, I: 'Privatizing' the State and Economy," in *Roads to the Temple: Truth, Memory, Ideas, and Ideals in the Making of the Russian Revolution, 1987–1991* (New Haven, CT: Yale University Press, 2012); and Leon Aron, "In Man's Image, II: The Empire, the 'Garrison State,' and the World," in *Roads to the Temple: Truth, Memory, Ideas, and Ideals in the Making of the Russian Revolution, 1987–1991* (New Haven, CT: Yale University Press, 2012).

145. Levada Center, "Dinamika otnsheniya k Stalinu" [The Changes in the Attitude Toward Stalin], April 16, 2019, https://www.levada.ru/2019/04/16/dinamika-otnosheniya-k-stalinu.

146. Levada Center, "41 protsent molodyozhi Rossii ne informirovany o stalinskikh repressiyakh" [41 Percent of Russian Young People Are Not Informed About Stalin's Repressions], June 24, 2020, https://www.levada.ru/2020/06/24/41-molodyozhi-rossii-ne-informirovany-o-stalinskih-repressiyah-11-o-sobytiyah-vtoroj-mirovoj-vojny.

147. Kolesknikov, "Russian Ideology After Crimea."

148. Levada Center, "22 iunya 2021 goda: 80 let posle nachala voyny" [June 22, 2021: 80 Years Since the Beginning of the War], June 22, 2021, https://www.levada.ru/2021/06/22/22-iyunya-2021-goda-80-let-posle-nachala-vojny.

149. Levada Center, "Dinamika otnsheniya k Stalinu" [The Changes in the Attitude Toward Stalin].

150. Levada Center, "Dinamika otnsheniya k Stalinu" [The Changes in the Attitude Toward Stalin]; and Levada Center, "Otnoshenie k Stalinu: Rossiya i Ukraina" [Attitudes Toward Stalin: Russia and Ukraine], June 23, 2021, https://www.levada.ru/2021/06/23/otnoshenie-k-stalinu-rossiya-i-ukraina.

151. Levada Center, "Samye vydayuushiesya lichnosti v istorii" [The Most Distinguished Figures in History], June 21, 2021, https://www.levada.ru/2021/06/21/samye-vydayushhiesya-lichnosti-v-istorii.

152. Joseph Stalin, "Slava Nashemu Velikomu Narodu, Narodu-Pobeditelyu!" [Glory to Our Great Nation—the Victorious Nation!], Istoria, May 8, 1945, https://histrf.ru/read/articles/slava-nashiemu-vielikomu-narodu-narodu-pobieditieliu.

153. In his 18 years in power, Leonid Brezhnev used the phrase once, in a speech on the 60th anniversary of the October Revolution in 1977. Aleksandr Khantskiy, "1974–1979 (Tret'ye Pyatiletie Brezhneva—Stranitsa 10)" [1974–1979 (Brezhnev's Third 5-Year Plan)—Page 10], Leninism, January 12, 2013, https://leninism.su/revolution-and-civil-war/4251-velikij-oktyabr-god-za-godom-1917-1990.html?start=9. Mikhail Gorbachev's minister of defense, Dmitry Yazov, praised *narod-pobeditel* at the 1990 Victory Parade. RedSamurai84, "HD Soviet Army Parade, Victory Day 1990," YouTube, May 18, 2016, https://www.youtube.com/watch?v=Yrj3vhrI7aY. Boris Yeltsin said it once in 1999. Stanislav Derkachev, "9 maya 1999g. Moskva. Krasnaya Ploshchad'. Voyenniy Parad." [May 9, 1999. Moscow. Red Square. Military Parade.], 2011, https://www.youtube.com/watch?v=dc4qNXDenK0. In the 18 speeches he delivered on May 9 between 2000 and 2022, Putin used the phrase 13 times.

154. Joshua Yaffa, "Dmitry Kiselev Is Redefining the Art of Russian Propaganda," *New Republic*, July 1, 2014, https://newrepublic.com/article/118438/dmitry-kiselev-putins-favorite-tv-host-russias-top-propogandist.

155. Volkov and Medvedev, "Vozvrashchenie generalissimusa" [The Return of the Generalissimo].

156. Kirill Rogov, "Krepost' vrastaet v zemlyu" [The Fortress Grows Down into the Soil], Liberal Mission Foundation, https://liberal.ru/files/articles/7335/krepost.pdf.

157. Levada Center, "Nasha glavnaya strana" [Our Most Important Country], June 1, 2021, https://www.levada.ru/2021/06/01/nasha-glavnaya-strana.

158. Levada Center, "Nasha glavnaya strana" [Our Most Important Country].

159. Vladimir Putin, "Polnyy tekst vystupleniya prezidenta RF Vladimira Putina v Gosdume 10 marta 2020 goda" [Speech Delivered to the State Duma], *Nezavisimaya Gazeta*, March 10, 2020, https://www.ng.ru/politics/2020-03-10/100_putin10032020.html.

160. Kiev v Gorode, "Press-konferentsia Putina: Kratkoe Soderzhanie" [Putin's Press Conference: A Short Summary], March 4, 2014, https://kiev.vgorode.ua/news/sobytyia/213662-putyn-hovoryt-o-krysakh-yanukovyche-uchenyiakh-v-krymu-y-vyvode-voisk-yz-ukrayny.

161. Pavel Felgenhauer, "Russia's Direct Action 'Black Ops' in Europe," *Eurasia Daily Monitor*, April 29, 2021, https://jamestown.org/program/russias-direct-action-black-ops-in-europe.

162. Paul Goble, "Moscow Says US Waging Biological War Against Russia," *Eurasia Daily Monitor*, July 28, 2021, https://jamestown.org/program/moscow-says-us-waging-biological-war-against-russia.

163. Nikolai Patrushev, "Nadeemsya, chto v Vashingtone vsyo zhe vozobladayet zdravyy smysl" [We Are Hoping That Sanity Will Prevail in Washington], *Kommersant*, April 7, 2021, https://www.kommersant.ru/doc/4762137.

164. *Red Star*, "Voyennaya Nauka Smotrit v Budushcheye" [Military Science Looks to the Future], March 26, 2018, http://archive.redstar.ru/index.php/component/k2/item/36626-voennaya-nauka-smotrit-v-budushchee.

165. *Red Star*, "Voyennaya Nauka Smotrit v Budushcheye" [Military Science Looks to the Future].

166. Dmitry Kiselev, "Rossiya Mozhet Prevratit' SShA v Padioaktivniy Pepel" [Russia Can Turn the USA into Radioactive Ash], YouTube, March 17, 2014, https://www.youtube.com/watch?v=TA9mVLomYo8.

167. Daisy Sindelar, "In Choosing Kiselyov, Media Critics Say Putin Opts for Personal Propagandist," Radio Free Europe/Radio Liberty, December 10, 2013, https://www.rferl.org/a/russia-media-kiselyov-propagandist/25195932.html.

168. Alexei Levinson and Stepan Goncharov, "Voyna vmesto budyshchego—vykhod iz anomicheskogo soznaniya" [War Instead of the Future—an Exit from the Anomie-Affected Consciousness], *Vestnik obshchestvennogo mneniya* 121, no. 3–4 (July–December 2015), https://cyberleninka.ru/article/n/voyna-vmesto-buduschego-vyhod-dlya-anomicheskogo-soznaniya/viewer.

169. Levada Center, "Pochemu voyna tak prityagatel'na dlya Rossiyan?" [Why Is War So Appealing to Russians?], November 17, 2015, https://www.levada.ru/2015/11/17/pochemu-vojna-tak-prityagatelna-dlya-rossiyan; and Levada Center, "Nasha glavnaya strana" [Our Most Important Country].

170. Putin, "Obrashcheniye Prezidenta Rossiyskoy Federatsii" [Speech Delivered in Moscow Announcing the Beginning of Russia's Invasion of Ukraine].

171. Vladimir Putin, "Obrashcheniye Prezidenta Rossiyskoy Federatsii" [Speech Delivered to State Duma Deputies, Members of the Federal Assembly, Heads of Russian Regions, and Representatives of Civil Society in the Kremlin], March 18, 2014, http://kremlin.ru/events/president/news/20603.

172. Putin, "Zasedaniye kollegii FSB Rossii" [Speech Delivered in Moscow at a Meeting of the Collegium of the FSB].

173. Vladimir Putin, "Zasedaniye Mezhdunarodnogo diskussionnogo kluba 'Valday'" [Speech Delivered at the Concluding Session of the Valdai Club], October 22, 2015, http://kremlin.ru/events/president/news/50548.

174. Valery Gerasimov, "Vektory razvitiya voyennoy strategii" [Key Directions of the Development of Military Strategy, Speech at the Meeting of the Academy of Military Science], *Red Star*, March 4, 2019, https://web.archive.org/web/20190810143322/http://redstar.ru/vektory-razvitiya-voennoj-strategii.

175. Gerasimov, "Vektory razvitiya voyennoy strategii" [Key Directions of the Development of Military Strategy, Speech at the Meeting of the Academy of Military Science].

176. Gerasimov, "Vektory razvitiya voyennoy strategii" [Key Directions of the Development of Military Strategy, Speech at the Meeting of the Academy of Military Science].

177. Gerasimov, "Vektory razvitiya voyennoy strategii" [Key Directions of the Development of Military Strategy, Speech at the Meeting of the Academy of Military Science].

178. International Memorial, "Russia's Supreme Court Approves Liquidation of International Memorial," February 28, 2022, https://www.memo.ru/en-us/memorial/departments/intermemorial/news/690.

179. Daria Skibo, "Inostrannykh agentov stanet bol'she" [There Will Be More Foreign Agents], Eurasianet, February 25, 2020, https://russian.eurasianet.org/иностранных-агентов-статет-больше.

180. Ivan Nechepurenko, "Meeting a Russian Scientist? He Might Need to Report on You," *New York Times*, August 14, 2019, https://www.nytimes.com/2019/08/14/world/europe/russia-science-rules.html.

181. Nechepurenko, "Meeting a Russian Scientist?" These guidelines put one in the mind of a passage in Alexander Solzhenitsyn's *In the First Circle*, which I read in the Samizdat version while still in the Soviet Union. A Soviet diplomat attempted to protect a family doctor from being arrested for passing an experimental cancer drug to a foreign colleague. (In the full, 96-chapter version of the book, published abroad, the diplomat calls the American embassy to warn about the hand-off of nuclear secrets to a Soviet spy in New York.) Aleksandr Solzhenitsyn, *In the First Circle* (1968; New York: Harper Perennial, 2009).

182. Victor Kudryavtsev, who worked at the Central Scientific Research Institute of Machine Construction, died after 14 months in pretrial detention. Professor Valery Mitko, a corresponding member of the St. Petersburg Academy of Engineering, has been awaiting trial under house arrest since February 2020, as has been Valery Golubkin of the Central Aerohydrodynamic Institute since April 2021. Anatoly Gubanov of the Central Aerohydrodynamic Institute has been in pretrial detention in the infamous Lefortovo prison since December 2020.

183. *Kommersant*, "Chislo uezzhayushchikh iz Rossii uchyonykh vyroslo v pyat raz s 2012 goda" [The Number of Scientists Leaving Russia Increased Five-Fold Since 2012], April 20, 2021, https://www.kommersant.ru/doc/4782133.

184. Nechepurenko, "Meeting a Russian Scientist?"

185. Irina Tumakova, "Rossiya na izmene" [The Treasonous Russia], *Novaya Gazeta*, July 10, 2020, https://novayagazeta.ru/articles/2020/07/09/86211-rossiya-na-izmene.

186. Radio Svoboda, "Protiv advocate Pavlova vosbuzhdeno delo o gosudarstvennoy izmene" [The Lawyer Pavlov Was Charged with State Treason], December 21, 2021, https://www.svoboda.org/a/protiv-advokata-ivana-pavlova-vozbuzhdeno-ugolovnoe-delo-o-gosizmene/31619740.html.

187. Tumakova, "Rossiya na izmene" [The Treasonous Russia].

188. Radio Svoboda, "Protiv advocate Pavlova vosbuzhdeno delo o gosudarstvennoy izmene" [The Lawyer Pavlov Was Charged with State Treason].

189. Alexander Golts, *Military Reform and Militarism in Russia* (Washington, DC: Jamestown Foundation, December 2018), https://jamestown.org/product/military-reform-and-militarism-in-russia.

190. Golts, *Military Reform and Militarism in Russia*.

191. Golts, *Military Reform and Militarism in Russia*.

192. Andrei Kondrashov, "Krym. Put' na rodinu, dokumentalniy fil'm Andreya Kondrashova" [Crimea: The Way Home, Documentary Film by Andrei Kondrashov], YouTube, October 4, 2020, https://www.youtube.com/watch?v=PGGNXIQXlcU.

193. Kondrashov, "Krym. Put' na rodinu, dokumentalniy fil'm Andreya Kondrashova" [Crimea: The Way Home, Documentary Film by Andrei Kondrashov].

194. Kondrashov, "Krym. Put' na rodinu, dokumentalniy fil'm Andreya Kondrashova" [Crimea: The Way Home, Documentary Film by Andrei Kondrashov].

195. Alexander Tsipko, "Istoki i sud'ba sakralizatsii vlasti Putina" [The Origins and the Fate of the Sacralization of Putin's Authority], *Nezavisimaya Gazeta*, May 20, 2020, http://www.ng.ru/ideas/2020-05-20/7_7865_sacralization.html.

196. Alexander Gamov, "25 dekabrya 1991 goda: kak v Kremle khoronili Sovetskii Soyuz" [25th of December 1991: How the Kremlin Buried the Soviet Union], *Komsomolskaya Pravda*, December 25, 2021, https://www.kp.ru/daily/28374.5/4524245.

197. Vladimir Putin, "Vladimir Putin posetil Natsional'nyy tsentr upravleniya oboronoy Rossii, gde provol soveshchaniye o deystviyakh Vozdushno-kosmicheskikh sil Rossiyskoy Federatsii v Siriyskoy Arabskoy Respublike" [Remarks at the National Defense Center, Where He Conducted a Meeting on the Activities of the Airspace Forces of the Russian Federation in the Syrian Arab Republic], November 17, 2015, http://kremlin.ru/events/president/news/50714.

198. Vladimir Putin, "Vladimir Putin prinyal uchastiye v yezhegodnom rasshirennom zasedanii kollegii Ministerstva vnutrennikh del Rossiyskoy Federatsii" [Speech Delivered at an Expanded Meeting of Colleagues of the Ministry of Interior Affairs of Russia in Moscow], March 3, 2021, http://kremlin.ru/events/president/news/65090.

199. *Morskoi Sbornik*, "Glavny Voenno-Morskoy Parad" [Main Naval Parade], 2019, https://heritage-institute.ru/wp-content/uploads/2019/10/mc_9-2019_%D0%BB%D0%B5%D0%BD%D0%B8%D0%BD%D0%BA%D0%B0_s-1_compressed.pdf.

200. Alexander Golts, "Putin's Militarized Election Campaign," *Eurasia Daily Monitor* 15, no. 40 (March 15, 2018), https://jamestown.org/program/putins-militarized-election-campaign.

201. Putin did not attend the Victory Day Parades during Dmitry Medvedev's place-holding from 2008 to 2012.

202. Pavel Baev, "Naval Parade Plays into Putin's Dangerous Vanity," *Eurasia Daily Monitor* 18, no. 118 (July 26, 2021), https://jamestown.org/program/naval-parade-plays-into-putins-dangerous-vanity.

203. Vladimir Soldatkin, "Putin Marks 63rd Birthday with Ice Hockey Match, Syria War Briefing," Reuters, October 7, 2015, https://www.reuters.com/article/us-russia-putin-birthday-idUSKCN0S121720151007; and *RBK*, "Minoborony obnarodovalo video puska raket Kaspiyskoy flotilii po Syrii" [The Ministry of Defense Made Public the Video of the Launching of Missiles into Syria by the Caspian Fleet], October 7, 2015, https://www.rbc.ru/politics/07/10/2015/5615172a9a7947c1ce9d0346.

204. Valery Gerasimov, "Vstrecha s nachal'nikom Genshtaba Vooruzhonnykh Sil Valeriyem Gerasimovym" [Meeting with Chief of the General Staff of the Russian Armed Forces Valery Gerasimov], October 7, 2020, http://kremlin.ru/events/president/news/64169.

205. Vladimir Putin, "Vstrecha s nachal'nikom Genshtaba Vooruzhonnykh Sil Valeriyem Gerasimovym" [Remarks Delivered in a Virtual Meeting with Chief of the General Staff of the Russian Armed Forces Valery Gerasimov].

Chapter 4. Worshipping the Nukes

1. Vladimir Putin, "Yezhegodnie poslania prezidenta RF federal'nomu sobraniyu" [The Yearly Addresses of the President of the Russian Federation to the Federation Council], TASS, February 28, 2018, https://tass.ru/info/4995125; and Andrey Veselov, "Chto rasskazal Vladimir Putin strane i miru v poslanii Federal'nomu Sobraniyu" [What Putin Told the Country and the World in His Message to the Federal Assembly], RIA Novost, March 1, 2018, https://ria.ru/20180301/1515574957.html.

2. Putin, "Yezhegodnie poslania prezidenta RF federal'nomu sobraniyu" [The Yearly Addresses of the President of the Russian Federation to the Federation Council].

3. Vladimir Putin, "Poslaniye Prezidenta Federal'nomu Sobraniyu" [Presidential Address to the Federal Assembly], Kremlin.ru, March 1, 2018, http://kremlin.ru/events/president/news/56957.

4. Putin, "Poslaniye Prezidenta Federal'nomu Sobraniyu" [Presidential Address to the Federal Assembly].

5. Putin, "Poslaniye Prezidenta Federal'nomu Sobraniyu" [Presidential Address to the Federal Assembly].

6. Neil MacFarquhar and David E. Sanger, "Putin's 'Invincible' Missile Is Aimed at U.S. Vulnerabilities," *New York Times*, March 1, 2018, https://www.nytimes.com/2018/03/01/world/europe/russia-putin-speech.html.

7. Putin, "Poslaniye Prezidenta Federal'nomu Sobraniyu" [Presidential Address to the Federal Assembly].

8. Putin, "Poslaniye Prezidenta Federal'nomu Sobraniyu" [Presidential Address to the Federal Assembly].

9. Putin, "Poslaniye Prezidenta Federal'nomu Sobraniyu" [Presidential Address to the Federal Assembly].

10. Sarmat had its first test flight four years later, in April 2022. See Mike Wall, "Russia Conducts 1st Full Flight Test of New 'Sarmat' Intercontinental Ballistic Missile," April 22, 2022, Space.com, https://www.space.com/russia-test-launch-sarmat-icbm.

11. Putin, "Poslaniye Prezidenta Federal'nomu Sobraniyu" [Presidential Address to the Federal Assembly].

12. Putin, "Poslaniye Prezidenta Federal'nomu Sobraniyu" [Presidential Address to the Federal Assembly].

13. Russia did deploy two versions of the older SS-27 ICBM: 78 single-warhead Topol-Ms and 72 four-warhead Yars. Hans Kristensen and Matt Korda, "Russian Nuclear

Forces, 2019," *Bulletin of the Atomic Scientists* 75, no. 2 (March 4, 2019): 73–84, https://doi.org/10.1080/00963402.2019.1580891.

14. The missile was not nearly as successful over Kyiv on May 16, 2023, when six Kinzhals were shot down by the US-supplied MIM-104 Patriot battery.

15. Aleksandr Khrolenko, "Sarmat gotovitsya letat'" [Sarmat Is Getting Ready to Fly], Sputnik Belarus, May 17, 2022, https://sputnik.by/20200528/Raketa-Sarmat-gotovitsya-letat-dlya-chego-Rossii-novaya-Satana-1044749111.html.

16. According to top Russian independent experts, both the US and the Soviet Union had looked into a nuclear-powered missile in the 1950s and eventually abandoned the project because a nuclear reactor would be too heavy to combine with any kind of anti-radiation protection. In flight, such a rocket would contaminate everything below and was thus impossible to test. In addition, it was much slower and more expensive than a regular intercontinental ballistic missile (ICBM). See Alexander Golts, "V pogone za sverkhoruzhiem. Pomogut li Rossii noveyshie rakety vernut' status superderzhavy" [In Search of a Superweapon. Will the Newest Rockets Help Russia Return to the Status of a Superpower?], Republic, November 26, 2019, https://republic.ru/posts/95309. A former Russian nuclear weapons engineer confirmed much of this in an interview with the now banned *Novaya Gazeta*. See Andrey Gorbachevsky and Irina Tumakova, "Eto prosto opasno" [This Is Simply Dangerous], *Novaya Gazeta*, September 27, 2019, https://novayagazeta.ru/articles/2019/09/25/82114-eto-prosto-opasno. An expert from the Nuclear Information Project at the Federation of American Scientists, too, described the weapon as "a kind of flying Chernobyl," an "unshielded nuclear reactor that's essentially just flying around pumping out radiation." See Ann Simmons, "Blast, Radiation Unnerve Russians Living near Test Site," *Wall Street Journal*, September 5, 2019, https://www.wsj.com/articles/blast-radiation-unnerve-russians-living-near-test-site-11569403801. Half a year later, experts concluded that an explosion at the Nyonoksa weapons testing site northwest of Arkhangelsk, in which at least seven people were killed and radiation spiked in the area, was connected to this project. At a meeting with the families of the killed engineers and scientists, Vladimir Putin vowed to "continue to perfect this weapon no matter what happens." See Christina Levieva, "Prezident Rossii vruchil nagrady vdovam pogibshikh pri ispytanii noveishego oruzhiya pod Severodvinskom" [The President of Russia Handed Out Awards to the Widows of Those Who Died While Testing Cutting Edge Weaponry near Severodvinsk], Perviiy Kanal, 2019, https://www.1tv.ru/news/2019-11-22/376180-prezident_rossii_vruchil_nagrady_vdovam_pogibshih_pri_ispytanii_noveyshego_oruzhiya_pod_severodvinskom. For Ukrainian air defenses, see Gleb Garanich and Sergiy Karazy, "Kyiv Says It Shoots Down Volley of Russian Hypersonic Missiles," Reuters, March 16, 2023, https://www.reuters.com/world/europe/air-defence-systems-repelling-attacks-ukraine-early-tuesday-officials-2023-05-16.

17. Sergei Karakaev, "Noviy raketniy kompleks 'Sarmat.' Mnenie rossiiskogo eksperta" [The New Rocket System 'Sarmat.' The Opinion of a Russian Expert], Nauka i Tekhnika, December 17, 2019, https://naukatehnika.com/raketnyj-kompleks-sarmat.html. The author was at the time commander of the Strategic Rocket Force.

18. Kristensen and Korda, "Russian Nuclear Forces, 2019."

19. Vladimir Putin, "Poslaniye Prezidenta Federal'nomu Sobraniyu" [Speech Delivered to the Federal Assembly in Moscow], Kremlin.ru, February 20, 2021, http://kremlin.ru/events/president/news/59863.

20. Vladimir Putin, "S'yezd partii 'Yedinaya Rossiya'" [Speech Delivered at the 19th Congress of the United Russia Party in Moscow], November 23, 2019, http://kremlin.ru/events/president/news/62105.

21. Steven Simon, "Hypersonic Missiles Are a Game Changer," *New York Times*, January 2, 2020, https://www.nytimes.com/2020/01/02/opinion/hypersonic-missiles.html.

22. Simon, "Hypersonic Missiles Are a Game Changer."

23. Julian Cooper, "The Funding of Nuclear Weapons in the Russian Federation," University of Oxford, Changing Character of War Centre, October 2018, https://static1.squarespace.com/static/55faab67e4b0914105347194/t/5bb1ea3ee4966 b5320fa197c/1538386496442/The+funding+of+nuclear+weapons+in+the+Russian+ Federation.pdf.

24. Premier.gov.ru, "V. V. Putin vstretilsya v g. Sarove s ekspertami po global'nym ugrozam natsional'noy bezopasnosti, ukrepleniyu oboronosposobnosti i povysheniyu boyegotovnosti Vooruzhonnykh sil Rossiyskoy Federatsii" [Vladimir Vladimirovich Putin Met in the City of Sarov with Experts on Global Threats to National Security, Strengthening Defense Capabilities and Increasing the Combat Readiness of the Armed Forces of the Russian Federation], February 24, 2012, https://web.archive.org/ web/20230202113229/http://archive.premier.gov.ru/events/news/18248. For a detailed list of new or upgraded nuclear weapons added to the Russian arsenal in the past decade, see Stephen Blank, "Putin's 'Asymmetric Strategy': Nuclear and New-Type Weapons in Russian Defense Policy," in *Russia's Military Strategy and Doctrine*, ed. Glen E. Howard and Matthew Czekaj (Washington, DC: Jamestown Foundation, February 2019), https://jamestown.org/wp-content/uploads/2019/02/Russias-Military-Strategy-and-Doctrine-web-1.pdf.

25. Vladimir Putin, "Stenograficheskiy otchyot o press-konferentsii dlya rossiiskikh i inostrannykh zhurnalistov" [Transcribed Account of the Press Conference for Russian and International Journalists], February 1, 2007, http://kremlin.ru/events/president/ transcripts/24026. "Traditional denominations" are those officially recognized: Buddhism, Islam, Judaism, and Orthodoxy.

26. Kremlin.ru, "Prezident prinyal uchastie v prazdnichnykh torzhestvakh po sluchaiyu 100-letiya kanonizatsii prepodobnogo Serafima Sarovskogo" [The President Took Part in the Celebratory Activities in Honor of the 100 Year Anniversary of the Canonization of the Venerable Seraphim of Sarov], July 31, 2003, http://kremlin.ru/events/ president/news/29121.

27. Vladimir Putin, "Vystupleniye na tseremonii blagosloveniya krestnogo khoda" [Address at the Ceremony of the Blessing of the Procession of the Cross], Kremlin.ru, July 31, 2003, http://www.special.kremlin.ru/events/president/transcripts/22071; and Vladimir Putin, "Vstupitel'noye slovo na vstreche s uchenymi Rossiyskogo federal'nogo yadernogo tsentra" [Introductory Remarks at the Meeting with Scientists of the Russian Federal Nuclear Center], Kremlin.ru, July 31, 2003, http://kremlin.ru/events/president/ transcripts/22073.

28. Dmitry Adamsky, *Russian Nuclear Orthodoxy* (Stanford, CA: Stanford University Press, 2019), 190.

29. Viktor Yuzbashev, "Moleben Yadernomu Oruzhiyu" [A Public Prayer for Nuclear Weapons], *Nezavisimoie Voennoe Obrozrenie*, September 7, 2007, https://nvo.ng.ru/forces/2007-09-07/3_moleben.html; and *Blagovest*, "V khrame Khrista Spasitelya nachalis' torzhestva po sluchayu 60-letiya osnovaniya yadernogo kompleksa Rossii" [Services on the Occasion of the 60th Anniversary of the Foundation of the Russian Nuclear Complex Began in the Church of Christ the Savior], September 4, 2007, http://blagovest-info.ru/index.php?ss=2&s=3&id=15605.

30. Patriarchia.ru, "Patriarshee privetstvie uchastnikam prazdnovaniya 60-letiya so dnya osnovaniya 12-go Glavnogo upravleniya ministerstva oborony RF" [Patriarch's Greeting to the Participants of the Celebration of the 60th Anniversary of the Main Department of the Ministry of Defense], September 4, 2007, http://www.patriarchia.ru/db/text/290432.html.

31. Yuzbashev, "Moleben Yadernomu Oruzhiyu" [A Public Prayer for Nuclear Weapons].

32. Vladimir Putin, "Zasedanie diskussionnogo kluba 'Valdai'" [Remarks at a Session of the "Valdai" Discussion Club], Kremlin.ru, October 18, 2018, http://kremlin.ru/events/president/news/58848.

33. Azattyq TV, "Putin: 'My, kak mucheniki popadyom v ray. A oni sdokhnut'" [Putin: "We, Like Martyrs, Will End Up in Paradise. And They Will Just Croak"], YouTube, 2018, https://www.youtube.com/watch?v=IO_AjWjjfCo.

34. Sarmat's US counterpart, the silo-based Minuteman III, is half the size and six times lighter. Although capable of carrying three warheads of 335 kilotons each, the Minutemen are deployed with a single warhead. The other US strategic missile, the submarine-launched Trident II, could be armed with a maximum of eight 455 kiloton warheads but is believed to be equipped with four or five. Minuteman III entered service in 1970 and is projected to stay on until at least 2030. Trident II was first deployed in 1990 and under current Navy plans may be in service as far as 2084 after a "life extension program." The software, engines, and guidance components of both systems have been updated over the years, but the only truly new addition to the US arsenal in decades has been the tactical 5 kiloton W76-2 warhead, which can be mounted on the Trident II. Center for Strategic and International Studies, Missile Defense Project, "Minuteman III," August 2, 2021, https://missilethreat.csis.org/missile/minuteman-iii; Hans M. Kristensen and Matt Korda, "United States Nuclear Forces, 2020," *Bulletin of the Atomic Scientists* 76, no. 1 (January 13, 2020): 46–60, https://www.tandfonline.com/doi/figure/10.1080/00963402.2019.1701286?scroll=top&needAccess=true; Center for Strategic and International Studies, Missile Defense Project, "Trident II," July 30, 2021, https://missilethreat.csis.org/missile/trident; Congressional Research Service, "U.S. Strategic Nuclear Forces: Background, Developments, and Issues," December 13, 2021, https://sgp.fas.org/crs/nuke/RL33640.pdf; CBS News, "The U.S. Makes the First Addition to Its Arsenal in Decades," February 4, 2020, https://www.cbsnews.com/news/w76-2-us-first-major-addition-nuclear-arsenal-decades-low-yield-long-range; and William Arkin and Hans M. Kristensen, "US Deploys New Low-Yield Nuclear Submarine

Warhead," Federation of American Scientists, January 29, 2020, https://fas.org/blogs/security/2020/01/w76-2deployed.

35. Hans M. Kristensen and Matt Korda, "Russian Nuclear Weapons, 2022," *Bulletin of the Atomic Scientists* 78, no. 2 (2022): 98–121, https://www.tandfonline.com/doi/full/10.1080/00963402.2022.2038907.

36. Golts, "V pogone za sverkhoruzhiem. Pomogut li Rossii noveyshie rakety vernut' status superderzhavy" [In Search of a Superweapon. Will the Newest Rockets Help Russia Return to the Status of a Superpower?].

37. Golts, "V pogone za sverkhoruzhiem. Pomogut li Rossii noveyshie rakety vernut' status superderzhavy" [In Search of a Superweapon. Will the Newest Rockets Help Russia Return to the Status of a Superpower?].

38. Pavel Felgenhauer, "Strategic War Games Zapad Has Begun," *Eurasia Daily Monitor* 14, no. 112 (September 14, 2017), https://jamestown.org/program/strategic-war-game-zapad-2017-has-begun.

39. Kremlin.ru, "Strategicheskie voyennye ucheniya 'Zapad'" [Strategic Military Exercises "Zapad"], September 26, 2013, http://kremlin.ru/events/president/news/19290; and Vladimir Putin, "Vstupitel'noye slovo na soveshchanii o predvaritel'nykh itogakh sovmestnykh rossiysko-belorusskikh ucheniy 'Zapad-2013'" [Opening Remarks Delivered at the Conference on the Preliminary Results of the Joint Russian-Belorussian Military Exercise "Zapad 2013"], Kremlin.ru, September 26, 2013, http://kremlin.ru/events/president/transcripts/19292.

40. Kremlin.ru, "Vladimir Putin Took Part in Strategic Nuclear Forces' Training," October 27, 2017, http://en.kremlin.ru/events/president/news/55929; and Dmitry Kiselev, "Putin nazhal na 'krasnuyu knopku'" [Putin Pressed the "Red Button"], *Vesti Nedeli*, October 29, 2017, https://www.vesti.ru/article/1601485.

41. *RBK*, "Minoboroniy Provelo Ispytanie Ballisticheskikh Raket 'Yars' i 'Sineva'" [The Ministry of Defense Carried Out a Test of the Ballistic Missiles "Yars" and "Sineva"], December 9, 2020, https://www.rbc.ru/rbcfreenews/5fd0f7589a79476997997e6b.

42. Federation of American Scientists, "Russian Military Doctrine, November 1993," November 2, 1993, https://nuke.fas.org/guide/russia/doctrine/russia-mil-doc.html.

43. *Nezavisimaya Gazeta*, "Voennaya doktrina Rossiyskoy Federatsii" [Military Doctrine of the Russian Federation], April 22, 2000, https://www.ng.ru/politics/2000-04-22/5_doktrina.html.

44. Nikolai Patrushev, "Menyaetsya Rossiya, menyaetsya i eyo voennaya doktrina" [As Russia Changes So Does Its Military Doctrine], *Izvestiya*, October 14, 2009, https://iz.ru/news/354178.

45. Kremlin.ru, "Voyennaya Doktrina Rossiyskoi Federatsii" [Military Doctrine of the Russian Federation], February 5, 2010, http://kremlin.ru/supplement/461. The current Military Doctrine, which Putin signed in 2014, repeats the same provisions. See *Rossiskaya Gazeta*, "Voennaya doktrina Rossiiskoi Federatsii" [Military Doctrine of the Russian Federation], December 30, 2014, https://rg.ru/documents/2014/12/30/doktrina-dok.html. So does the 2020 decree, "Foundations of State Policy in the Area of Nuclear Deterrence." See Kremlin.ru, "Ukaz Prezidenta Rossiiskoi Federatsii ot 02.06.2020 g. No. 355" [Decree of the President of the Russian Federation from 02.06.2020, No. 355], June

2, 2020, http://kremlin.ru/acts/bank/45562. As of this writing, the most recent Nuclear Posture Review of the United States foresees the "employment of nuclear weapons" in the case of "significant non-nuclear strategic attacks" and "in extreme circumstances," requiring the defense of "vital interests of the United States, its allies and partners." Office of the Secretary of Defense, "Nuclear Posture Review—February 2018," 2018, https://media.defense.gov/2018/Feb/02/2001872886/-1/-1/1/2018-NUCLEAR-POSTURE-REVIEW-FINAL-REPORT.PDF.

46. Vladimir Putin, "Poslaniye Prezidenta Federal'nomu Sobraniyu" [Speech Delivered to the Federal Assembly in Moscow], Kremlin.ru, March 1, 2018, http://kremlin.ru/events/president/news/56957.

47. Kondrashov, "Krym: Put' na Rodinu" [Crimea: The Way Home, Documentary Film by Andrei Kondrashov].

48. Vladimir Putin, "Obrashcheniye Prezidenta Rossiyskoy Federatsii" [Speech Delivered in Moscow Announcing the Beginning of Russia's Invasion of Ukraine], Kremlin.ru, February 24, 2022, http://kremlin.ru/events/president/news/67843. In their exchange two months after the invasion, two of Putin's favorite propagandists spun the boss's already fairly transparent hint to a stark conclusion. Recalling her conversation with an "expert" who had broached the possibility of Russia losing the war with Ukraine, the head of RT, Margarita Simonyan, said that "knowing our leader, Vladimir Vladimirovich Putin," there was no chance that Russia would just roll over, "folding its little hands." A nuclear strike and World War III looked more probable. In reply, Vladimir Solovyov, on whose popular talk show the conversation took place, quoted Putin: "We will go to heaven, but they [the West] will croak." Vladimir Solovyov, "Efir 26.04.2022—Margarita Simon'yan: Nyet Shansov, Chto My Prosto Slozhim Lapki" [Broadcast 26.04.2022—Margarita Simonyan: There Is No Chance That We Will Just Quietly Surrender], April 26, 2022, https://www.vsoloviev.ru/vecher/8108.

49. Vladimir Isachenkov, "Russia Holds Drills with Nuclear Subs, Land-Based Missiles," AP News, March 1, 2022, https://apnews.com/article/russia-ukraine-vladimir-putin-business-europe-moscow-563573526a93ea73a95698d8ddb61b9c.

50. Russia "crossed the nuclear threshold" at the final phase of the annual conventional exercises, concluded a leading expert. When faced with an imaginary attack by a superior enemy, it deployed strategic (long-range) aviation and surface-to-surface missiles. Russian strategists appeared to believe that a counterattack by nonstrategic nuclear weapons would restore the status quo ante and "terminate hostilities" without unleashing a large-scale nuclear exchange. Dmitry Adamsky, "If War Comes Tomorrow: Russian Thinking About 'Regional Nuclear Deterrence,'" Journal of Slavic Military Studies 27, no. 1 (March 10, 2014): 174.

51. See, for example, Dave Johnson, Russia's Conventional Precision Strike Capabilities, Regional Crises, and Nuclear Thresholds, Lawrence Livermore National Laboratory and Center for Global Security Research, February 2018, 67, 85, https://cgsr.llnl.gov/content/assets/docs/Precision-Strike-Capabilities-report-v3-7.pdf; Katarzyna Zysk, "Nonstrategic Nuclear Weapons in Russia's Evolving Military Doctrine," Bulletin of the Atomic Scientists, September 3, 2017, 323; Nikolai Sokov, "Why Russia Calls a Limited Nuclear Strike 'De-Escalation,'" Bulletin of the Atomic Scientists, March 13, 2014; and Blank, "Putin's 'Asymmetric Strategy,'" 281. If deterrence fails, hypothesized a group of

experts, the use of nonstrategic nuclear weapons could become "a means to de-escalate military actions." See Michael Kofman, Anya Fink, and Kasey Jeffrey Edmonds, *Russian Strategy for Escalation Management: Evolution of Key Concepts*, Center for Naval Analysis, April 2020, https://www.cna.org/archive/CNA_Files/pdf/drm-2019-u-022455-1rev.pdf; and Congressional Research Service, "Russia's Nuclear Weapons: Doctrine, Forces, and Modernization," January 2, 2020, 21, https://sgp.fas.org/crs/nuke/R45861.pdf. Russian analysts and generals call such an option a "de-escalatory strike." Yelena Rykovtseva, "Kto Razvyazhen Tret'yu Mirovuyu?" [Who Will Unleash the Third World War?], Radio Svoboda, https://www.svoboda.org/a/30942753.html. Facing the large numerical superiority of the Warsaw Pact during the Cold War, NATO signaled its intent to use nuclear weapons if it failed to halt a conventional attack from the East. As they assign varying degrees of plausibility to the "escalate to de-escalate" option, these and many other Western researchers note that the issue continues to be a subject of debate.

52. Johnson, *Russia's Conventional Precision Strike Capabilities, Regional Crises, and Nuclear Thresholds*; and Zysk, "Nonstrategic Nuclear Weapons in Russia's Evolving Military Doctrine."

53. The estimates of the numbers of Russian tactical nuclear weapons are from Kristensen and Korda, "Russian Nuclear Weapons, 2022"; Zysk, "Nonstrategic Nuclear Weapons in Russia's Evolving Military Doctrine"; and Union of Concerned Scientists, "Tactical Nuclear Weapons," June 1, 2022, https://www.ucsusa.org/resources/tactical-nuclear-weapons. Some estimates put Russia's tactical weapons at between 2,000 and 4,000 and as high as 5,000 warheads. Adamsky, "If War Comes Tomorrow," 167. The yields are from Union of Concerned Scientists, "Tactical Nuclear Weapons"; and Kristensen and Korda, "Russian Nuclear Weapons, 2022." The United States is estimated to have between 200 and "less than 500" tactical nuclear gravity bombs with yields ranging from 0.3 to 170 kilotons. The Pentagon is said to deploy about 100 of those bombs, called the B61, in five European countries: Belgium, Germany, Italy, the Netherlands, and Turkey. Union of Concerned Scientists, "Tactical Nuclear Weapons"; and Zysk, "Nonstrategic Nuclear Weapons in Russia's Evolving Military Doctrine," 322.

54. Kremlin.ru, "Ukaz Prezidenta Rossiyskoy Federatsii ot 20.7.2017 No.327 'Ob utverzhdenii Ostnov gosudarstvennoy politiki Rossiyskoy Federatsii v oblasti voenno-morskoy deyatel'nosti na period do 2030 goda'" [Decree of the President of the Russian Federation of July 20, 2017 No. 327 "On the Adoption of the Foundation of the State Policy of the Russian Federation in the Area of Naval Activity to 2030"], http://kremlin.ru/acts/bank/42117.

55. Novosti VPK, "Upravlyaemaya Operativno-Takticheskaya Raketa 9M723" [The Controlled Operational-Tactical Rocket 9M723], https://vpk.name/library/f/9m723.html.

56. See, for example, France 24, "Propaganda in Russia Arguing for Nuclear Weapons Use: Nobel Laureate," May 3, 2022, https://www.france24.com/en/live-news/20220503-propaganda-in-russia-arguing-for-nuclear-weapons-use-nobel-laureate; and Eric Schlosser, "What If Russia Uses Nuclear Weapons in Ukraine?," *Atlantic*, June 20, 2022, https://www.theatlantic.com/ideas/archive/2022/06/russia-ukraine-nuclear-weapon-us-response/661315.

57. Michael Birnbaum and David Filipov, "Russia Held a Big Military Exercise This Week. Here's Why the U.S. Is Paying Attention," *Washington Post*, September 23, 2017, https://www.washingtonpost.com/world/europe/russia-held-a-big-military-exercise-this-week-heres-why-the-us-is-paying-attention/2017/09/23/3a0d37ea-9a36-11e7-af6a-6555caaeb8dc_story.html.

58. France 24, "Propaganda in Russia Arguing for Nuclear Weapons Use."

Chapter 5. The Next War

1. Vladimir Putin, "Videoobrashcheniye po sluchayu Dnya rabotnika organov bezopasnosti" [Video Address on the Occasion of the Day of the Security Worker], Kremlin.ru, December 20, 2022, http://kremlin.ru/events/president/news/70146.

2. Brian Taylor, "Putin's Fourth Term: The Phantom Breakthrough," PONARS Eurasia, July 18, 2019, https://www.ponarseurasia.org/putin-s-fourth-term-the-phantom-breakthrough.

3. Konstantin Sonin, "Russia's Road to Economic Ruin," *Foreign Affairs*, November 15, 2022, https://www.foreignaffairs.com/russian-federation/russias-road-economic-ruin.

4. Natalia Zubarevich, "Natal'ya Zubarevich: 'Nado govorit' ne o gibeli, a o degradatsii nashey ekonomiki'" [Natalia Zubarevich: We Must Talk Not About the Death, but About the Degradation of Our Economy], *Novaya Izvestia*, November 16, 2022, https://newizv.ru/news/2022-11-16/natalya-zubarevich-nado-govorit-ne-o-gibeli-a-o-degradatsii-nashey-ekonomiki-372647.

5. Nikolai Petrov, "Period poluraspada. Nikolay Petrov o tom, kak voyna v Ukraine i sanktsii mogut privesti k dezintegratsii Rossii" [Half Life. Nikolai Petrov on How the War in Ukraine and Sanctions Can Lead to the Disintegration of Russia.], Insider, September 9, 2022, https://theins.ru/opinions/nikolai-petrov/254483.

6. Denis Kasyanchuk, "The Russian Labour Market and the Ukrainian War," N-IUSSP, November 7, 2022, https://www.niussp.org/education-work-economy/the-russian-labour-market-and-the-ukrainian-war.

7. Zubarevich, "Natal'ya Zubarevich: 'Nado govorit' ne o gibeli, a o degradatsii nashey ekonomiki" [Natalia Zubarevich: We Must Talk Not About the Death, but About the Degradation of Our Economy].

8. Vladislav Inozemtsev, "God Velikogo Nevozvrata" [The Year of Default], Riddle, December 21, 2022, https://ridl.io/ru/god-velikogo-nevozvrata.

9. Vadim Visloguzov, "Defitsit priros trillionom" [The Deficit Increased by a Trillion], Kommersant.ru, May 12, 2023, https://www.kommersant.ru/doc/5979272?mc_cid=0fc2f3c8d4&mc_eid=41e75d6c66.

10. Vladimir Putin, "Tekst obrashcheniya prezidenta Rossii Vladimira Putina" [Text of the Address of the President of Russia Vladimir Putin," RIA Novosti, February 24, 2022, https://ria.ru/20220224/obraschenie-1774658619.html.

11. NKVD stands for "People's Commissariat of Internal Affairs," and SMERSH translates to "Death to Spies."

12. Joseph Stalin, "Tost I.V. Stalina za 'zdorov'ye russkogo naroda': Vystupleniye na priyeme v Kremle v chest' komanduyushchikh voyskami Krasnoy Armii, 24 maya 1945 g"

[The Toast of Joseph Stalin to the "Health of the Russian People": Address at a Reception in the Kremlin in Honor of the Commanders of the Red Army, May 24, 1945], 100 Klyuchevykh dokumentov po rossiyskoy i sovetskoy istorii, https://www.1000dokumente.de/index.html?c=dokument_ru&dokument=0028_toa&object=translation&l=ru.

13. Vladimir Putin, "Videoobrashcheniye po sluchayu Dnya rabotnika organov bezopasnosti" [Video Address on the Occasion of the Day of the Security Worker].

14. In his June 24, 2023, address to the nation, Putin likened the Wagner mutiny to the "ruination of the armed forces" in 1917, followed by the "disintegration of the state and a civil war." Vladimir Putin "Obrashcheniye k grazhdanam Rossii" [Address to the Russian People], Kremlin.ru, June 24, 2023, http://kremlin.ru/events/president/news/71496.

15. Lev Gudkov, "Khvatit militarizma!" [Enough of Militarism!], *Novaya Gazeta*, February 19, 2020, https://novayagazeta.ru/articles/2020/02/19/83994-hvatit-naraschivat-voennuyu-mosch-daesh-rost-blagosostoyaniya.

16. Andrei Pertsev, "Putinskaya nestabil'nost'. Kak president stal istochnikom riskov dlya sistemy" [Putin Instability. How the President Became the Source of Risks for the System], Carnegie Endowment for International Peace, March 30, 2020, https://carnegie.ru/commentary/81397.

17. Alexander Nevzorov, "Nevzorov v programme "Gordon". Bol'shoye interv'yu pro Putina, vechnost' i perspektivy Rossii." [Nevzorov on "Gordon." A Big Interview About Putin, Eternity and the Perspective of Russia], YouTube, March 9, 2020, https://www.youtube.com/watch?v=453cUKleB5I.

18. Evan Gershkovich, "As the Coronavirus Contagion Grows in Russia, Putin's Strongman Image Weakens," *Moscow Times*, May 14, 2020, https://www.themoscowtimes.com/2020/05/14/as-the-coronavirus-contagion-grows-in-russia-putins-strongman-image-weakens-a70257.

19. Alexander Shunin, "Solovei na Baltkom: Putin schitaet sebya nepogreshimym messiei" [Solovei on Baltkom: Putin Considers Himself a Messiah Who Does Not Err], MixNews, June 20, 2019, https://mixnews.lv/exclusive/2019/06/20/solovej-na-baltkom-putin-schitaet-sebya-nepogreshimym-missiej.

20. Lev Tolstoy, "Khadzhi-Murat," in *Lev Nikolaevich Tolstoy: Povesti i rasskazy* [*Lev Nikolaevich Tolstoy, Novellas and Stories*] (Moscow, Russia: Eksmo, 2006); and Nikita Sergeyevich Khrushchev, "Special Report to the 20th Congress of the Communist Party of the Soviet Union," February 24–25, 1956, https://web.archive.org/web/20051107221432/http:/www.uwm.edu/Course/448-343/index12.html.

21. Leni Riefenstahl, dir., *Triumph of the Will* (Germany: Leni Riefenstahl-Produktion, 1935).

22. I am grateful to Paula Chang for this excellent observation.

23. Irina Borogan and Andrei Soldatov, "Putin Places Spies Under House Arrest," Center for European Policy Analysis, March 11, 2022, https://cepa.org/article/putin-places-spies-under-house-arrest. Col. Gen. Sergey Beseda was later released but was not restored to his former job. Calling the general's quick release "unprecedented" in Putin's practice, a top Russian expert on the security services, Andrei Soldatov, attributed it to the maintenance of the Kremlin narrative that "everything was going

according to the plan." The same pretense must have been Putin's letting Defense Minister Sergei Shoigu and Chief of General Staff Valery Gerasimov keep their jobs after the collapse of the blitzkrieg. One can almost hear the gnashing of teeth in Putin's office, yet such cat-and-mouse games with officials who slipped up was also very much Joseph Stalin's way of personnel management. See Reid Standish, "Interview: How Russia's Intelligence Agencies Have Adapted After Six Months of War," Radio Free Europe, August 24, 2022, https://www.rferl.org/a/russia-intelligence-agencies-ukraine-war-six-months/32003096.html.

24. Sarah Rainsford, "Russia's Putin Embraces Higher Pension Age but Softens Blow," BBC, August 29, 2018, https://www.bbc.com/news/world-europe-45347228; and World Bank, "Survival to Age 65, Male (% of Cohort)—Russian Federation," 2020, https://data.worldbank.org/indicator/SP.DYN.TO65.MA.ZS?locations=RU&most_recent_year_desc=false.

25. Levada Center, "Pensionnaya Reforma" [Pension Reform], September 9, 2018, https://www.levada.ru/2018/09/27/pensionnaya-reforma-4.

26. Levada Center, "Pensionnaya Reforma" [Pension Reform]; and Levada Center, "Odobrenie deyatel'nosti Vladimira Putina" [Vladimir Putin's Approval Rating], https://www.levada.ru/indikatory.

27. Pertsev, "Putinskaya nestabil'nost'. Kak president stal istochnikom riskov dlya sistemy" [Putin Instability. How the President Became the Source of Risks for the System].

28. Konstantin Simonov, "OPEK minus: zachem Sechin I Siluanov ubedili Putina vyiti iz neftyanoi sdelki" [OPEC Minus: Why Sechin and Siluanov Convinced Putin to Leave the Oil Deal], *Forbes*, April 23, 2020, https://www.forbes.ru/biznes/398841-opek-minus-zachem-sechin-i-siluanov-ubedili-putina-vyyti-iz-neftyanoy-sdelki.

29. US Energy Information Administration, "Crude Oil Prices Were Generally Lower in 2019 Than in 2018," January 7, 2020, https://www.eia.gov/todayinenergy/detail.php?id=42415; and *RBK*, "Minfin raskryl srednyuyu tsenu rossiiskoi nefti za mart" [The Ministry of Finance Revealed the Average Price of Russian Oil in March], *RBK*, April 8, 2020, https://www.rbc.ru/economics/01/04/2020/5e84cc099a7947889c4ba151.

30. Rosie Perper and Bill Bostock, "Oil Is Down 21% After Its Biggest Drop in Decades Following Saudi Price Cuts That Sparked a Race to the Bottom with Russia," Insider, March 9, 2020, https://www.businessinsider.com/oil-price-crash-market-drop-global-price-war-futures-coronavirus-2020-3.

31. Mikhail Krutikhin, "Neft' za $30?" [Oil for $30?], Republic, March 7, 2020, https://republic.ru/posts/96101; and Evegnia Pismennaya, Ilya Arkhipov, and Henry Meyer, "Russia Paid a Heavy Price to End the Oil Price War," World Oil, April 13, 2020, https://www.worldoil.com/news/2020/4/13/russia-paid-a-heavy-price-to-end-the-oil-price-war.

32. Vladimir Putin, "Polnyy tekst vystupleniya prezidenta RF Vladimira Putina v Gosdume 10 marta 2020 goda" [Speech Delivered to the State Duma], *Nezavisimaya Gazeta*, March 10, 2020, https://www.ng.ru/politics/2020-03-10/100_putin10032020.html.

33. Ben Noble, "Russia's 'Nationwide Vote' on Constitutional Reforms," Presidential Power, June 19, 2020, https://presidential-power.net/?p=11174.

34. Levada Center, "Obnulenie prezidentskikh srokov" [The Nullification of Presidential Terms], March 27, 2020, https://www.levada.ru/2020/03/27/obnulenie-prezidentskih-srokov.

35. Otkrytye Media, "Palatki, bagazhnik, penyok. Samye strannye mesta, gde prokhodit golosovanie po 'obnuleniyu' Putina" [Tents, Trunks, and Tree Stumps. The Strangest Places Where the Putin 'Nullification' Voting Occurred], June 25, 2020, https://openmedia.io/news/n1/palatki-bagazhnik-penyok-samye-strannye-mesta-gde-proxodit-golosovanie-po-obnuleniyu-putina.

36. Dary'ya Kozlova, "'Fantomnaya real'nost', kotoraya ne otrazhaet nichego" ["Phantom Reality" That Shows Nothing], Novaya Gazeta, July 1, 2020, https://novayagazeta.ru/articles/2020/07/01/86108-fantomnaya-realnost-kotoraya-ne-otrazhaet-nichego; and Viktor Vladimirov, "Dmitrii Oreshkin: 'Triumf Besstydstva'" [Dmitry Oreshkin: "The Triumph of Shamelessness"], Voice of America, July 3, 2020, https://www.golosameriki.com/a/putin-amendments-oreshkin-interview/5487913.html.

37. Mumin Shakirov, "Triumf ili bol'shaya afera Vladimira Putina" [A Triumph, or Putin's Big Scam], Radio Svoboda, July 4, 2020, https://www.svoboda.org/a/30705723.html.

38. Moscow Times, "Russian Bookstores Sell New Constitution Ahead of Vote on Putin's Reforms," June 16, 2020, https://www.themoscowtimes.com/2020/06/16/russian-bookstores-sell-new-constitution-ahead-of-vote-on-putins-reforms-a70593.

39. Olesya Zakharova, "How Does Putin Justify Resetting His Term-Limit Clock?," Riddle, April 28, 2020, https://ridl.io/how-does-putin-justify-resetting-his-term-limit-clock.

40. Andrei Kondrashov, "Krym: Put' na Rodinu" [Crimea: The Way Home, Documentary Film by Andrei Kondrashov], YouTube, October 4, 2020, 2:25:49, https://www.youtube.com/watch?v=PGGNXIQXlcU.

41. Ben Judah, "Behind the Scenes in Putin's Court: The Private Habits of a Latter-Day Dictator," Newsweek, July 23, 2014, https://www.newsweek.com/2014/08/01/behind-scenes-putins-court-private-habits-latter-day-dictator-260640.html.

42. Economist, "Emmanuel Macron in His Own Words (English)," November 7, 2019, https://www.economist.com/europe/2019/11/07/emmanuel-macron-in-his-own-words-english.

43. Munich Security Conference, "Westlessness," February 16, 2020, https://securityconference.org/en/news/full/westlessness-the-munich-security-conference-2020.

44. Moira Fagan and Jacob Poushter, "NATO Seen Favourably Across Member States," RealClearPublicAffairs, February 9, 2020, https://www.realclearpublicaffairs.com/public_affairs/2020/02/13/nato_seen_favorably_across_member_states_484081.html.

45. RIA Novosti, "Putin prokommentiroval zayavleniya Zapada o bor'be do 'poslednego ukraintsa'" [Putin Commented on the Statements of the West About "Fighting to the Last Ukrainian"], July 7, 2022, https://ria.ru/20220707/putin-1801063012.html.

46. Vladimir Putin, "Poslaniye Prezidenta Federal'nomu Sobraniyu" [Presidential Address to the Federal Assembly], Kremlin.ru, March 1, 2018, http://kremlin.ru/events/president/news/56957.

47. Radio Baltkom, "Zamdirektora 'Levada-Tsentr' o sotsiologii, Putine I VTsIOM" [The Deputy Director of the Levada Center on Sociology, Putin, and VTsIOM], YouTube, February 3, 2020, 41:34, https://www.youtube.com/watch?v=mslAwEM5ZX0.

48. Radio Baltkom, "Zamdirektora 'Levada-Tsentr' o sotsiologii, Putine I VTsIOM" [The Deputy Director of the Levada Center on Sociology, Putin, and VTsIOM].

49. Mironov, "Predatelyam poshchady byt' ne dolzhno!" [There Should Be No Mercy for Traitors!], May 19, 2015, https://mironov.ru/moya-pozitsiya/predatelyam-poshhady-byt-ne-dolzhno.

50. David Remnick, "Echo in the Dark," New Yorker, September 15, 2008, https://www.newyorker.com/magazine/2008/09/22/echo-in-the-dark.

51. Vladimir Putin, "The Real Lessons of the 75th Anniversary of World War II," National Interest, June 18, 2020, https://nationalinterest.org/feature/vladimir-putin-real-lessons-75th-anniversary-world-war-ii-162982.

52. Alexandra Odynova, "WikiLeaks: Putin's 'Personal Gripe' with Estonia Result of WWII Betrayal," Moscow Times, September 5, 2011, https://www.themoscowtimes.com/2011/09/05/wikileaks-putins-personal-gripe-with-estonia-result-of-wwii-betrayal-a9358.

53. Natalya Gevorkyan, Natalya Timakova, and Andrei Kolesnikov, "Syn" [Son], in Ot Pervogo Litsa [From the First Person. Conversations with Vladimir Putin] (Moscow, Russia: Vagrius, 2000), http://lib.ru/MEMUARY/PUTIN/razgowor.txt.

54. RIA Novosti, "Pervaya mashina sem'i Putina" [The Putin Family's First Car], May 2, 2009, https://ria.ru/20090205/161002448.html.

55. Vladimir Putin, "Vstrecha s molodymi predprinimatelyami, inzhenerami i uchonymi" [Meeting with Young Entrepreneurs, Engineers and Scientists], Kremlin.ru, June 9, 2022, http://kremlin.ru/events/president/news/68606.

56. Vladimir Putin, "Vstrecha s molodymi predprinimatelyami, inzhenerami i uchonymi" [Meeting with Young Entrpreneurs, Engineers and Scientists].

57. Steven Lee Meyers, "Estonia Removes Soviet-Era War Memorial After a Night of Violence," New York Times, April 27, 2007, https://www.nytimes.com/2007/04/27/world/europe/27iht-estonia.4.5477141.html; and Baltic Times, "Tallinn Erupts in Deadly Riot, Bronze Soldier Removed," April 28, 2007, https://www.baltictimes.com/news/articles/17774. For more detail, see Ivo Juuree and Mariita Mattiisen, The Bronze Soldier Crisis of 2007 ((Tallinn, Estonia: International Centre for Defense and Security, 2020), https://icds.ee/wp-content/uploads/2020/08/ICDS_Report_The_Bronze_Soldier_Crises_of_2007_Juurvee_Mattiisen_August_2020.pdf.

58. The share of those who "viewed Putin positively" shrank in Latvia from 31 percent in 2021 to 14 percent in 2022, from 13 percent to 6 percent in Lithuania, and from 30 percent to 22 percent in Estonia. Dominika Hajdu, "GLOBSEC Trends 2022: Central and Eastern Europe amid the War in Ukraine," GLOBSEC, May 31, 2022, https://www.globsec.org/what-we-do/publications/globsec-trends-2022-central-and-eastern-europe-amid-war-ukraine.

59. LRT.lt, "Lithuania Bans Russian, Belarusian TV Channels over War Incitement," February 25, 2022, https://www.lrt.lt/en/news-in-english/19/1626345/lithuania-bans-russian-belarusian-tv-channels-over-war-incitement; ERR.ee, "Four Russian TV Channels Banned from Estonian Airwaves," February 25, 2022, https://news.err.ee/1608512162/four-russian-tv-channels-banned-from-estonian-airwaves; and Chris Dziadul, "Latvia Bans Russian Channels," Broadband TV News, February 24, 2023, https://www.broadbandtvnews.com/2022/02/24/latvia-bans-russian-channels-2.

60. Sune Engel Rasmussen, "Putin's War in Ukraine Tests Allegiances of Russian Speakers in Former Soviet Latvia," *Wall Street Journal*, March 28, 2022, https://www.wsj.com/articles/putins-war-in-ukraine-tests-allegiances-of-russian-speakers-in-former-soviet-latvia-11648459800.

61. Although the GLOBSEC poll did not provide an ethnic breakdown, we can safely assume that the 14 percent of Latvians (259,000) and 22 percent of Estonians (292,000) who, according to the GLOBSEC poll, viewed Putin positively were overwhelmingly ethnic Russians.

62. A shorter version of this scenario was published in Leon Aron, "Putin's Next War," *National Review*, February 13, 2023, https://www.nationalreview.com/2023/02/putins-next-war.

63. David A. Shlapank and Michael W. Johnson, "Reinforcing Deterrence on NATO's Eastern Flank," RAND Corporation, 2016, https://www.rand.org/content/dam/rand/pubs/research_reports/RR1200/RR1253/RAND_RR1253.pdf.

64. I am grateful to Fred Kagan, director of the Critical Threats Project at the American Enterprise Institute, for the details of the Western Military District's depredation.

65. North Atlantic Treaty Organization, "NATO's Forward Presence," June 2022, https://www.nato.int/nato_static_fl2014/assets/pdf/2022/6/pdf/2206-factsheet_efp_en.pdf.

66. Janis Laizans, "U.S. Apache Helicopters Arrive in Latvia," Reuters, February 24, 2022, https://www.reuters.com/world/europe/us-apache-helicopters-arrive-latvia-2022-02-24.

67. North Atlantic Treaty Organization, "NATO's Forward Presence."

68. North Atlantic Treaty Organization, "NATO's Eastern Flank: Stronger Defense and Deterrence," July 2022, https://www.nato.int/nato_static_fl2014/assets/pdf/2022/3/pdf/2203-map-det-def-east.pdf.

69. Anna Bruschetta, Maria Vitoria Santana, and Gilles de Valk, "Europe's Role in the Very High Readiness Joint Task Force," European Army Interoperability Center, August 2021, https://finabel.org/wp-content/uploads/2021/09/27.-Europes-Role-in-the-Very-High-Readiness-Joint-Task-Force-3-2.pdf.

70. Bruschetta, Santana, and de Valk, "Europe's Role in the Very High Readiness Joint Task Force."

71. Haley Britzky, "'We're Always Ready'—Meet the Soldiers of America's Go-To Rapid Response Force," Task & Purpose, January 27, 2022, https://taskandpurpose.com/news/army-82nd-airborne-division-immediate-response; and US Army, "82nd Airborne Division," https://home.army.mil/bragg/index.php/units-tenants/82nd-airborne-division.

72. Robert Killebrew, "Rapid Deployment: The Army and American Strategy," War on the Rocks, December 9, 2013, https://warontherocks.com/2013/12/rapid-deployment-the-army-and-american-strategy.

73. Richard Milne, "Estonia's PM Says Country Would Be 'Wiped from Map' Under Existing Nato Plans," *Financial Times*, June 22, 2022, https://www.ft.com/content/a430b191-39c8-4b03-b3fd-8e7e948a5284.

74. Michael Moran, "Modern Military Force Structure," Council on Foreign Relations, October 26, 2006, https://www.cfr.org/backgrounder/modern-military-force-structures.

75. Meghann Meyers, "Most Troops Deployed for Ukraine Response Still in Europe," *Military Times*, November 1, 2022, https://www.militarytimes.com/news/your-military/2022/11/01/most-troops-deployed-for-ukraine-response-still-in-europe; and John Vandiver, "Army 10th Mountain, 101st Airborne Division Soldiers Deploying to NATO's Southeast Flank," *Stars and Stripes*, March 8, 2023, https://www.stripes.com/branches/army/2023-03-08/101st-airborne-10th-mountain-romania-9421840.html.

76. Estonian Foreign Intelligence Service, "Exercise Zapad 2017 Versus Zapad 2021," February 15, 2022, https://raport.valisluureamet.ee/2022/en/russian-armed-forces/zapad-2017-vs-zapad-2021.

77. Michael Kofman, "Zapad 2021: What We Learned from Russia's Massive Military Drills," *Moscow Times*, September 23, 2021, https://www.themoscowtimes.com/2021/09/23/zapad-2021-what-we-learned-from-russias-massive-military-drills-a75127; and Vladimir Putin, "Zasedaniye kollegii Ministerstva oborony" [Meeting of the Collegium of the Ministry of Defense], Kremlin.ru, December 21, 2022, http://kremlin.ru/events/president/news/70159.

78. George Barros, "Belarus Warning Update: Russia and Belarus Launch Military Exercises," Institute for the Study of War, August 17, 2020, https://www.understandingwar.org/backgrounder/belarus-warning-update-russia-and-belarus-launch-military-exercises; AFP, "Putin Orders Massive Snap Military Drills," *Moscow Times*, July 17, 2020, https://www.themoscowtimes.com/2020/07/17/putin-orders-massive-snap-military-drills-a70908; Dominik P. Jankowski, "The Dangerous Tool of Russian Military Exercises," Foreign Policy Association, June 7, 2017, https://foreignpolicyblogs.com/2017/06/07/dangerous-tool-russian-military-exercises; and Congressional Research Service, "Russian Military Exercises," October 4, 2021, https://sgp.fas.org/crs/row/IF11938.pdf.

79. *Rossiskaya Gazeta*, "Voyennaya doktrina Rossiyskoy Federatsii" [Military Doctrine of the Russian Federation], December 30, 2014, https://rg.ru/documents/2014/12/30/doktrina-dok.html.

80. Hans M. Kristensen and Matt Korda, "Russian Nuclear Weapons, 2021," *Bulletin of the Atomic Scientists* 77, no. 2 (March 18, 2021): 90–108, https://www.tandfonline.com/doi/full/10.1080/00963402.2021.1885869.

81. Hans M. Kristensen and Matt Korda, "Nuclear Notebook: How Many Nuclear Weapons Does Russia Have in 2022?," *Bulletin of the Atomic Scientists* 78, no. 2 (February 23, 2022): 98–121, https://thebulletin.org/premium/2022-02/nuclear-notebook-how-many-nuclear-weapons-does-russia-have-in-2022.

82. Jānis Bārzinŝ, "Latvia: The Potential Modes and Venues of Russian Aggression," in *To Have and to Hold: Putin's Quest for Control in the Former Soviet Empire*, ed. Leon Aron (Washington, DC: American Enterprise Institute, 2018), 56.

83. *Moscow Times*, "Russia Simulates Nuclear Strikes near EU," May 5, 2022, https://www.themoscowtimes.com/2022/05/05/russia-simulates-nuclear-capable-strikes-near-eu-a77586.

84. Kremlin.ru, "Prezident prinyal uchastiye v prazdnichnykh torzhestvakh po sluchayu 100-letiya kanonizatsii prepodobnogo Serafima Sarovskogo" [The President Took Part in Celebrations on the Occasion of the 100th Anniversary of the Canonization of Saint Seraphim of Sarov], July 31, 2003, http://kremlin.ru/events/president/news/29121.

85. Andrei Kondrashov, "Krym: Put' na Rodinu" [Crimea: The Road to the Motherland], YouTube, October 4, 2020, 2:25:49, https://www.youtube.com/watch?v=PGGNXIQXlcU.

86. Mykola Bielieskov, "Russia's Managed Escalation in Ukraine," *Eurasia Daily Monitor* 19, no. 168 (November 10, 2022), https://jamestown.org/program/russias-managed-escalation-in-ukraine-part-one.

87. RIA Novosti, "Putin prikazal perevesti sily sderzhivaniya v ocobiy rezhim dezhurstva" [Putin Ordered Russia's (Strategic Nuclear) Deterrence Forces to Be Brought into a Special Regime of Readiness], February 27, 2022, https://ria.ru/20220227/putin-1775389742.html. Three weeks before the invasion, Yars intercontinental ballistic missiles (ICBMs) were moved out of permanent bases to "war-time firing positions" across Russia. In another two weeks, Putin "directed" exercises of the "forces of strategic deterrence." Aimed at dealing a potential enemy "a certain defeat," the games included the launching of the ballistic missiles Yar and a Sineva (Blue Sky), Iskanders, hypersonic missiles Kinzhal (Dagger) and Tsirkon (Zircon), and the Kalibr cruise missiles. Pavel Felgengauer, "Kremlin Must Make Final Decisions on War Soon as Diplomatic Runway Grows Short," *Eurasian Daily Monitory* 19, no. 13 (February 3, 2022), https://jamestown.org/program/kremlin-must-make-final-decision-on-war-soon-as-diplomatic-runway-grows-short; and TASS, "Ucheniya sil strategitecheskogo sderzhivaniya proydut v Rossii v dva etapa" [The Exercises of the Forces of Strategic Deterrence Will Be Conducted in Two Phases], February 19, 2022, https://tass.ru/armiya-i-opk/13766909.

88. Vladimir Putin, "Poslaniye Prezidenta Federal'nomu Sobraniyu" [Presidential Address to the Federal Assembly].

89. Vladimir Putin, "Poslaniye Prezidenta Federal'nomu Sobraniyu" [Presidential Address to the Federal Assembly].

90. Vladimir Putin, "Poslaniye Prezidenta Federal'nomu Sobraniyu" [Speech Delivered to the Federal Assembly in Moscow], Kremlin.ru, February 20, 2019, http://kremlin.ru/events/president/news/59863.

91. Vladimir Putin, "Poslaniye Prezidenta Federal'nomu Sobraniyu" [Speech Delivered to the Federal Assembly in Moscow].

92. Vladimir Solovyov, "Miroporyadok 2018" [World Order 2018], YouTube, April 2, 2018, https://www.youtube.com/watch?v=uC2bWSbZdQ4.

93. Vladimir Putin, "Obrashcheniye Prezidenta Rossiyskoy Federatsii" [Speech Delivered in Moscow on the Situation in Donbass], September 21, 2022, http://kremlin.ru/events/president/news/69390.

94. James Politi, Andy Bounds, and Valentina Pop, "Joe Biden Warns Vladimir Putin Is 'Not Joking' About Nuclear Threat," *Financial Times*, October 6, 2022, https://www.ft.com/content/2f4ab252-8eaa-4328-9c2e-18fad985a65c.

95. David Sanger et al., "Ukraine Wants More Powerful Weapons. Biden Is Not So Sure.," *New York Times*, September 17, 2022, https://www.nytimes.com/2022/09/17/us/politics/ukraine-biden-weapons.html.

96. Politi, Bounds, and Pop, "Joe Biden Warns Vladimir Putin Is 'Not Joking' About Nuclear Threat."

97. David E. Sanger, Anton Troianovaski, and Julian E. Barnes, "In Washington, Putin's Nuclear Threats Stir Growing Alarm," *New York Times*, October 1, 2022, https://www.nytimes.com/2022/10/01/world/europe/washington-putin-nuclear-threats.html.

Bibliography

Adamsky, Dmitry. 2019. *Russian Nuclear Orthodoxy*. Stanford, CA: Stanford University Press.

———. 2014. "If War Comes Tomorrow: Russian Thinking About 'Regional Nuclear Deterrence.'" *Journal of Slavic Military Studies* 27, no. 1 (March 10): 163–88. https://doi.org/10.1080/13518046.2014.874852.

AFP. 2020. "Putin Orders Massive Snap Military Drills." *Moscow Times*. July 17. https://www.themoscowtimes.com/2020/07/17/putin-orders-massive-snap-military-drills-a70908.

Aleksei, Kudrin. 2013. "Former Russian Finance Minister Alexei Kudrin: 'We Have to Take a Chance with More Democracy.'" *Der Spiegel*. January 23. https://www.spiegel.de/international/world/interview-with-putin-ally-alexei-kudrin-on-democracy-in-russia-a-878873.html.

Anton, Vyacheslav. 2017. "Deputat GosDumy Anna Kuvychko i volgogradskiye kadety" [State Duma Deputy Anna Kuvychko and Vologograd Cadets]. YouTube. November 14. https://www.youtube.com/watch?v=ZpKS0B6gzuc.

Arkin, William, and Hans M. Kristensen. 2020. "US Deploys New Low-Yield Nuclear Submarine Warhead." Federation of American Scientists. January 29. https://fas.org/blogs/security/2020/01/w76-2deployed.

Aron, Leon. 2023. "Putin's Next War." *National Review*. February 13. https://www.nationalreview.com/2023/02/putins-next-war.

———. 2012. *Roads to the Temple: Truth, Memory, Ideas, and Ideals in the Making of the Russian Revolution, 1987–1991*. New Haven, CT: Yale University Press.

———. 2008. "The Problematic Pages." *New Republic*. September 24. https://newrepublic.com/article/62070/the-problematic-pages.

Associated Press. 2023. "1st US Army Garrison on NATO's East Flank Formed in Poland." March 21. https://apnews.com/article/poland-us-security-military-nato-garrison-base-57a3db8e7e9073ed8fe7eb5b67e5f115.

Associated Press Newsroom. 2007. "Estonia War Memorial." April 27. https://newsroom.ap.org/editorial-photos-videos/detail?itemid=35de588bfd2a4ef3917ecfc4a3b7f309&mediatype=photo.

Azattyq TV. 2018. "Putin: 'My, kak mucheniki popadyom v ray. A oni sdokhnut'" [Putin: "We, Like Martyrs, Will End Up in Paradise. And They Will Just Croak"]. YouTube. October 19. https://www.youtube.com/watch?v=IO_AjWjjfCo.

Baev, Pavel. 2021. "Naval Parade Plays into Putin's Dangerous Vanity." *Eurasia Daily Monitor* 18, no. 118 (July 26). https://jamestown.org/program/naval-parade-plays-into-putins-dangerous-vanity.

Baltic Times. 2007. "Tallinn Erupts in Deadly Riot, Bronze Soldier Removed." April 28. https://www.baltictimes.com/news/articles/17774.

Barbashin, Anton, and Hannah Thoburn. 2015. "Putin's Philosopher: Ivan Ilyin and the Ideology of Moscow's Rule." *Foreign Affairs*. September 20.

Barros, George. 2020. "Belarus Warning Update: Russia and Belarus Launch Military Exercises." Institute for the Study of War. August 17. https://www.understandingwar.org/backgrounder/belarus-warning-update-russia-and-belarus-launch-military-exercises.

Barry, Ellen. 2014. "Foes of America in Russia Crave Rupture in Ties." *New York Times*. March 15. https://www.nytimes.com/2014/03/16/world/europe/foes-of-america-in-russia-crave-rupture-in-ties.html.

Barzins, Janis. 2018. "Latvia: The Potential Modes and Venues of Russian Aggression." In *To Have and to Hold: Putin's Quest for Control in the Former Soviet Empire*, ed. Leon Aron, 53–58. Washington, DC: American Enterprise Institute.

Baumgardner, Will. 2022. "Guns and God: Russian Orthodox Conservatism and the Militarization of Masculinity in Contemporary Russia." (bachelor's thesis, Pennsylvania State University, April 6). https://honors.libraries.psu.edu/files/final_submissions/7946.

Bayley, John. 2005. *The Power of Delight: A Lifetime in Literature: Essays 1962–2002*. New York: W. W. Norton & Co.

Bazanova, Elizaveta. 2019. "Pochemu za 20 let Rossiya tak i ne pereshla ot stagnatsii k razvitiyu" [Why for 20 Years Russia Never Moved from Stagnation to Development]. *Vedomsti*. October 8. https://www.vedomosti.ru/economics/articles/2019/10/08/813068-20-let-stagnatsii.

BBC News. 2012. "Pussy Riot Members Jailed for Two Years for Hooliganism." August 17. https://www.bbc.com/news/world-europe-19297373.

BBC Russian Service. 2017. "Opros: bol'shinstvo rossiyan rady tomu, chto Rossiyu v mire boyatsya" [Poll: The Majority of Russians Are Glad That Russia Is Feared in the World]. January 14. https://www.bbc.com/russian/news-38621441.

———. 2014. "Udal'tsov i Razvozzhayev prigovoreny k 4,5 godam kolonii" [Udaltsov and Razvozzhayev Were Sentenced to 4.5 Years of Labor Camp]. July 24. https://www.bbc.com/russian/russia/2014/07/140724_udaltsov_sentence_verdict.

Bekbulatova, Taisiya, Ivan Safronov, and Maksim Ivanov. 2013. "Na Strazhe dukhovnoi bezopasnosti" [Guarding Spiritual Security]. April 25. https://www.kommersant.ru/doc/2178141.

Belkovsky, Stanislav. 2015. "'Ya uberu vsekh, kto posmeyet posyagnut' na russkiy yazyk'" ["I Will Wipe Out All Who Dare Imperil the Russian Language"]. *Afisha Daily*. April 23. https://daily.afisha.ru/archive/vozduh/books/ya-uberu-vseh-kto-posmeet-posyagnut-na-russkiy-yazyk-belkovskiy-o-slovesnosti.

Belsat. 2022. "Rossiyane v Estonii: vmeste, no po otdel'nosti" [Russians in Estonia: Together, but at a Distance]. February 24. https://naviny.belsat.eu/ru/news/rossiyane-v-estonii-vmeste-no-po-otdelnosti.

Berdyaev, Nikolas. 1976. *The Origins of Russian Communism*. Ann Arbor, MI: University of Michigan Press.

Bielieskov, Mykola. 2022. "Russia's Managed Escalation in Ukraine." *Eurasia Daily Monitor* 19, no. 168 (November 10). https://jamestown.org/program/russias-managed-escalation-in-ukraine-part-one.

Birnbaum, Michael, and David Filipov. 2017. "Russia Held a Big Military Exercise This Week. Here's Why the U.S. Is Paying Attention." *Washington Post*. September 23. https://www.washingtonpost.com/world/europe/russia-held-a-big-military-exercise-this-week-heres-why-the-us-is-paying-attention/2017/09/23/3a0d37ea-9a36-11e7-af6a-6555caaeb8dc_story.html.

BK55.ru. 2014. "Posle sravneniya s Gitlerom Putina sravnili so Stalinym" [After Being Compared to Hitler, Putin Was Compared to Stalin]. June 6. https://bk55.ru/news/article/33781.

Blagovest. 2007. "V khrame Khrista Spasitelya nachalis' torzhestva po sluchayu 60-letiya osnovaniya yadernogo kompleksa Rossii" [Services on the Occasion of the 60th Anniversary of the Foundation of the Russian Nuclear Complex Began in the Church of Christ the Savior]. September 4. http://blagovest-info.ru/index.php?ss=2&s=3&id=15605.

Boffey, Daniel. 2022. "'I'm Always Looking over My Shoulder': Anxiety Among Estonia's Russians." *Guardian*. August 22. https://www.theguardian.com/world/2022/aug/22/always-looking-shoulder-anxiety-estonia-russians-tallinn.

Borogan, Irina, and Andrei Soldatov. 2022. "Putin Places Spies Under House Arrest." Center for European Policy Analysis. March 11. https://cepa.org/article/putin-places-spies-under-house-arrest.

Britzky, Haley. 2022. "'We're Always Ready'—Meet the Soldiers of America's Go-To Rapid Response Force." Task & Purpose. January 27. https://taskandpurpose.com/news/army-82nd-airborne-division-immediate-response.

Brumfiel, Geoff. 2013. "Megatons to Megawatts: Russian Warheads Fuel U.S. Power Plants." National Public Radio. December 11. https://www.npr.org/2013/12/11/250007526/megatons-to-megawatts-russian-warheads-fuel-u-s-power-plants.

Bruschetta, Anna, Maria Vitoria Santana, and Gilles de Valk. 2021. "Europe's Role in the Very High Readiness Joint Task Force." European Army Interoperability Center. August. https://finabel.org/wp-content/uploads/2021/09/27.-Europes-Role-in-the-Very-High-Readiness-Joint-Task-Force-3-2.pdf.

Burton, Tara Isabella. 2022. "The Far-Right Mystical Writer Who Helped Shape Putin's View of Russia." *Washington Post*. May 12. https://www.washingtonpost.com/outlook/2022/05/12/dugin-russia-ukraine-putin.

Cazac, Dumitru. 2018. "Patriotic Mobilisation in Russia." Scribd. July 4. https://www.scribd.com/document/538962923/251-Patriotic-Mobilisation-in-Russia.

CBS News. 2020. "U.S. Makes First Major Addition to Its Nuclear Arsenal in Decades." February 4. https://www.cbsnews.com/news/w76-2-us-first-major-addition-nuclear-arsenal-decades-low-yield-long-range.

Center for Strategic and International Studies. Missile Defense Project. 2021a. "Minuteman III." August 2. https://missilethreat.csis.org/missile/minuteman-iii.

———. 2021b. "Trident II." July 30. https://missilethreat.csis.org/missile/trident.

Chan, Paula. 2014. "I za belykx, i za krasnykh" [For Both the Whites and the Reds]. (Unpublished paper, December 17).

Cherny, Milan. 2023. "Ekzamen s avtomatom. Kak 'voyenno-patrioticheskoye' obucheniye zakhvatyvayet shkoly, detsady i tvorcheskiye kruzhki" [The Exam with Machine Guns. How "Military-Patriotic" Education Captures Schools,

Kindergartens and After-School Programs]. Theins.ru. March 25. https://theins.ru/politika/260134.

CIA Office of Russian and European Analysis. 2014. "Ivan Ilyin: National Philosopher of Putin's Russia." November 24.

Civil Initiatives Committee. 2013. "Vystuplenie Alexeya Kudrina na zasedanii Komiteta Grazhdanskikh Initsiatives" [Remarks by Alexei Kudrin at the Meeting of the Committee for Civil Initiatives]. Facebook. September 23. https://www.facebook.com/watch/?v=413413462097038.

Cohen, Roger. 2022. "The Making of Vladimir Putin." *New York Times*. March 26. https://www.nytimes.com/2022/03/26/world/europe/vladimir-putin-russia.html.

Congressional Research Service. 2020. "Russia's Nuclear Weapons: Doctrine, Forces, and Modernization." January 2. https://sgp.fas.org/crs/nuke/R45861.pdf.

———. 2021a. "Russian Military Exercises." October 4. https://sgp.fas.org/crs/row/IF11938.pdf.

———. 2021b. "U.S. Strategic Nuclear Forces: Background, Developments, and Issues." https://sgp.fas.org/crs/nuke/RL33640.pdf.

Connolly, Richard, and Mathieu Boulègue. 2018. *Russia's New State Armament Programme: Implications for the Russian Armed Forces and Military Capabilities to 2027*. Chatham House. May. https://www.chathamhouse.org/sites/default/files/publications/research/2018-05-10-russia-state-armament-programme-connolly-boulegue-final.pdf.

Cooper, Julian. 2018. "The Funding of Nuclear Weapons in the Russian Federation." University of Oxford. Changing Character of War Centre. October. https://static1.squarespace.com/static/55faab67e4b0914105347194/t/5bb1ea3ee4966b5320fa197c/1538386496442/The+funding+of+nuclear+weapons+in+the+Russian+Federation.pdf.

Daily Mail. 2019. "Little Troopers: Russian Children as Young as Four Are Taught Marching in Military Uniforms as Putin's 'Youth Army' Tops Half a Million." https://www.dailymail.co.uk/news/article-7007211/Russian-children-taught-march-military-uniforms-Putins-youth-army-tops-half-million.html.

Davis Center for Russian and Eurasian Studies. 2021. "The Use and Abuse of Soviet History in Putin's Russia." YouTube. April 6. https://www.youtube.com/watch?v=AhVxzHTFJsI.

Derkachev, Stanislav. 2011. "9 maya 1999g. Moskva. Krasnaya Ploshchad'. Voyenniy Parad" [May 9th, 1999. Moscow. Red Square. Military Parade]. YouTube. https://www.youtube.com/watch?v=dc4qNXDenKo.

Dostoevsky, Fyodor. 2012. *Humiliated and Insulted*. 1861; Richmond, London: Alma Books.

———. 1994. *Notes from Underground*. 1864; New York City: Vintage.

Druzhinin, Alexey. 2012. "Russia's Prime Minister and President-Elect Vladimir Putin Aims at a Target with a Replica of Kalashnikov Assault Rifle in Moscow, on April 26, 2012, While Visiting a Shooting Gallery at an Exhibition of Russian Railways' Research Center." Getty Images. April 26. https://www.gettyimages.com/detail/news-photo/russias-prime-minister-and-president-elect-vladimir-putin-news-photo/143437306?adppopup=true.

Dugin, Alexander. 2014. "Konets liberalizma i nachalo patriotizma v Rossii" [The End of

Liberalism and the Beginning of Patriotism in Russia]. VKontakte.com. March 22. http://vk.com/wall-2789767_9761.

Dziadul, Chris. 2022. "Latvia Bans Russian Channels." Broadband TV News. February 24. https://www.broadbandtvnews.com/2022/02/24/latvia-bans-russian-channels-2.

Economist. 2019. "Emmanuel Macron in His Own Words (English)." November 7. https://www.economist.com/europe/2019/11/07/emmanuel-macron-in-his-own-words-english.

———. 2008. "A Parade of Power in Russia." May 9. https://www.economist.com/europe/2008/05/09/a-parade-of-power-in-russia.

ERR.ee. 2022. "Four Russian TV Channels Banned from Estonian Airwaves." February 25. https://news.err.ee/1608512162/four-russian-tv-channels-banned-from-estonian-airwaves.

Estonian Foreign Intelligence Service. 2022. "Exercise Zapad 2017 Versus Zapad 2021." February 15. https://raport.valisluureamet.ee/2022/en/russian-armed-forces/zapad-2017-vs-zapad-2021.

Fagan, Moira, and Jacob Poushter. 2020. "NATO Seen Favourably Across Member States." RealClearPublicAffairs. February 9. https://www.realclearpublicaffairs.com/public_affairs/2020/02/13/nato_seen_favorably_across_member_states_484081.html.

Federation of American Scientists. 1993. "Russian Military Doctrine, November 1993." November 2. https://nuke.fas.org/guide/russia/doctrine/russia-mil-doc.html.

Felgenhauer, Pavel. 2021. "Russia's Direct Action 'Black Ops' in Europe." *Eurasia Daily Monitor*. April 29. https://jamestown.org/program/russias-direct-action-black-ops-in-europe.

———. 2017. "Strategic War Games Zapad Has Begun." *Eurasia Daily Monitor* 14, no. 112 (September 14). https://jamestown.org/program/strategic-war-game-zapad-2017-has-begun.

Finn, Pat. n.d. "The Power of Tradition: Russia's Massive Cathedral Dedicated to the Military." Architizer. https://architizer.com/blog/inspiration/stories/russia-military-cathedral.

France 24. 2022. "Propaganda in Russia Arguing for Nuclear Weapons Use: Nobel Laureate." May 3. https://www.france24.com/en/live-news/20220503-propaganda-in-russia-arguing-for-nuclear-weapons-use-nobel-laureate.

Freaking News. 2019. "Putin & Stalin." September 25. https://web.archive.org/web/20190925133145/http://www.freakingnews.com/Putin-Stalin-Pics-63259.asp.

Fried, Daniel, and Kurt Volker. 2022. "The Speech in Which Putin Told Us Who He Was." *Politico*. February 18. https://www.politico.com/news/magazine/2022/02/18/putin-speech-wake-up-call-post-cold-war-order-liberal-2007-00009918.

Galochka, Ekaterina. 2014. "Volodin:' Est' Putin, est' Rossya, net Putina, net Rossii" [If There Is Putin, There Is Russia, No Putin, No Russia]. *Moskovskiy Komsomolets*. October 23. https://www.mk.ru/politics/2014/10/23/volodin-est-putin-est-rossiya-net-putina-net-rossii.html.

Gamov, Alexander. 2021. "25 dekabrya 1991 goda: kak v Kremle khoronili Sovetskii Soyuz" [25th of December 1991: How the Kremlin Buried the Soviet Union]. *Komsomolskaya Pravda*. December 25. https://www.kp.ru/daily/28374.5/4524245.

Garanich, Gleb and Sergiy Karazy. 2023. "Kyiv Says It Shoots Down Volley of Russian Hypersonic Missiles." Reuters. May 16. https://www.reuters.com/world/europe/air-defence-systems-repelling-attacks-ukraine-early-tuesday-officials-2023-05-16.

Gavrilov, Yuri. 2021. "Minoborony: Chislennost' 'Yunarmii' Do Kontsa Goda Dolzhna Uvelichit'sya Do 1 Mln" [Ministry of Defense: The Number of "Yunarmia" Members Will Increase to 1 Million by the End of the Year]. *Rossiiskaya Gazeta*. July 5. https://rg.ru/2021/07/05/minoborony-chislennost-iunarmii-do-konca-goda-dolzhna-uvelichitsia-do-1-mln.html.

Gazeta. 2019a. "Eto pozor: Kudrin nazval sverkhostruyu problemu Rossii" [It Is a Shame: Kudrin Named the Most Acute Problem for Russia]. June 19. https://www.gazeta.ru/business/2019/06/19/12425227.shtml.

———. 2019b. "Ne umeret's golodu: skol'ko deneg nuzhno rossiyanam" [Not to Starve to Death: How Much Money Russians Need]. April 3. https://www.gazeta.ru/business/2019/04/03/12281539.shtml.

Gerasimov, Valery. 2020. "Vstrecha s nachal'nikom Genshtaba Vooruzhonnykh Sil Valeriyem Gerasimovym" [Meeting with Chief of the General Staff of the Russian Armed Forces Valery Gerasimov]. October 7. http://kremlin.ru/events/president/news/64169.

———. 2019. "Vektory razvitiya voyennoy strategii" [Key Directions of the Development of Military Strategy, Speech at the Meeting of the Academy of Military Science]. *Red Star.* March 4. https://web.archive.org/web/20190810143322/http://redstar.ru/vektory-razvitiya-voennoj-strategii.

Gershkovich, Evan. 2020. "As the Coronavirus Contagion Grows in Russia, Putin's Strongman Image Weakens." *Moscow Times*. May 14. https://www.themoscowtimes.com/2020/05/14/as-the-coronavirus-contagion-grows-in-russia-putins-strongman-image-weakens-a70257.

Gevorkyan, Natalya, Natalya Timakova, and Andrei Kolesnikov. 2000. *Ot pervogo litsa: Razgovory s Vladimirom Putinym* [*From the First Person. Conversations with Vladimir Putin*]. Moscow, Russia: Vagrius.

Goble, Paul. 2021. "Moscow Says US Waging Biological War Against Russia." *Eurasia Daily Monitor*. July 8. https://jamestown.org/program/moscow-says-us-waging-biological-war-against-russia.

Golos Kubani. 2018. "V krasnodarskoy shkole detey zastavlyayut pet' pesnyu "Dyadya Vova, my s toboy"" [Children Are Forced to Sing the Song "Uncle Vova, We Are with You" in a Krasnodar School]. January 26. https://golos-kubani.ru/v-krasnodarskoj-shkole-detej-zastavlyayut-pet-pesnyu-dyadya-vova-my-s-toboj-video.

Golts, Alexander. 2019a. "Istoki 'pobedobesiya'" [The Sources of "Victory Run Amok"]. *Ezhednevniy Zhurnal*. May 7. https://www.ej2020.ru/?a=note&id=33726.

———. 2019b. "Kak den' pobedy prevrashchayut v voenno-patrioticheskiy maskarad" [How Victory Day Is Being Made into a Military-Patriotic Masquerade]. Otkrytye Media. May 8. https://openmedia.io/news/kak-den-pobedy-prevrashhayut-v-voenno-patrioticheskij-maskarad.

———. 2019c. "V pogone za sverkhoruzhiem. Pomogut li Rossii noveyshie rakety vernut' status superderzhavy" [In Search of a Superweapon. Will the Newest Rockets Help Russia Return to the Status of a Superpower?]. Republic. November 26. https://republic.ru/posts/95309.

———. 2018a. *Military Reform and Militarism in Russia*. Washington, DC: Jamestown Foundation. December. https://jamestown.org/product/military-reform-and-militarism-in-russia.

———. 2018b. "Putin's Militarized Election Campaign." *Eurasia Daily Monitor* 15, no. 40 (March 15). https://jamestown.org/program/putins-militarized-election-campaign.

Gontmakher, Evgeny. 2013. "Esli ne sdelaesh vybor ty, ego sdelaet dzhinn'" [If You Don't Make a Choice, the Genie Will Make It for You]. *Vedomosti*. February 18. https://www.vedomosti.ru/opinion/articles/2013/02/18/sygrat_na_predrassudkah.

Gorbachevsky, Andrey, and Irina Tumakova. 2019. "Eto prosto opasno" [This Is Simply Dangerous]. *Novaya Gazeta*. September 27. https://novayagazeta.ru/articles/2019/09/25/82114-eto-prosto-opasno.

Gosudarstvennaya Duma. 2020. "Noviy tekst Konstitutsii RF s popravkami 2020" [The New Text of the Constitution of the Russian Federation with the 2020 Amendments]. March. http://duma.gov.ru/news/48953.

Govorkov, Viktor. 1948. "Ne balui!" [Don't You Fool Around!]. https://calisphere.org/item/4c976b48277958c2e6c8c5975523090a.

Gov.pl. "Increasing the US Military Presence in Poland." https://www.gov.pl/web/national-defence/increasing-the-us-military-presence-in-poland.

Gromyko, Andrei. 1971. Rech na 240m s'ezde Kommunisticheskoy partii Sovetskogo soyuza [Speech at the 24th Congress of the Communist Party of the Soviet Union]. In *XXIV S'yezd Kommunisticheskoy Partii Sovetskogo Soyuza. Stenographicheskiy Otchet* [*24th Congress of the Communist Party of the Soviet Union*]. Moscow, Soviet Union: Politicheskaya Literatura. https://istmat.org/files/uploads/52749/24_sezd._chast_1._1971.pdf.

GTO.ru. n.d. "Vserossiyskiy fizkul'turno-sportivniy compleks GTO" [The National Physical Fitness and Sports Complex GTO]. https://www.gto.ru.

Gudkov, Lev. 2020a. "Khvatit militarizma!" [Enough of Militarism!]. *Novaya Gazeta*. February 19. https://novayagazeta.ru/articles/2020/02/19/83994-hvatit-naraschivat-voennuyu-mosch-daesh-rost-blagosostoyaniya.

———. 2020b. "Tyaga k Stalinu—moral'nya tupost' obshchestva" [The Appeal of Stalin Is the Moral Torpor of Society]. Fontanka.ru. January 8. https://www.fontanka.ru/2020/01/08/020.

———. 2019. "Epokha razvitogo militarizma" [The Era of Developed Militarism]. *Novaya Gazeta*. May 8. https://novayagazeta.ru/articles/2019/05/09/80447-epoha-razvitogo-militarizma.

Gudkov, Lev, Nina Khrushcheva, and Sergei Medvedev. 2021. "Zuby proch ot Rossii" [Teeth off from Russia!]. Radio Svoboda. June 2. https://www.svoboda.org/a/31272653.html.

Guriev, Sergei, and Aleh Tsyvinski. 2010. "Challenges Facing the Russian Economy After the Crisis." In *Russia After the Global Economic Crisis*, ed. Anders Aslund and Andrew Kuchins. Washington, DC: Peterson Institute for International Economics.

Hajdu, Dominika. 2022. "GLOBSEC Trends 2022: Central and Eastern Europe amid the War in Ukraine." GLOBSEC. May 31. https://www.globsec.org/what-we-do/publications/globsec-trends-2022-central-and-eastern-europe-amid-war-ukraine.

Hankewitz, Sten. 2020. "Estonian Foreign Intelligence, We're Particularly Threatened by Russia." Estonian World. February 14. https://estonianworld.com/security/estonian-foreign-intelligence-were-particularly-threatened-by-russia.

Harding, Luke. 2008. "Signs of Dispute on Moscow's Solzhenitsyn Street." *Guardian*. December 12. https://www.theguardian.com/world/2008/dec/12/russia.

Higgins, Andrew. 2020. "He Found One of Stalin's Mass Graves. Now He's in Jail." *New York Times*. April 27. https://www.nytimes.com/2020/04/27/world/europe/russia-historian-stalin-mass-graves.html.

Hopkins, Valerie. 2021. "Putin Tries to Erase History of Gulag Atrocities." *New York Times*. November 23. https://www.nytimes.com/2021/11/22/todayspaper/quotation-of-the-day-putin-tries-to-erase-history-of-gulag-atrocities.html.

Howard, Glen E., and Matthew Czekaj, eds. 2019. *Russia's Military Strategy and Doctrine*. Washington, DC: Jamestown Foundation. https://jamestown.org/wp-content/uploads/2019/02/Russias-Military-Strategy-and-Doctrine-web-1.pdf.

Hurska, Alla. 2019. "Putin Seeks to Garner Support of Russian Youth Through Military-Patriotic Upbringing (Part One)." *Eurasia Daily Monitor* 16, no. 51 (April 10). https://jamestown.org/program/putin-seeks-to-garner-support-of-russian-youth-through-military-patriotic-upbringing-part-one.

Ilyin, Ivan. 1993. *Nashi zadachi: Istoricheskaya sud'ba i budushchee rossii. Stat'I 1948–1954* [*Our Tasks: Historic Fate and Future of Russia. Essays 1948–1954*]. Moscow, Russia: Russkaya Kniga. 1:327–28. https://imwerden.de/publ-11960.html.

InfoResist. 2019. "Novosti Krymnasha. Chem YUNARMIYA vam ne terroristy-smertniki?" [News of Crimea-Is-Ours. Aren't Yunarmia a Lot like Not Suicide Bombers?]. October 17. https://inforesist.org/chem-yunarmiya-vam-ne-terroristy-smertniki.

Inozemtsev, Vladislav. 2022. "God Velikogo Nevozvrata" [The Year of Default]. Riddle. December 21. https://ridl.io/ru/god-velikogo-nevozvrata.

———. 2017. "Zachem v Kremle Govoryat o Voennoy Ekonomike" [Why Does the Kremlin Talk About the War Economy]. *RBK*. November 28.

Insider. 2014. "Anatomiya propagandy: Chto podtverdila pochta rabotayushchey na AP Kristiny Potupchik" [The Anatomy of Propaganda: What Confirmed the Email of Kristina Potupchik Who Works for the Presidential Administration]. December 26. https://theins.info/politika/2320.

Intelros. 2007. "Minutes of the Meeting with the Delegates of an All-Russian Conference of the Teachers of Social Sciences in Novo-Ogaryovo on June 21, 2007." http://www.intelros.ru/2007/06/21/stenograficheskijj_otchet_o_vstreche_s_delegatami_vserossijjskojj_konferencii_prepodavatelejj_gumanitarnykh_i_obshhestvennykh_nauk_novoogarevo_21_ijunja_2007_g.html.

Interfax. 2021. "Rosstat otmetil sokrashchenie urovnya bednosti v yanvare-sentyabre 2021 goda" [Rosstat Noted the Lowering of the Poverty Level from January-September of 2021]. December 3. https://www.interfax.ru/business/806527.

International Federation for Human Rights. 2021. "Russia: 'Crimes Against History.'" June. https://www.fidh.org/IMG/pdf/russie-_pad-uk-web.pdf.

International Memorial. 2022. "Russia's Supreme Court Approves Liquidation of International Memorial." February 28. https://www.memo.ru/en-us/memorial/departments/intermemorial/news/690.

Investigative Committee of the Russian Federation. 2020. "Alexandr Bastrykin prinyal uchastie v meropriyatii posvyashchyonnom pamyati zhertv fashizma" [Alexandr Bastrykin Participated in an Event Devoted to the Memory of the Victims of Fascism]. September 10. https://sledcom.ru/news/item/1498218.

Isachenkov, Vladimir. 2022. "Russia Holds Drills with Nuclear Subs, Land-Based Missiles." AP News. March 1. https://apnews.com/article/russia-ukraine-vladimir-putin-business-europe-moscow-563573526a93ea73a95698d8ddb61b9c.

Izdatel'stvo Politicheskoi Literatury. 1971. "XXIV Syezd Kommunisticheskoi Partii Sovetskogo Soyuza" [XXIV Congress of the Communist Party of the Soviet Union]. March 30. https://istmat.org/files/uploads/52749/24_sezd._chast_1._1971.pdf.

Jankowski, Dominik P. 2017. "The Dangerous Tool of Russian Military Exercises." Foreign Policy Association. June 7. https://foreignpolicyblogs.com/2017/06/07/dangerous-tool-russian-military-exercises.

Johnson, Dave. 2018. *Russia's Conventional Precision Strike Capabilities, Regional Crises, and Nuclear Thresholds*. Lawrence Livermore National Laboratory and Center for Global Security Outreach. February. 67, 85. https://cgsr.llnl.gov/content/assets/docs/Precision-Strike-Capabilities-report-v3-7.pdf.

Judah, Ben. 2014. "Behind the Scenes in Putin's Court: The Private Habits of a Latter-Day Dictator." *Newsweek*. July 23. https://www.newsweek.com/2014/08/01/behind-scenes-putins-court-private-habits-latter-day-dictator-260640.html.

Juuree, Ivo, and Mariita Mattiissen. 2020. *The Bronze Soldier Crisis of 2007*. Tallinn, Estonia: International Centre for Defense and Security. https://icds.ee/wp-content/uploads/2020/08/ICDS_Report_The_Bronze_Soldier_Crises_of_2007_Juurvee_Mattiisen_August_2020.pdf.

Kaftan, Larisa. 2004. "Putin ukreplyaet gosudarstvo, a ne sebya" [Putin Is Strengthening the State, Not Himself]. *Komsomolskaya Pravda*. September 28. https://www.kp.ru/daily/23370/32473.

Kahneman, Daniel. 2013. *Thinking, Fast and Slow*. New York: Farrar, Strauss and Giroux.

Kalikh, Aleksandr. 2015. "'Perm-36': Unichtozkenie Pamyati" ["Perm-36": The Destruction of Memory]. Grani.ru. March 4. https://graniru.org/blogs/free/entries/238693.html.

Kamenskiy, Il'ya. 2018. "Smotr detsadovskikh voisk; parad kolyasok v Pyatigorske" [An Inspection Kindergarten Troops; the Parade of Strollers in Pyatigorsk]. YouTube. https://www.youtube.com/watch?v=c4KTLKoYzGw.

Kantchev, Georgi. 2023. "Russian Deficit Soars to $25 Billion on War Spending, Oil Embargo." *Wall Street Journal*. February 6. https://www.wsj.com/articles/russian-deficit-soars-to-25-billion-on-war-spending-oil-embargo-11675706249.

Karakaev, Sergei. 2019. "Noviy raketniy kompleks 'Sarmat.' Mnenie rossiiskogo eksperta" [The New Rocket System "Sarmat." The Opinion of a Russian Expert]. Nauka i Tekhnika. December 17. https://naukatehnika.com/raketnyj-kompleks-sarmat.html.

Karpukhin, Sergei. 2003. "Russian President Vladimir Putin Crosses Himself as Patriarch Alexey II Conducts a Service Outside the Newly Restored Cathedral of St. Seraphim of Sarov in Sarov July 31, 2003." Reuters Pictures. July 31. https://pictures.reuters.com/CS.aspx?VP3=SearchResult&VBID=2C0FCIX47S79CY&SMLS=1&RW=1920&RH=969&POPUPPN=3&POPUPIID=2C040824LYK2.

Kasyanchuk, Denis. 2022. "The Russian Labour Market and the Ukrainian War." N-IUSSP. November 7. https://www.niussp.org/education-work-economy/the-russian-labour-market-and-the-ukrainian-war.

Kendall-Taylor, Anna, and Maria Snegovaya. 2022. "Supporting Russian Civil Society: A Report of the Transatlantic Forum on Russia." Center for a New American Security. December 1. https://www.cnas.org/publications/reports/supporting-russian-civil-society.

Khanskiy, Aleksandr. 2013. "1974–1979 (Tret'ye Pyatiletie Brezhneva—Stranitsa 10)" [1974–1979 (Brezhnev's Third 5-Year Plan)—Page 10]. Leninism. January 12. https://leninism.su/revolution-and-civil-war/4251-velikij-oktyabr-god-za-godom-1917-1990.html?start=9.

Khodzhaeva, Ekaterina, and Irina Meyer. 2017. "Mobilizing Patriotism in Russia: Federal Programs of Patriotic Education." *Russian Analytical Digest*, no. 207 September): 2–7. https://css.ethz.ch/content/dam/ethz/special-interest/gess/cis/center-for-securities-studies/pdfs/RAD_207.pdf.

Khozhateleva, Yulia. 2014. "Anna Semenovich: 'Sanktsii? Ne smeshite moi 'Iskandery'!" [Anna Semenovich: "Sanctions? Don't Make My Iskanders Laugh!]. *Komsomolskaya Pravda*. September 24. https://www.kp.ru/daily/26286/3164120.

Khrolenko, Aleksandr. 2020. "Raketa 'Sarmat' gotovitsya letat'" [Sarmat Is Getting Ready to Fly]. T Sputnik Belarus. May 28. https://sputnik.by/20200528/Raketa-Sarmat-gotovitsya-letat-dlya-chego-Rossii-novaya-Satana-1044749111.html.

Khruschev, Nikita. 1956. "Special Report to the 20th Congress of the Communist Party of the Soviet Union." https://web.archive.org/web/20051107221432/http://www.uwm.edu/Course/448-343/index12.html.

Kiev v Gorode. 2014. "Press-konferentsia Putina: Kratkoe Soderzhanie" [Putin's Press Conference: A Short Summary]. March 4. https://kiev.vgorode.ua/news/sobytiya/213662-putyn-hovoryt-o-krysakh-yanukovyche-uchenyiakh-v-krymu-y-vyvode-voisk-yz-ukrayny.

Killebrew, Robert. 2013. "Rapid Deployment: The Army and American Strategy." War on the Rocks. December 9. https://warontherocks.com/2013/12/rapid-deployment-the-army-and-american-strategy.

Kiselev, Dmitry. 2014. "Rossiya Mozhet Prevratit' SShA v Padioaktivniy Pepel" [Russia Can Turn the USA into Radioactive Ash]. YouTube. March 17. https://www.youtube.com/watch?v=TA9mVLomYo8.

Kodeks Zakonov. n.d. "Stat'ya 354.1 UK RF Reabilitatsiya Natsizma" [Article 354.1 of the Legal Code of the Russian Federation "On the Rehabilitation of Nazism"]. https://www.zakonrf.info/uk/354.1.

Kofman, Michael. 2021. "Zapad 2021: What We Learned from Russia's Massive Military Drills." *Moscow Times*. September 23. https://www.themoscowtimes.com/2021/09/23/zapad-2021-what-we-learned-from-russias-massive-military-drills-a75127.

Kofman, Michael, Anya Fink, and Jeffrey Edmonds. 2020. *Russian Strategy for Escalation Management: Evolution of Key Concepts*. Center for Naval Analysis. April. https://www.cna.org/archive/CNA_Files/pdf/drm-2019-u-022455-1rev.pdf.

Kolesnikov, Andrei. 2015. "Russian Ideology After Crimea." Carnegie Moscow Center. September. https://carnegieendowment.org/files/CP_Kolesnikov_Ideology2015_web_Eng.pdf.

Kolesnikov, Andrei, and Aleksei Polukhin. 2013. "Alexei Kudrin: 'My uperlis' v stenu effiktivnosti'" [Alexei Kudrin: "We Hit the Wall of Effectiveness"]. *Novaya Gazeta*. October 10. https://novayagazeta.ru/articles/2013/10/10/56683-aleksey-kudrin-171-my-uperlis-v-stenu-effiktivnosti-187.

Kommersant. 2021. "Chislo uyezzhayushikh iz Rossii uchenykh vyroslo v pyat' raz s 2012 goda" [The Number of Scientists Leaving Russia Increased Five-Fold Since 2012]. April 20. https://www.kommersant.ru/doc/4782133.

Kondrashov, Andrei. 2020. "Krym. Put' na rodinu, dokumentalniy fil'm Andreya Kondrashova" [Crimea: The Way Home, Documentary Film by Andrei Kondrashov]. YouTube. October 4. https://www.youtube.com/watch?v=PGGNXIQXlcU.

Korniyenko, Eduard. 2015. "Boys Dressed in a Historical Military Uniform Attend the So-Called Parade of Children's Troops in Rostov-on-Don, Southern Russia." Reuters Pictures. May 14. https://pictures.reuters.com/CS.aspx?VP3=SearchResult&VBID=2C0FCIX47S9IFL&SMLS=1&RW=1920&RH=969&POPUPPN=4&POPUPIID=2C0BF1OO5WE0U.

Kostereva, Milena. 2015. "Putin podpisal zakon o realizatsii kompleksa GTO" [Vladimir Putin Signed a Law on the Implementation of the GTO Complex]. *Kommersant*. October 6. https://www.kommersant.ru/doc/2825951.

Kotubey, Olesya. 2022. "'Nikoli Znovu' i 'Mozhem Povtorit'"—Dvi Kontseptsii Pam'iati i Ikhnia Funktsional'na Vidminnist'" ["Never Again" and "We Can Repeat It"—Two Concepts of Memory and Their Functional Difference]. Suspil'ne Kultura. May 7. https://suspilne.media/235124- nikoli-znovu-i-mozem-povtorit-dvi-koncepcii-pamati-i-ihna-funkcionalna-vidminnist.

Kozlova, Dary'ya. 2020. "'Fantomnaya real'nost', kotoraya ne otrazhaet nichego" ["Phantom Reality" That Shows Nothing]. *Novaya Gazeta*. July 1. https://novayagazeta.ru/articles/2020/07/01/86108-fantomnaya-realnost-kotoraya-ne-otrazhaet-nichego.

Kremlin.ru. 2023. "Ukaz ob utverzhdenii Konstsepsii vneshney politiki Rossiyskoy Federatsii" [Concept of the Foreign Policy of the Russian Federation]. March 31. http://kremlin.ru/events/president/news/70811.

———. 2022. "Strategic Deterrence Forces Exercise." February 19. http://www.en.kremlin.ru/events/president/news/67814/photos.

———. 2021a. "Expanded Meeting of the Defence Ministry Board." December 21. http://en.kremlin.ru/events/president/news/67402/photos.

———. 2021b. "Unveiling of Monument to Emperor Alexander III." June 5. http://en.kremlin.ru/events/president/news/65751.

———. 2020. "Ukaz Prezidenta Rossiiskoi Federatsii ot 02.06.2020 g. № 355" [Decree of the President of the Russian Federation from 02.06.2020, No. 355]. June 2. http://kremlin.ru/acts/bank/45562.

———. 2019a. "Grom-2019 Strategic Command-Post Exercises." October 17. http://www.en.kremlin.ru/events/president/news/61845.

———. 2019b. "Vladimir Putin provyol otdykh v Sibiri" [Vladimir Putin Spent His Holiday in Siberia]. October 7. http://kremlin.ru/events/president/news/61732/photos.

———. 2018a. "Laying Flowers at the Monument to Kuzma Minin and Dmitry Pozharsky." November 4. http://www.en.kremlin.ru/events/president/news/59041/photos.

———. 2018b. "Voyennyy parad na Krasnoy ploshchadi" [Military Parade on Red Square]. May 9. http://www.kremlin.ru/events/president/news/57436.

———. 2017a. "Sovmestnyye rossiysko-belorusskiye strategicheskiye ucheniya 'Zapad-2017'" [Joint Russian-Belarusian Strategic Exercises "West-2017"]. September 18. http://www.kremlin.ru/events/president/news/55644/photos.

———. 2017b. "Ukaz Prezidenta Rossiyskoy Federatsii ot 20.7.2017 No.327 'Ob utverzhdenii Ostnov gosudarstvennoy politiki Rossiyskoy Federatsii v oblasti voenno-morskoy deyatel'nosti na period do 2030 goda" [Decree of the President of the Russian Federation of July 20, 2017 No. 327 "On the Adoption of the Foundation of the State Policy of the Russian Federation in the Area of Naval Activity to 2030"]. July 20. http://kremlin.ru/acts/bank/42117.

———. 2017c. "Vladimir Putin Took Part in Strategic Nuclear Forces' Training." October 27. http://en.kremlin.ru/events/president/news/55929.

———. 2017d. "Voyennyy parad na Krasnoy ploshchadi" [Military Parade on Red Square]. May 9. http://www.kremlin.ru/events/president/news/54467.

———. 2015a. "Strategiya natsional'noy bezopasnosti Rossiyskoy Federatsii" [The National Security Strategy of the Russian Federation]. http://static.kremlin.ru/media/acts/files/0001201512310038.pdf.

———. 2015b. "Vladimir Putin vozlozhil tsvety k pamyatniku Kuz'me Mininu i Dmitriyu Pozharskomu na Krasnoy ploshchadi" [Vladimir Putin Laid Flowers at the Monument to Kuzma Minin and Dmitry Pozharsky on Red Square]. November 4. http://www.kremlin.ru/events/president/news/50619/photos.

———. 2014. "Vladimir Putin Observed Western and Central Military District Forces Exercises." March 3. http://en.kremlin.ru/events/president/news/20362.

———. 2013a. "Strategicheskie voyennye ucheniya 'Zapad'" [Strategic Military Exercises "Zapad"]. September 26. http://kremlin.ru/events/president/news/19290.

———. 2013b. "Vladimir Putin Spent a Weekend in Tyva and Krasnoyarsk Territory." July 26. http://www.en.kremlin.ru/events/president/news/18957/photos.

———. 2010. "Voyennaya Doktrina Rossiyskoi Federatsii" [Military Doctrine of the Russian Federation]. February 5. http://kremlin.ru/supplement/461.

———. 2003. "Prezident prinyal uchastie v prazdnichnykh torzhestvakh po sluchaiyu 100-letiya kanonizatsii prepodobnogo Serafima Sarovskogo" [The President Took Part in the Celebratory Activities in Honor of the 100 Year Anniversary of the Canonization of the Venerable Seraphim of Sarov]. July 31. http://kremlin.ru/events/president/news/29121.

Kristensen, Hans M. 2020. "US Deploys New Low-Yield Nuclear Submarine Warhead." Federation of American Scientists. January 29. https://fas.org/blogs/security/2020/01/w76-2deployed.

Kristensen, Hans M., and Matt Korda. 2022a. "Nuclear Notebook: How Many Nuclear Weapons Does Russia Have in 2022?" *Bulletin of the Atomic Scientists* 78, no. 2 (February 23): 98–121, https://thebulletin.org/premium/2022-02/nuclear-notebook-how-many-nuclear-weapons-does-russia-have-in-2022.

———. 2022b. "Russian Nuclear Weapons, 2022." *Bulletin of the Atomic Scientists* 78, no. 2. https://doi.org/10.1080/00963402.2022.2038907.

———. 2021. "Russian Nuclear Weapons, 2021." *Bulletin of the Atomic Scientists* 77, no. 2 (March 18): 90–108, https://www.tandfonline.com/doi/full/10.1080/00963402.2021.1885869.

———. 2020. "United States Nuclear Forces, 2020." *Bulletin of the Atomic Scientists* 76, no. 1 (January 2): 46–60. https://doi.org/10.1080/00963402.2019.1701286.

———. 2019. "Russian Nuclear Forces, 2019." *Bulletin of the Atomic Scientists* 75, no. 2 (March 4): 73–84. https://doi.org/10.1080/00963402.2019.1580891.

Krutikhin, Mikhail. 2020. "Neft' za $30?" [Oil for $30?]. Republic. March 7. https://republic.ru/posts/96101.

Kryminform. 2017. "Nagrada Krymskoy vesny: skol'ko stoit medal' 'Za vozvrashcheniye Kryma'" [Crimean Spring Award: How Much the Medal "For the Return of Crimea" Costs]. November 29. https://www.c-inform.info/comments/id/298.

Kuzmin, Vitaly. 2016. "Military-Technical Forum ARMY-2016—Demonstration." September 6. https://www.vitalykuzmin.net/Military/ARMY-2016-Demonstration/i-JgHQvQP/A.

Laizans, Jeff. 2022. "U.S. Apache Helicopters Arrive in Latvia." Reuters. February 24. https://www.reuters.com/world/europe/us-apache-helicopters-arrive-latvia-2022-02-24.

Lally, Kathy. 2013. "Trial of Bolotnaya 12 Seen as a Warning Against Challenging the Kremlin." *Washington Post*. October 30. https://www.washingtonpost.com/world/trial-of-bolotnaya-12-seen-as-a-warning-against-challenging-the-kremlin/2013/10/29/5e1dec92-381f-11e3-89db-8002ba99b894_story.html.

Lashov, Yuri. 2014. "A Russian Orthodox Priest Blesses a SU-27 SM Fighter Jet on the Airfield of Belbek Military Airport Outside Sevastopol on November 26, 2014." Getty Images. November 26. https://www.gettyimages.com/detail/news-photo/russian-orthodox-priest-blesses-a-su-27-sm-fighter-jet-on-news-photo/459606800?adppopup=true.

Lenin, Vladimir. 1944. O natsional'noy gordosti velikorossov [On the National Pride of the Great Russians]. Moscow, Soviet Union: OGIZ. https://www.booksite.ru/fulltext/179758/text.pdf.

Lenta. 2019. "Genshtab Rossii obyasnil sut' amerikanskogo 'Troyanskogo konya'" [The General Staff Explained the Meaning of the American "Trojan Horse"]. March 2. https://lenta.ru/news/2019/03/02/kon.

Lermontov, Mikhail. 1964. "Izmail-Bey." In *Sobranie sochineniy v chetyryokh tomakh. Tom vtoroy, Poemy I povesti v stikhakh* [*Collected Works in Four Volumes. Volume II, Poems and Novellas in Verse*], 288. Moscow, Soviet Union: Khudozhestvennaya literatura.

Levada Center. n.d. "Odobrenie deyatel'nosti Vladimira Putina" [Vladimir Putin's Approval Rating]. https://www.levada.ru/indikatory.

———. 2022. "Strakhi" [Fears]. January 12. https://www.levada.ru/2022/01/12/strahi-5.

———. 2021a. "22 iunya 2021 goda: 80 let posle nachala voiny [June 22, 2021: 80 Years Since the Beginning of the War]. June 22. https://www.levada.ru/2021/06/22/22-iyunya-2021-goda-80-let-posle-nachala-vojny.

———. 2021b. "Nasha glavnaya strana" [Our Most Important Country]. June 1. https://www.levada.ru/2021/06/01/nasha-glavnaya-strana.

———. 2021c. "Otnoshenie k Stalinu: Rossiya i Ukraina" [Attitudes Toward Stalin: Russia and Ukraine]. June 23. https://www.levada.ru/2021/06/23/otnoshenie-k-stalinu-rossiya-i-ukraina.

———. 2021d. "Prezidentskie reitingi i polozhenie del v strane" [The President's Ratings and the State of the Country]. February 4. https://www.levada.ru/2021/02/04/prezidentskie-rejtingi-i-polozhenie-del-v-strane.

———. 2021e. "Rossiya i Evropa" [Russia and Europe]. March 18. https://www.levada.ru/2021/03/18/rossiya-i-evropa-2.

———. 2021f. "Samye vydayushchiesya lichnosti v istorii" [The Most Distinguished Figures in History]. June 21. https://www.levada.ru/2021/06/21/samye-vydayushhiesya-lichnosti-v-istorii.

———. 2020a. "41 protsent molodyozhi Rossii ne informirovany o stalinskikh repressiyakh" [41 Percent of Russian Young People Are Not Informed About Stalin's Repressions]. June 24. https://www.levada.ru/2020/06/24/41-molodyozhi-rossii-ne-informirovany-o-stalinskih-repressiyah-11-o-sobytiyah-vtoroj-mirovoj-vojny.

———. 2020b. "Doverie institutam" [Trust in Institutions]. September 21. https://www.levada.ru/2020/09/21/doverie-institutam.

———. 2020c. "Obnulenie prezidentskikh srokov" [The Nullification of Presidential Terms]. March 27. https://www.levada.ru/2020/03/27/obnulenie-prezidentskih-srokov.

———. 2020d. "Struktura i vosproizvodstvo pamyati o Sovetskom Soyuze" [The Structure and the Reproduction of Memory of the Soviet Union]. March 24. https://www.levada.ru/2020/03/24/struktura-i-vosproizvodstvo-pamyati-o-sovetskom-soyuze.

———. 2020e. "Velikaya derzhava" [A Great Power]. January 28. https://www.levada.ru/2020/01/28/velikaya-derzhava.

———. 2019a. "Approval Ratings." December 16. https://www.levada.ru/en/2019/12/16/approval-ratings-10.

———. 2019b. "Dinamika otnosheniya k Stalinu" [The Changes in the Attitude Toward Stalin]. April 16. https://www.levada.ru/2019/04/16/dinamika-otnosheniya-k-stalinu.

———. 2018a. "Institutional Trust." October 22. https://www.levada.ru/en/2018/10/22/institutional-trust-4.

———. 2018b. "Pensionnaya Reforma" [Pension Reform]. September 9. https://www.levada.ru/2018/09/27/pensionnaya-reforma-4.

———. 2015. "Pochemu voyna tak prityagatel'na dlya Rossiyan?" [Why Is War So Appealing to Russians?]. November 17. https://www.levada.ru/2015/11/17/pochemu-vojna-tak-prityagatelna-dlya-rossiyan.

———. 2013a. "Dekabr'skie reitingi odobroniya i doveriya" [The December Ratings of Approval and Trust]. December 25. https://www.levada.ru/2013/12/25/dekabrskie-rejtingi-odobreniya-i-doveriya-3.

———. 2013b. "Russian Public Opinion—2012–2013." 2013. https://www.levada.ru/sites/default/files/2012_eng.pdf.

Levieva, Christina. 2019. "Prezident Rossii vruchil nagrady vdovam pogibshikh pri ispytanii noveishego oruzhiya pod Severodvinskom" [The President of Russia Handed Out Awards to the Widows of Those Who Died While Testing Cutting Edge Weaponry near Severodvinsk]. Perviiy Kanal. https://www.1tv.ru/news/2019-11-22/376180-prezident_rossii_vruchil_nagrady_vdovam_pogibshih_pri_ispytanii_noveyshego_oruzhiya_pod_severodvinskom.

Levinson, Alexei. 2014. "Mental'naya yama" [Mental Abyss]. *Novaya Gazeta*. June 3. https://novayagazeta.ru/articles/2014/06/04/59831-mentalnaya-yama.

———. 2011. "Nevelikaya imperiya?" [A Not So Great Empire?]. Russia in Global Affairs. June 11. https://globalaffairs.ru/articles/nevelikaya-imperiya.

Levinson, Alexei, and Stepan Goncharov. 2015. "Voyna vmesto budyshchego—vykhod iz anomicheskogo soznaniya" [War Instead of the Future—an Exit from the Anomie-Affected Consciousness]. *Vestnik Obshchestvennogo Mneniya* 121, no. 3–4 (July–December). https://cyberleninka.ru/article/n/voyna-vmesto-buduschego-vyhod-dlya-anomicheskogo-soznaniya/viewer.

Lewis, Michael. 2016. "How Two Trailblazing Psychologists Turned the World of Decision Science Upside Down." *Vanity Fair*. November 14. www.vanityfair.com/news/2016/11/decision-science-daniel-kahneman-amos-tversky.

Library of Congress. 2012. "Russia: Espionage and State Treason Concepts Revised." November 28. https://www.loc.gov/item/global-legal-monitor/2012-11-28/russia-espionage-and-state-treason-concepts-revised.

Lindner, Evelin. 2006. *Making Enemies: Humiliation and International Conflict*. Westport, CT: Praeger Security International, 2006.

LRT.lt. 2022. "Lithuania Bans Russian, Belarusian TV Channels over War Incitement." February 25. https://www.lrt.lt/en/news-in-english/19/1626345/lithuania-bans-russian-belarusian-tv-channels-over-war-incitement.

Lurie, Vadim. 2012. "Azbuka protesta" [The ABCS of the Protest]. Polit.ru. https://polit.ru/media/files/2012/04/27/Azbuka_Blok_Internet.pdf.

L'vov, Yury. 2001. "Tridtsat' tri putinskikh bogatyrya" [Putin's Thirty-Three Knights]. *Kommersant*. November 13. https://www.kommersant.ru/doc/290986.

MacFarquhar, Neil, and David E. Sanger. 2018. "Putin's 'Invincible' Missile Is Aimed at U.S. Vulnerabilities." *New York Times*. March 1. https://www.nytimes.com/2018/03/01/world/europe/russia-putin-speech.html.

Makarkin, Aleksei. 2013. "Politicheskayasituatsiya i obshchestvennye nastroeniya v Rossii. God posle vyborov: Nachalo zastoya ili vremennoe zatish'e?" [The Political Situation and Societal Mood in Russia. One Year After the Elections: The Beginning of a Stagnation, or a Temporary Lull?]. Politkom. June 23. http://politcom.ru/15953.html.

Malinovna, Ol'ga. 2015. *Aktual'noe Proshloe: Simvolicheskaya Politika Vlastvuyushchei Eliti i Dilemmy Rossiiskoi Identichnosti* [*The Urgent Past: Symbolic Politics of the Ruling Elite and the Dilemmas of Russian Identity*]. Moscow, Russia: Politicheskaya entsiklopedia.

Masyuk, Elena. 2015. "Boris Nemtsov: 'Oni ne smogut zastavit menya zamolchat', prosto ne smogut" [Boris Nemtsov: They Will Not Force Me to Be Silent, They

Simply Will Not]. *Novaya Gazeta*. February 28. https://novayagazeta.ru/articles/2015/02/28/63231-boris-nemtsov-171-oni-ne-smogut-zastavit-menya-zamolchat-prosto-ne-smogut-187.

Medinsky, Vladimir. 2019. "Diplomatichiskiy triumf SSSR" [The Diplomatic Triumph of the USSR]. RIA Novosti. August 23. https://ria.ru/20190823/1557826932.html.

Meduza. 2015. "Russia's Only Gulag Memorial Is Redesigned to Celebrate the Gulag." March 4. https://meduza.io/en/news/2015/03/05/russia-s-only-gulag-memorial-is-redesigned-to-celebrate-the-gulag.

Medvedev, Sergei. 2021. "Nas zhdyot strashnaya i smeshnaya diktatura" [A Strange and Ridiculous Dictatorship Awaits Us]. Grani.ru. July 23. https://graniru.org/Society/m.282183.html.

———. 2017. *Park Krymskogo perioda. Khroniki tretego sroka* [*The Crimean Era Park. Chronicles of* [*Putin's*] *Third Term*]. Moscow, Russia: Individuum.

Meyers, Meghann. 2022. "Most Troops Deployed for Ukraine Response Still in Europe." *Military Times*. November 1. https://www.militarytimes.com/news/your-military/2022/11/01/most-troops-deployed-for-ukraine-response-still-in-europe.

Meyers, Steven Lee. 2007. "Estonia Removes Soviet-Era War Memorial After a Night of Violence." *New York Times*. April 27. https://www.nytimes.com/2007/04/27/world/europe/27iht-estonia.4.5477141.html.

Milne, Richard. 2022. "Estonia's PM Says Country Would Be 'Wiped from Map' Under Existing Nato Plans." *Financial Times*. June 22. https://www.ft.com/content/a430b191-39c8-4b03-b3fd-8e7e948a5284.

Ministry of Defense of the Russian Federation. 2019. "V Moskve proshel parad v chest' 74-y godovshchiny Pobedy v Velikoy Otechestvennoy voyne" [A Parade Was Held in Moscow in Honor of the 74th Anniversary of Victory in the Great Patriotic War]. May 9. https://мультимедиа.минобороны.рф/multimedia/photo/gallery.htm?id=65550@cmsPhotoGallery.

Ministry of Finance of the Russian Federation. 2021. "Osnovnye napravleniya byudzhetnoi nalogovoi i tamozhenno tarifnoi politiki na 2022 god i na planovyi period 2023 i 2024 godov" [The Main Directions of the Budget, Tax and Customs Tariff Policy for 2022 and for the Planning Period of 2023 and 2024]. September 30. https://minfin.gov.ru/ru/document/?id_4=134362-osnovnye_napravleniya_byudzhetnoi_nalogovoi_i_tamozhenno-tarifnoi_politiki_na_2022_god_i_na_planovyi_period_2023_i_2024_godov.

Mironov. 2015. "Predatelyam poshchady byt' ne dolzhno!" [There Should Be No Mercy for Traitors!]. May 19. https://mironov.ru/moya-pozitsiya/predatelyam-poshhady-byt-ne-dolzhno.

Moran, Michael. 2006. "Modern Military Force Structure." Council on Foreign Relations. October 26. https://www.cfr.org/backgrounder/modern-military-force-structures.

Morskoi Sbornik. 2019. "Glavny Voenno-Morskoy Parad" [Main Naval Parade]. https://heritage-institute.ru/wp-content/uploads/2019/10/mc_9-2019_%D0%BB%D0%B5%D0%BD%D0%B8%D0%BD%D0%BA%D0%B0_s-1_compressed.pdf.

Moscow Times. 2022. "Russia Simulates Nuclear Strikes near EU." May 5. https://www.themoscowtimes.com/2022/05/05/russia-simulates-nuclear-capable-strikes-near-eu-a77586.

———. 2020a. "Russia Is a 'Distinct Civilization,' Putin Says." May 18. https://www.the-moscowtimes.com/2020/05/18/russia-is-a-distinct-civilization-putin-says-a70295.

———. 2020b. "Russian Bookstores Sell New Constitution Ahead of Vote on Putin's Reforms." June 16. https://www.themoscowtimes.com/2020/06/16/russian-bookstores-sell-new-constitution-ahead-of-vote-on-putins-reforms-a70593.

———. 2019a. "Putin Orders Monitoring of Youth Behavior Online." October 17. https://www.themoscowtimes.com/2019/10/17/putin-orders-monitoring-youth-behavior-online-a67776.

———. 2019b. "Russia Launches World War II–Themed TV Channel Targeting Youth." April 10. https://www.themoscowtimes.com/2019/04/10/russia-launches-world-war-ii-themed-tv-channel-targeting-youth-a65175.

———. 2019c. "Russia Marks Victory Day with Red Square Military Parade." May 9. https://www.themoscowtimes.com/2019/05/09/russia-marks-victory-day-with-red-square-military-parade-a65534.

———. 2019d. "Siberian Communists Unveil Stalin Monument amid Controversy." May 10. https://www.themoscowtimes.com/2019/05/10/siberian-communists-unveil-stalin-monument-amid-controversy-a65539.

———. 2017. "Russian Activist Navalny Given 5-Year Suspended Sentence in Kirovles Retrial." February 8. https://www.themoscowtimes.com/2017/02/08/russian-activist-navalny-sentenced-in-kirovles-case-a57038.

Moskovskiy Komsomolets. 2019. "Kreml' ne poveril, chto u rossiyan nyet deneg na obuv" [The Kremlin Did Not Believe That Russians Have No Money for Shoes]. April 3. https://www.mk.ru/politics/2019/04/03/kreml-ne-poveril-chto-u-rossiyan-net-deneg-na-obuv.html.

Moskva News Agency. 2015. "Obryad blagosloveniya uchastnikov Parada Pobedy i osvyashcheniya puskovykh ustanovok na Khodynskom pole" [Ritual of the Blessing of the Participants of the Victory Parade and the Consecration of Launchers on Khodynka Field]. May 6. https://web.archive.org/web/20220517193838/https://www.mskagency.ru/photobank/147993.

Munich Security Conference. 2020. "Westlessness." February 16. https://securityconference.org/en/news/full/westlessness-the-munich-security-conference-2020.

Naipaul, V. S. 1988. *The Enigma of Arrival*. New York: Vintage.

National News Service. 2021a. "Putin raskryl chislo agentov TsRU sredi sovetnikov pravitel'stva v nachale 90-kh" [Putin Revealed the Number of CIA Agents Among Government Advisers in the Early '90s]. November 12. https://nsn.fm/policy/putin-raskryl-chislo-agentov-tsru-sredi-sovetnikov-pravitelstva-v-nachale-90-h.

———. 2021b. "Putin soobshchil, chto v pravitel'stve RF rabotali kadrovie sotrudniki TsRU" [Putin Said That CIA Personnel Worked in the Russian Government]. December 9. https://nsn.fm/policy/putin-soobschil-chto-v-pravitelstve-rf-rabotali-kadrovye-sotrudniki-tsru.

Nechepurenko, Ivan. 2019. "Meeting a Russian Scientist? He Might Need to Report on You." *New York Times*. August 14. https://www.nytimes.com/2019/08/14/world/europe/russia-science-rules.html.

Nevzorov, Alexander. 2020. "Nevzorov v programme «Gordon». Bol'shoye interv'yu pro Putina, vechnost' i perspektivy Rossii" [Nevzorov on "Gordon." A Big Interview About Putin, Eternity and the Perspective of Russia]. YouTube. March 9. https://www.youtube.com/watch?v=453cUKleB5I.

Nezavisimaya Gazeta. 2000. "Voennaya doktrina Rossiyskoy Federatsii" [Military Doctrine of the Russian Federation]. April 22. https://www.ng.ru/politics/2000-04-22/5_doktrina.html.

Nikolaev, Igor. 2020. "Chto ne tak s vospitaniem rossiyskogo patriotizma" [What Is Wrong with the Rearing of Russian Patriotism]. *Moskovskiy Komsomolets.* January 23. https://www.mk.ru/politics/2020/01/23/chto-ne-tak-s-vospitaniem-rossiyskogo-patriotizma.html.

Nikolsky, Alexey. 2018. "Russian President Vladimir Putin Looks Through the Scope as He Shoots a Chukavin Sniper Rifle (SVC-380) During a Visit to the Military Patriot Park in Kubinka, Outside Moscow, on September 19, 2018." Getty Images. September 19. https://www.gettyimages.com/detail/news-photo/russian-president-vladimir-putin-looks-through-the-scope-as-news-photo/1035946814.

Nisametdinov, Timur. 2007. "Estonia War Memorial." AP Newsroom. April 26. https://newsroom.ap.org/editorial-photos-videos/detail?itemid=55cae7356d7e4527886df-6d266222291&mediatype=photo.

Noble, Ben. 2020. "Russia's 'Nationwide Vote' on Constitutional Reforms." Presidential Power. June 19. https://presidential-power.net/?p=11174.

North Atlantic Treaty Organization. 2022a. "NATO's Eastern Flank: Stronger Defense and Deterrence." July. https://www.nato.int/nato_static_fl2014/assets/pdf/2022/3/pdf/2203-map-det-def-east.pdf.

———. 2022b. "NATO's Forward Presence." June. https://www.nato.int/nato_static_fl2014/assets/pdf/2022/6/pdf/2206-factsheet_efp_en.pdf

Nove Izvestiya. 2011. "Putin predlozhil zhestche nakazyvat' prispeshnikov Zapada" [Putin Suggested Tougher Punishments for the Lackeys of the West]. December 8. https://newizv.ru/news/politics/08-12-2011/155943-putin-predlozhil-zhestche-nakazyvat-prispeshnikov-zapada.

Novoselova, Elena. 2021. "Pochti polovina Rossiyan schitayut, chto Vtoraya mirovaya voyna nachalas' v 1941-m" [Nearly Half of Russians Think That World War II Began in 1941]. *Rossiyskaya Gazeta.* September 2. https://rg.ru/2020/09/02/pochti-polovina-rossiian-schitaiut-chto-vtoraia-mirovaia-vojna-nachalas-v-1941-m.html.

Novosti VPK. n.d. "Upravlyaemaya Operativno-Takticheskaya Raketa 9M723" [The Controlled Operational-Tactical Rocket 9M723]. https://vpk.name/library/f/9m723.html.

Odynova, Alexandra. 2011. "WikiLeaks: Putin's 'Personal Gripe' with Estonia Result of WWII Betrayal." *Moscow Times.* September 5. https://www.themoscowtimes.com/2011/09/05/wikileaks-putins-personal-gripe-with-estonia-result-of-wwii-betrayal-a9358.

Office of the Secretary of Defense. 2018. "Nuclear Posture Review—February 2018." https://media.defense.gov/2018/Feb/02/2001872886/-1/-1/1/2018-NUCLEAR-POSTURE-REVIEW-FINAL-REPORT.PDF.

Otkrytye Media. 2020a. "Palatki, bagazhnik, penyok. Samye strannye mesta, gde prok-hodit golosovanie po 'obnuleniyu' Putina" [Tents, Trunks, and Tree Stumps. The Strangest Places Where the Putin 'Nullification' Voting Occurred]. June 25. https://openmedia.io/news/n1/palatki-bagazhnik-penyok-samye-strannye-mesta-gde-proxodit-golosovanie-po-obnuleniyu-putina.

———. 2020b. "V moskovskom detsadu povesili kalendar's okrovavlennymi det'mi' k 75-letiyu Pobedy" [For the 75th Anniversary of the Victory, They Hung Cal-endar 'with Bloodstained Children' in a Moscow Kindergarten]. February 11. https://origin.openmedia.io/news/n2/v-moskovskom-detsadu-povesili-kalendar-s-okrovavlennymi-detmi-k-75-letiyu-pobedy.

Pajula, Raigo. 2007a. "Estonia-Russia Unrest." AFP Photo. April 28. https://www.afpforum.com/AFPForum/Search/Results.aspx?pn=1&smd=8&mui=3&q=3207998675175097208_0&fst=Tallinn+riot&fto=3&t=2&cck=a1aff2#pn=1&smd=8&mui=3&q=3207998674126672361_0&fst=Tallinn+riot&fto=3&t=2&cck=a1aff2.

———. 2007b. "Police Face Demonstrators." Getty Images. April 27. https://www.gettyimages.com/detail/news-photo/police-face-demonstrators-27-april-2007-in-tallin-at-least-news-photo/73987127.

Patriarchia.ru. 2007. "Patriarshee privetstvie uchastnikam prazdnovaniya 60-letiya so dnya osnovaniya 12-go Glavnogo upravleniya ministerstva oborony RF" [Patri-arch's Greeting to the Participants of the Celebration of the 60th Anniversary of the Main Department of the Ministry of Defense]. September 4. http://www.patriarchia.ru/db/text/290432.html.

Patriot Park. n.d. "Tekhnicheskiy Tsentr—Park Patriot" [Technical Center—Patriot Park]. https://patriotp.ru/obekty/restavratsionno-tekhnicheskiy-tsentr.

———. n.d. "Trenezhurniy Kompleks Parka Patriot" [Training Complex of Park Patriot]. https://patriotp.ru/uslugi/igrovoy-tsentr-parka-patriot.

———. n.d. "Uslugi Mnogofunktsional'nogo Ognevogo Tsentra—Park Patriot" [The Services of the Multifunctional Firing Center—Patriot Park]. https://patriotp.ru/uslugi/mnogofunktsionalnyy-ognevoy-tsentr.

Patrushev, Nikolai. 2021a. "Nadeemsya, chto v Vashingtone vsyo zhe vozobladayet zdra-vyy smysl" [We Are Hoping That Sanity Will Prevail in Washington]. *Kommersant*. April 7. https://www.kommersant.ru/doc/4762137.

———. 2021b. "Patrushev znayet o planakh Zapada po razlozheniyu Rossii" [Patrushev Knows About the West's Plans for Russia. Speech at a Conference on the National Security, Khanty-Mansiysk]. *Nezavisimaya Gazeta*. March 23. https://www.ng.ru/politics/2021-03-23/3_8109_west.html.

———. 2014. "Nikolai Patrushev: Otrezvlenie ukraintsev budet zhestkim i boleznenym" [Nikolai Patrushev: The "Morning After" Will Be Tough and Painful for Ukrai-nians]. Interview with Ivan Yegorov. *Rossiiskaya Gazeta*. October 15. https://rg.ru/2014/10/15/patrushev.html.

———. 2009. "Menyaetsya Rossiya, menyaetsya i yeyo voennaya politika" [As Russia Changes So Does Its Military Doctrine]. *Izvestiya*. October 14. https://iz.ru/news/354178.

Perper, Rosie, and Bill Bostock. 2020. "Oil Is Down 21% After Its Biggest Drop in Decades Following Saudi Price Cuts That Sparked a Race to the Bottom with

Russia." Insider. March 9. https://www.businessinsider.com/oil-price-crash-market-drop-global-price-war-futures-coronavirus-2020-3.

Pertsev, Andrei. 2020. "Putinskaya nestabil'nost'. Kak president stal istochnikom riskov dlya sistemy" [Putin Instability. How the President Became the Source of Risks for the System]. Carnegie Endowment for International Peace. March 30. https://carnegie.ru/commentary/81397.

Petrov, Nikolai. 2022. "Period poluraspada. Nikolay Petrov o tom, kak voyna v Ukraine i sanktsii mogut privesti k dezintegratsii Rossii" [Half Life. Nikolai Petrov on How the War in Ukraine and Sanctions Can Lead to the Disintegration of Russia]. Insider. September 9. https://theins.ru/opinions/nikolai-petrov/254483.

Philotheus. n.d. "Poslaniye velikomu knyazu Vasiliyu, v kotorom ob ispravlenii krestnogo znameniya I o sodomskom blude" [Address to Grand Prince Vasily on the Improvement of the Sign of the Cross and the Sodom Lust]. Museum of Historical Russian Reforms Named After P. A. Stolypin. http://museumreforms.ru/node/13626.

Pikabu.ru. 2014. "7-metrovyy plakat '5-ya kolonna. Chuzhiye sredi nas' poyavilsya naprotiv redaktsii 'Ekha Moskvy' na Novom Arbate, na fasade Moskovskogo doma knigi" [7-Meter Poster "5th Column. Aliens Among Us" Appeared on the Façade of the Moscow House of Books Across the Street from the Editorial Office of "Echo Moscow" on Novy Arbat]. https://pikabu.ru/story/7metrovyiy_plakat_5ya_kolonna_chuzhie_sredi_nas_poyavilsya_naprotiv_redaktsii_yekha_moskvyi_na_novom_arbate_na_fasade_moskovskogo_doma_knigi_2168315.

Pinkham, Sophie. 2022. "A Hotter Russia." *New York Review of Books*. June 23. https://www.nybooks.com/articles/2022/06/23/a-hotter-russia-klimat-thane-gustafson.

Pismennaya, Evgenia, Ilya Arkhipov, and Henry Meyer. 2020. "Russia Paid a Heavy Price to End the Oil Price War." *World Oil*. April 13. https://www.worldoil.com/news/2020/4/13/russia-paid-a-heavy-price-to-end-the-oil-price-war.

Pitalev, Iliya. 2020. "Russia's Young Army Cadets March During the Victory Day Parade in Red Square in Moscow, Russia, June 24, 2020." Reuters Pictures. June 24. https://pictures.reuters.com/CS.aspx?VP3=SearchResult&VBID=2C0FCIXRDX0CP2&SMLS=1&RW=1920&RH=969&POPUPPN=1&POPUPIID=2C0FQEXKFIAWL%20.

Pivovarov, Sergey. 2019a. "Children, Wearing Military Uniforms March During a Parade Held by Pupils of Infant and Primary Schools and Russian Servicemen, Which Is a Public Event to Honour World War Two Veterans, in Rostov-on-Don, Russia May 16, 2018." Reuters Pictures. May 16. https://pictures.reuters.com/CS.aspx?VP3=SearchResult&VBID=2C0FCIX47SP8AC&SMLS=1&RW=1920&RH=969&POPUPPN=18&POPUPIID=2C0FQE38E2F7Z.

———. 2019b. "Children Wearing Military Uniforms Ride Kick Scooters During a Parade, Held by Russian Servicemen; Children from Infant and Toddler Day Care Centers and Grade Schools at a Public Event Devoted to World War II Veterans and to Marking the Upcoming Victory Day, in Rostov-on-Don, Russia." Reuters Pictures. April 25. https://pictures.reuters.com/CS.aspx?VP3=SearchResult&VBID=2C0FCIX47SP8AC&SMLS=1&RW=1920&RH=969&POPUPPN=1&POPUPIID=2C0BF1QW1G765.

Politi, James, Andy Bounds, and Valentina Pop. 2022. "Joe Biden Warns Vladimir Putin Is 'Not Joking' About Nuclear Threat." *Financial Times*. October 6. https://www.ft.com/content/2f4ab252-8eaa-4328-9c2e-18fad985a65c.

Pravo. 2002. "Federal'niy Zakon o Vyborakh Prezidenta Rossiskoi Federatsii" [Federal Law on Russian Federal Presidential Elections]. December 27. https://web.archive.org/web/20220122162250/http://pravo.gov.ru/proxy/ips/?docbody=&nd=102079674.

Pressmania.pl. 2020 "Największe kłamstwo Putina" [Putin's Biggest Lie]. June 21. http://pressmania.pl/najwieksze-klamstwo-putina.

Priemier.gov.ru. 2012. "V. V. Putin vstretilsya v g. Sarove s ekspertami po global'nym ugrozam natsional'noy bezopasnosti, ukrepleniyu oboronosposobnosti i povysheniyu boyegotovnosti Vooruzhonnykh sil Rossiyskoy Federatsii" [Vladimir Vladimirovich Putin Met in the City of Sarov with Experts on Global Threats to National Security, Strengthening Defense Capabilities and Increasing the Combat Readiness of the Armed Forces of the Russian Federation]. February 24. https://web.archive.org/web/20230202113229/http://archive.premier.gov.ru/events/news/18248.

Putin, Vladimir. 2023. "Obrashcheniye k grazhdanam Rossii" [Address to the Russian People]. Kremlin.ru. June 24, 2023. http://kremlin.ru/events/president/news/71496.

———. 2022a. "Zasedaniye kollegii Ministerstva oborony" [Meeting of the Collegium of the Ministry of Defense]. Kremlin.ru. December 21. http://kremlin.ru/events/president/news/70159

———. 2022b. "Obrashchenie Prezidenta Rossiyskoy Federatsii" [An Address by the President of the Russian Federation]. Kremlin.ru. February 24. http://kremlin.ru/events/president/news/67843.

———. 2022c. "Obrashchenie Prezidenta Rossiyskoy Federatsii" [Speech Delivered in Moscow on the Situation in Donbass]. Kremlin.ru. September 21. http://kremlin.ru/events/president/news/69390.

———. 2022d. "Videoobrashcheniye po sluchayu Dnya rabotnika organov bezopasnosti" [Video Address on the Occasion of the Day of the Security Worker]. Kremlin.ru. December 20. http://kremlin.ru/events/president/news/70146.

———. 2022e. "Vstrecha s molodymi predprinimatelyami, inzhenerami i uchonymi" [Meeting with Young Entrepreneurs, Engineers and Scientists]. Kremlin.ru. June 9. http://kremlin.ru/events/president/news/68606.

———. 2021a. "Bol'shaya press-konferentsiya Vladimira Putina" [Vladimir Putin's Big Press Conference]. Kremlin.ru. December 23. http://kremlin.ru/events/president/news/67438.

———. 2021b. "Parad Pobedy na Krasnoy ploshchadi" [Speech Delivered at the Victory Parade on Red Square]. Kremlin.ru. May 9. http://kremlin.ru/events/president/news/65544.

———. 2021c. "Poslaniye Prezidenta Federal'nomu Sobraniyu" [Speech Delivered to the Federal Assembly in Moscow]. Kremlin.ru. April 21. http://kremlin.ru/events/president/news/65418.

———. 2021d. "Rasshirennoye zasedaniye kollegii Minoborony" [Speech Delivered at an Expanded Meeting of the Collegium of the Ministry of Defense]. Kremlin.ru. December 21. http://kremlin.ru/events/president/news/67402.

———. 2021e. "Vladimir Putin prinyal uchastiye v yezhegodnom rasshirennom zase-danii kollegii Ministerstva vnutrennikh del Rossiyskoy Federatsii" [Speech Deliv-ered at an Expanded Meeting of Colleagues of the Ministry of Interior Affairs of Russia in Moscow]. Kremlin.ru. March 3. http://kremlin.ru/events/president/news/65090.

———. 2021f. "Zasedaniye kollegii FSB Rossii" [Speech Delivered in Moscow at a Meet-ing of the Collegium of the FSB]. Kremlin.ru. February 24. http://kremlin.ru/events/president/news/65068.

———. 2021g. "Zasedaniye Rossiyskogo organizatsionnogo komiteta 'Pobeda'" [Speech Delivered at a Meeting of the Russian Organizational Committee "Victory" in Mos-cow]. Kremlin.ru. http://kremlin.ru/events/president/news/65618.

———. 2020a. "Polnyy tekst vystupleniya prezidenta RF Vladimira Putina v Gosdume 10 marta 2020 goda" [Speech Delivered to the State Duma]. *Nezavisimaya Gazeta*. March 10. https://www.ng.ru/politics/2020-03-10/100_putin10032020.html.

———. 2020b. "The Real Lessons of the 75th Anniversary of World War II." National Interest. June 18. https://nationalinterest.org/feature/vladimir-putin-real-lessons-75th-anniversary-world-war-ii-162982.

———. 2019a. "Bol'shaya press-konferentsia Vladimira Putina" [Vladimir Putin's Big Press Conference]. Kremlin.ru. December 19. http://kremlin.ru/events/president/news/62366.

———. 2019b. "Neformal'nyy sammit SNG" [Informal CIS Summit]. Kremlin.ru. December 20. http://kremlin.ru/events/president/news/62376.

———. 2019c. "Parad Pobedy na Krasnoy ploshchadi" [Speech Delivered at the Vic-tory Parade on Red Square]. Kremlin.ru. May 9. http://kremlin.ru/events/president/news/60490.

———. 2019d. "Poslaniye Prezidenta Federal'nomu Sobraniyu" [Speech Delivered to the Federal Assembly in Moscow]. Kremlin.ru. February 20. http://kremlin.ru/events/president/news/59863.

———. 2019e. "S'yezd partii 'Yedinaya Rossiya'" [Speech at the 19th Congress of the United Russia Party]. Kremlin.ru. November 23. http://kremlin.ru/events/president/news/62105.

———. 2019f. "Vladimir Putin vyskazalsya za patrioticheskoye vospitanie molodyozhi bez ideologizatsii takoi roboty" [Putin Supported Patriotic Upbringing of the Young Without Ideologization of This Process]. TASS. March 18. https://tass.ru/politika/6230692.

———. 2018a. "Poslaniye Prezidenta Federal'nomu Sobraniyu" [Presidential Address to the Federal Assembly]. Kremlin.ru. March 1. http://kremlin.ru/events/president/news/56957.

———. 2018b. "Voyennyy parad na Krasnoy ploshchadi" [Speech Delivered at the Victory Day Parade on Red Square]. Kremlin.ru. May 9. http://kremlin.ru/events/president/news/57436.

———. 2018c. "Yezhegodnie poslania prezidenta RF federal'nomu sobraniyu" [The Yearly Addresses of the President of the Russian Federation to the Federation Council]. TASS. February 28. https://tass.ru/info/4995125.

———. 2018d. "Zasedanie diskussionnogo kluba 'Valdai'" [Remarks at a Session of the "Valdai" Discussion Club]. Kremlin.ru. October 18. http://kremlin.ru/events/president/news/58848.

———. 2017a. "Otkrytiye memoriala pamyati zhertv politicheskikh repressiy 'Stena skorbi'" [Speech Delivered at the Opening Ceremony of the Wall of Sorrow Memorial to Victims of Political Repression in Moscow]. Kremlin.ru. October 30. http://kremlin.ru/events/president/news/55948.

———. 2017b. "Otkrytiye pamyatnika Aleksandru III" [Opening of the Monument to Alexander III]. Kremlin.ru. November 18. http://special.kremlin.ru/catalog/regions/CR/events/56125.

———. 2017c. "Torzhestvennyy vecher, posvyashchonnyy Dnyu rabotnika organov bezopasnosti" [Speech Delivered at the Gala Evening to Mark the Day of the Worker of State Security Organs in Moscow]. Kremlin.ru. December 20. http://kremlin.ru/events/president/news/56452.

———. 2016. "Putin o patrioticheskom vospitanii" [Putin on the Patriotic Upbringing]. Odnako.ru. September 3. https://web.archive.org/web/20160903084517/http:/www.odnako.org/blogs/putin-o-patrioticheskom-vospitanii-dopolneno-goszakaz-i-kontrol-v-kulture-obrazovanie.

———. 2015a. "Vladimir Putin posetil Natsional'nyy tsentr upravleniya oboronoy Rossii, gde provol soveshchaniye o deystviyakh Vozdushno-kosmicheskikh sil Rossiyskoy Federatsii v Siriyskoy Arabskoy Respublike" [Remarks at the National Defense Center, Where He Conducted a Meeting on the Activities of the Airspace Forces of the Russian Federation in the Syrian Arab Republic]. Kremlin.ru. November 17. http://kremlin.ru/events/president/news/50714.

———. 2015b. "Vystupleniye na tseremonii otkrytiya Mezhdunarodnogo voyenno-tekhnicheskogo foruma 'Armiya-2015'" [Speech Delivered at the Opening of the International Military-Technological Forum "Army-2015" in Moscow]. Kremlin.ru. June 16. http://kremlin.ru/events/president/transcripts/49712.

———. 2015c. ""Zasedaniye Mezhdunarodnogo diskussionnogo kluba 'Valday'" [Speech at the Concluding Session of the Valdai Club]. Kremlin.ru. October 22. http://kremlin.ru/events/president/news/50548.

———. 2014a. "'Na Miru i Smert Krasna'" [With One's Own Around You, Death Itself Is Good]. Obshchestvenni Kontrol. April 18. https://ok-inform.ru/tribuna/12084-vladimir-putin-na-miru-i-smert-krasna.html.

———. 2014b. "Obrashcheniye Prezidenta Rossiyskoy Federatsii" [Speech Delivered to State Duma Deputies, Members of the Federal Assembly, Heads of Russian Regions, and Representatives of Civil Society in the Kremlin]. Kremlin.ru. March 18. http://kremlin.ru/events/president/news/20603.

———. 2014c. "Putin: Russkii narod shire dushoi, chem predstaviteli drugikh narodov" [Putin: The Russian People's Souls Are Larger Than Those of Other Peoples]. RIA Novosti. April 17. https://ria.ru/20140417/1004339422.html.

———. 2013a. "Interv'yu Pervomu kanalu i agentstvu Assoshieyted Press" [Interview to the Channel One and the Associated Press]. Kremlin.ru. September 4. http://www.kremlin.ru/events/president/transcripts/interviews/19143/photos.

———. 2013b. "Vstupitel'noye slovo na soveshchanii o predvaritel'nykh itogakh sovmestnykh rossiysko-belorusskikh ucheniy 'Zapad-2013'" [Opening Remarks Delivered at the Conference on the Preliminary Results of the Joint Russian-Belorussian Military Exercise "Zapad 2013"]. Kremlin.ru. September 26. http://kremlin.ru/events/president/transcripts/19292.

———. 2013c. "Zasedaniye mezhdunarodnogo diskussionnogo kluba 'Valday'" [Speech Delivered at the Valdai Club]. Kremlin.ru. November 19. http://kremlin.ru/events/president/news/19243.

———. 2012a. "Byt sil'nymi—garantii natsionalnoy bezopasnosti dlya Rossii" [To Be Strong Is a Guarantee of the National Security of Russia]. *Rossiyskaya Gazeta*. February 20. https://rg.ru/2012/02/20/putin-armiya.html.

———. 2012b. "Poslaniye Prezidenta Federal'nomu Sobraniyu" [Speech to the Federal Assembly in Moscow]. Kremlin.ru. December 12. http://kremlin.ru/events/president/news/17118.

———. 2012c. "Rossiya: Natsional'niy Vopros" [Russia: The National Question]. *Nezavisimaya Gazeta*. January 23. https://www.ng.ru/politics/2012-01-23/1_national.html.

———. 2012d. "Rossiya sosredotatchivaetsya—vyzovy, na kotorye my dolzhny otvetit'" [Russia Is Getting Ready for Action: The Challenges That We Have to Meet]. *Izvestia*. January 12. https://iz.ru/news/511884.

———. 2012e. "Vstrecha s predstavitelyami obshchestvennosti po voprosam patrioticheskogo vospitaniya molodozhi" [Remarks Delivered to Representatives of the Public at a Meeting on the Patriotic Upbringing of Russian Youth]. Kremlin.ru. September 12. http://kremlin.ru/events/president/news/16470.

———. 2012f. "Vystupleniye Vladimira Putina na mitinge v Luzhnikakh" [Speech Delivered at a Rally in Luzhniki Stadium in Moscow]. RIA Novosti. February 23. https://ria.ru/20120223/572995366.html.

———. 2011a. "Polnyy tekst interv'yu Putina rossiyskim telekanalam" [A Complete Transcript of the Interview with Russia's Major TV Channels]. RIA Novosti. October 17. https://ria.ru/20111017/462204254.html.

———. 2011b. "Stenogramma programmy 'Razgovor s Vladimirom Putinym. Prodolzheniye'" [Transcript of "A Conversation with Vladimir Putin. Continued"]. *Rossiyskaya Gazeta*. December 15. https://rg.ru/2011/12/15/stenogramma.html.

———. 2007a. "Stenograficheskiy otchyot o press-konferentsii dlya rossiiskikh i inostrannykh zhurnalistov" [Transcribed Account of the Press Conference for Russian and International Journalists]. Kremlin.ru. February 1. http://kremlin.ru/events/president/transcripts/24026.

———. 2007b. "Vystuplenie i discussiya na Myunkhenskoy konferentsii po voprosam politiki bezopasnosti" [Speech and Discussion at the Munich Conference on International Security Policy]. Kremlin.ru. February 10. http://kremlin.ru/events/president/transcripts/24034.

———. 2006. "Annual Address to the Federal Assembly." Kremlin.ru. May 10. http://en.kremlin.ru/events/president/transcripts/23577.

———. 2005. "Poslaniye Federal'nomu Sobraniyu Rossiyskoy Federatsii" [Address to the Federal Assembly]. Kremlin.ru. April 25. http://kremlin.ru/events/president/transcripts/22931.

———. 2004. "Obrashcheniye Prezidenta Rossii Vladimira Putina" [Speech Delivered in Moscow in the Wake of the Beslan Hostage Crisis]. Kremlin.ru. September 4. http://kremlin.ru/events/president/transcripts/22589.

———. 2003a. "Vstupitel'noye slovo na vstreche s uchenymi Rossiyskogo federal'nogo yadernogo tsentra" [Introductory Remarks at the Meeting with Scientists of the Russian Federal Nuclear Center]. Kremlin.ru. July 31. http://kremlin.ru/events/president/transcripts/22073.

———. 2003b. "Vystupleniye na tseremonii blagosloveniya krestnogo khoda" [Address at the Procession of the Blessing of the Cross]. Kremlin.ru. July 31. http://www.special.kremlin.ru/events/president/transcripts/22071.

———. 2001. "Vystuplenie v Bundestage FRG" [Speech in the Bundestag of the Federal Republic of Germany]. Kremlin.ru. September 25. http://kremlin.ru/events/president/transcripts/21340.

Pyatigorsk City Administration. 2019. "Parad doshkol'nykh voysk vpervyye proshel v Pyatigorske" [A Parade of Preschool Soldiers Was Held for the First Time in Pyatigorsk]. June 5. https://pyatigorsk.org/16693.

Radio Baltkom. 2020. "Zamdirektora 'Levada-Tsentr' o sotsiologii, Putine I VTsIOM" [The Deputy Director of the Levada Center on Sociology, Putin, and VTsIOM]. YouTube. February 3. 41:34. https://www.youtube.com/watch?v=mslAwEM5ZX0.

Radio Svoboda. 2021a. "Protiv advokata Pavlova vozbuzhdeno delo o gosudarstvennoy izmene" [The Lawyer Pavlov Was Charged with State Treason]. December 21. https://www.svoboda.org/a/protiv-advokata-ivana-pavlova-vozbuzhdeno-ugolovnoe-delo-o-gosizmene/31619740.html.

———. 2021b. "Putin na vstreche so SMI: 'Idite vy so svoimi ozabochenostyami'" [Putin at a Meeting with Mass Media: 'Go to Hell with Your Preoccupations]. https://www.svoboda.org/a/idite-vy-so-svoimi-ozabochennostyami-o-chyom-govoril-putin-na-vstreche-so-smi/31623010.html.

Rainsford, Sarah. 2018. "Russia's Putin Embraces Higher Pension Age but Softens Blow." BBC. August 29. https://www.bbc.com/news/world-europe-45347228.

Rasmussen, Sune Engel. 2022. "Putin's War in Ukraine Tests Allegiances of Russian Speakers in Former Soviet Latvia." *Wall Street Journal*. March 28. https://www.wsj.com/articles/putins-war-in-ukraine-tests-allegiances-of-russian-speakers-in-former-soviet-latvia-11648459800.

RBK. 2020a. "Minfin raskryl srednyuyu tsenu rossiiskoi nefti za mart" [The Ministry of Finance Revealed the Average Price of Russian Oil in March]. April 8. https://www.rbc.ru/economics/01/04/2020/5e84cc099a7947889c4ba151.

———. 2020b. "Minoboroniy Provelo Ispytanie Ballisticheskikh Raket 'Yars' i 'Sineva'" [The Ministry of Defense Carried out a Test of the Ballistic Missiles "Yars" and "Sineva"]. December 9. https://www.rbc.ru/rbcfreenews/5fd0f7589a79476997997e6b.

———. 2016. "Putin nazval yedinstvenno vozmozhnuyu dlya Rossii natsional'nuyu ideyu" [Putin Named the Only Possible National Idea for Russia]. February 3. https://www.rbc.ru/politics/03/02/2016/56b1f8a79a7947060162a5a7.

———. 2015. "Minoborony obnarodovalo video puska raket Kaspiyskoy flotilii Po Syrii" [The Ministry of Defense Made Public—the Video of the

Launching of Missiles into Syria by the Caspian Fleet]. October 7. https://www.rbc.ru/politics/07/10/2015/5615172a9a7947c1ce9d0346.

RedSamurai84. 2016a. "HD Russian Army Parade, Victory Day 2015." YouTube. May 16. https://www.youtube.com/watch?app=desktop&v=kDFVNhlBE7U&t=859s.

———. 2016b. "HD Soviet Army Parade, Victory Day 1990." YouTube. https://www.youtube.com/watch?v=Yrj3vhrI7aY.

Red Star. 2018. "Voyennaya Nauka Smotrit v Budushcheye" [Military Science Looks to the Future]. March 26. http://archive.redstar.ru/index.php/component/k2/item/36626-voennaya-nauka-smotrit-v-budushchee.

Remnick, David. 2008. "Echo in the Dark." *New Yorker.* September 15. https://www.newyorker.com/magazine/2008/09/22/echo-in-the-dark.

Reuters. 2018. "Putin, Before Vote, Says He'd Reverse Soviet Collapse If He Could." March 2. https://www.reuters.com/article/us-russia-election-putin-idUSKCN1GE2TF.

———. 2007. "Putin's Speech Showed Why NATO Must Enlarge." February 11. https://www.reuters.com/article/uk-russia-usa-czech-idUSL1126843820070211.

Reznik, Il'ya. n.d. "Nasha armiya" [Our Army]. http://www.ilya-reznik.ru/txt/102_nasha_armiya.html.

RIA Novosti. 2022a. "Putin prikazal perevesti sily sderzhivaniya v ocobiy rezhim dezhurstva" [Putin Ordered Russia's (Strategic Nuclear) Deterrence Forces to Be Brought into a Special Regime of Readiness]. February 27. https://ria.ru/20220227/putin-1775389742.html.

———. 2022b. "Putin prokommentiroval zayavleniya Zapada o bor'be do 'poslednego ukraintsa'" [Putin Commented on the Statements of the West About "Fighting to the Last Ukrainian"]. July 7. https://ria.ru/20220707/putin-1801063012.html.

———. 2021. "V 'Yunarmiyu' vstupil millionnyy uchastnik" [The Millionth Participant Joined Yunarmia]. December 5. https://ria.ru/20211205/yunarmiya-1762239903.html.

———. 2020. "Voyennyy svyashchennik: nam predlagayut otkazat'sya ot osvyashcheniya oruzhiya" [Military Priest: We Are Urged to Refuse the Consecration of Weapons]. February 20. https://ria.ru/20200220/1564984970.html?rcmd_alg=&rcmd_id=1564984970.

———. 2018. "Putin poobeshchal dal'neysheye ukrepleniye vooruzhennykh sil" [Putin Promised to Further Strengthen the Armed Forces]. September 13. https://ria.ru/20180913/1528445508.html.

———. 2017a. "'Chto ty glaza otvodish?' Safronov otvetil predstavitelyu Britanii v OON" ["Why Are You Looking Away?" Safronov Answered the British Representative in the UN]. April 12. https://ria.ru/20170412/1492116042.html.

———. 2017b. "Ryabkov: nyneshnei ritorike SShA svoistvenny primitive i khamstvo" [Ryabkov: The Current Rhetoric of the USA Is Typically Primitive and Boorish]. April 12. https://ria.ru/20170412/1492057665.html.

———. 2009. "Pervaya mashina sem'i Putina" [The Putin Family's First Car]. May 2. https://ria.ru/20090205/161002448.html.

Riefenstahl, Leni. 1935. *Triumph of the Will.* Germany: Leni Riefenstahl-Produktion.

Rogov, Kirill. n.d. "Krepost' vrastart v zemlyu" [The Fortress Grows down into the Soil]. Liberal Mission Foundation. https://liberal.ru/files/articles/7335/krepost.pdf.

Romanoffsky, Stas. 2014. "Vystupleniie Putina 18 marta 2014 goda federalnym sobraniem po krymskomu voprosu (polnaya versia)" [The March 18th 2014 Address of Putin to the Federal Assembly on the Crimean Question (Full Version)]. YouTube. March 18. https://www.youtube.com/watch?v=dEXPXj3xvWY.

Rossiyskaya Gazeta. 2014. "Voyennaya doktrina Rossiyskoy Federatsii" [Military Doctrine of the Russian Federation]. December 30. https://rg.ru/documents/2014/12/30/doktrina-dok.html.

———. 2007. "Vladimir Putin: U tekh, kto khochet vernut' oligarkhicheskiy rezhim, nichego ne poluchitsya" [Vladimir Putin: Those Who Want to Return the Oligarchic Regime Will Utterly Fail]. November 22. https://rg.ru/2007/11/22/putin-forum.html.

Rosstat. 2021. "O Znachenii Granits Bednosti i Chislennosti Naseleniya s Denezhnymi Dokhodami Nizhe Granitsi Bednosti za 1-3 kvartaly 2021 Goda v Tselom Po Rossiiskoi Federatsii" [The Significance of the Limits of Poverty and the Number of People with Incomes Lower Than the Poverty Level in the First Through Third Quarters of 2021 in the Russian Federation]. https://rosstat.gov.ru/storage/mediabank/218_03-12-2021.htm.

Rothrock, Kevin [@KevinRothrock]. 2022a. "Apparently, This Happened in the Pskov Region, Too. One Parent Shared the Permission Request Slip Sent Home with His Daughter from School with Local Journalists. Https://Vk.Com/Wall-75765180_17136 Https://T.Co/UopqjBJGay." Twitter. May 9. https://twitter.com/KevinRothrock/status/1523678454977228800.

———. 2022b. "Children in Chita Perform the 2017 Propaganda Hit 'Uncle Vova, We're with You,' Where They Vow to Take Up Arms in 'the Final Battle,' If Putin Sends Russia to War. (The Song Also Calls for Reconquering Alaska, by the Way.) Https://T.Co/2yDuxo2BUv." Twitter. May 9. https://twitter.com/KevinRothrock/status/1523658175525785601.

Ru.citaty. 2022. "Proshedsheye Rossii bylo udivitel'no, yeye nastoyashcheye boleye chem velikolepno, chto zhe kasayetsya do budushchego, to ono vyshe vsego, chto mozhet narisovat' sebe samoye smeloye voobrazheniye" [Russia's Past Was Extraordinary, Its Present Is Better Than Magnificent, and as to Its Future It Exceeds the Most Daring Imagination]. July 2. http://ru.citaty.net/tsitaty/653223-aleksandr-khristoforovich-benkendorf-proshedshee-rossii-bylo-udivitelno-ee-nastoiashchee-bo.

RT. 2015. "Vladimir Putin: Svyashchenniy Dolg Rossiyan—Byt' Vernymi Tsennostyam Patriotizma" [Vladimir Putin: A Sacred Duty of Russians: To Be Faithful to the Values of Patriorism]. June 22. https://russian.rt.com/article/98867.

RT International. n.d. "Nuclear Deterrence Ready: Putin Presides over Mega Missile Exercise Involving Submarines, Bombers & Ground Launchers (VIDEOS)." https://www.rt.com/russia/471143-mega-missile-exercise-russia.

Ryabkov, Sergei, and Evgeny Minibaev. 2012. "Voprosy raznye, rezul'tat resheniya odin" [The Questions Are Different but the Decision's Result Is the Same]. Topwar.ru. March 13. https://topwar.ru/12371-voprosy-raznye-rezultat-resheniya-odin.html.

Rykovtseva, Yelena. n.d. "Kto Razvyazhen Tret'yu Mirovuyu?" [Who Will Unleash the Third World War?]. Radio Svoboda. https://www.svoboda.org/a/30942753.html.

Samarina, Alexandra. 2014. "'Fultonskaya rech Putina'" [Putin's Fulton Speech]. *Nezavisimaya Gazeta*. March 19. https://www.ng.ru/politics/2014-03-19/1_speech.html.

Samotsety. 2011. "Moy adres—Sovetskiy Soyuz" [My Address Is the Soviet Union]. YouTube. May 5. https://www.youtube.com/watch?v=J9s7Zel1sm4.

Sanger, David E., Anton Troianovaski, and Julian E. Barnes. 2022. "In Washington, Putin's Nuclear Threats Stir Growing Alarm." *New York Times*. October 1. https://www.nytimes.com/2022/10/01/world/europe/washington-putin-nuclear-threats.html.

Sanger, David E., Anton Troianovski, Julian E. Barnes, and Eric Schmitt. 2022. "Ukraine Wants More Powerful Weapons. Biden Is Not So Sure." *New York Times*. September 17. https://www.nytimes.com/2022/09/17/us/politics/ukraine-biden-weapons.html.

Sanina, Anna. 2016. "Patriotizm i patrioticheskoye vospitanie v covremennoi Rossii" [Patriotism and Patriotic Upbringing in Modern Russia]. *Sotsialogicheskie Issledovaniya*, no. 5: 44–53. https://elibrary.ru/item.asp?id=26125604.

Schlosser, Eric. 2022. "What If Russia Uses Nuclear Weapons in Ukraine?" *Atlantic*. June 20. https://www.theatlantic.com/ideas/archive/2022/06/russia-ukraine-nuclear-weapon-us-response/661315.

Sebelev, Sergey. 2020. "Main Cathedral of the Russian Armed Forces Patriot." Wikimedia Commons. July 9. https://commons.wikimedia.org/wiki/File:Main_Cathedral_of_the_Russian_Armed_Forces_Patriot.jpg.

Severodvinsk.info. 2021. "V Severodvinske otkryli filial Parka 'Patriot'" [A Branch of the Patriot Park Was Opened in Severodvinsk]. March 12. https://www.severodvinsk.info/pr/24602.

Shakirov, Mumin. 2020. "Triumf ili bol'shaya afera Vladimira Putina" [A Triumph, or Putin's Big Scam]. Radio Svoboda. July 4. https://www.svoboda.org/a/30705723.html.

Shlapank, David A., and Michael W. Johnson. 2016. "Reinforcing Deterrence on NATO's Eastern Flank." RAND Corporation. https://www.rand.org/content/dam/rand/pubs/research_reports/RR1200/RR1253/RAND_RR1253.pdf.

Shunin, Alexander. 2019. "Solovei na Baltkom: Putin schitaet sebya nepogreshimym messiei" [Solovei on Baltkom: Putin Considers Himself a Messiah Who Does Not Err]. MixNews. June 20. https://mixnews.lv/exclusive/2019/06/20/solovej-na-baltkom-putin-schitaet-sebya-nepogreshimym-missiej.

Simmons, Ann M. 2019. "Blast, Radiation Unnerve Russians Living near Test Site." *Wall Street Journal*. September 5. https://www.wsj.com/articles/blast-radiation-unnerve-russians-living-near-test-site-11569403801.

Simon, Steven. 2020. "Hypersonic Missiles Are a Game Changer." *New York Times*. January 2. https://www.nytimes.com/2020/01/02/opinion/hypersonic-missiles.html.

Simonov, Konstantin. 2020. "OPEK minus: zachem Sechin I Siluanov ubedili Putina vyiti iz neftyanoi sdelki" [OPEC Minus: Why Sechin and Siluanov Convinced Putin to Leave the Oil Deal]. *Forbes*. April 23. https://www.forbes.ru/biznes/398841-opek-minus-zachem-sechin-i-siluanov-ubedili-putina-vyyti-iz-neftyanoy-sdelki.

Sindelar, Daisy. 2013. "In Choosing Kiselyov, Media Critics Say Putin Opts for Personal Propagandist." Radio Free Europe/Radio Liberty. December 10. https://www.rferl.org/a/russia-media-kiselyov-propagandist/25195932.html.

Skibo, Dariya. 2020. "Inostrannykh agentov stanet bol'she" [There Will Be More Foreign Agents]. Eurasianet. February 25. https://russian.eurasianet.org/иностранных-агентов-статет-больше.

Smirnov, Dmitry. 2017. "Bessmertnyy Polk Srazhayetsya" [The Immortal Regiment Is Fighting]. YouTube. https://www.youtube.com/watch?v=v7g6FdM2pgs.

Smirnov, Valery. 2019. "Monument to Russian Emperor Alexander III in Livadia Park on a Sunny Cloudless Day, Crimea." Alamy Stock Photo. https://www.alamy.com/monument-to-russian-emperor-alexander-iii-in-livadia-park-on-a-sunny-cloudless-day-crimea-image342439238.html.

Snyder, Timothy. 2018. "Ivan Ilyin, Putin's Philosopher of Russian Fascism." *New York Review of Books*. March 16. https://www.nybooks.com/online/2018/03/16/ivan-ilyin-putins-philosopher-of-russian-fascism.

Sokolrus. 2015. "RS-24 'Yars.'" Wikimedia Commons. May 9. https://commons.wikimedia.org/wiki/File:PC-24_%C2%AB%D0%AF%D1%80%D1%81%C2%BB.JPG.

Soldatkin, Vladimir. 2015. "Putin Marks 63rd Birthday with Ice Hockey Match, Syria War Briefing." Reuters. October 7. https://www.reuters.com/article/us-russia-putin-birthday-idUSKCN0S121720151007.

Solovyov, Vladimir. 2022. "Efir 26.04.2022—Margarita Simon'yan: Nyet Shansov, Chto My Prosto Slozhim Lapki" [Broadcast 26.04.2022—Margarita Simonyan: There Is No Chance That We Will Just Quietly Surrender]. April 26. https://www.vsoloviev.ru/vecher/8108.

———. 2018. "Miroporyadok 2018" [World Order 2018]. YouTube. April 2. https://www.youtube.com/watch?v=uC2bWSbZdQ4.

Solzhenitsyn, Aleksandr. *In the First Circle* (1968; New York: Harper Perennial, 2009).

Sonin, Konstantin. 2022. "Russia's Road to Economic Ruin." *Foreign Affairs*. November 15. https://www.foreignaffairs.com/russian-federation/russias-road-economic-ruin.

Sorokin, Vladimir. 2014. "Let the Past Collapse on Time." *New York Review*. August. https://www.nybooks.com/articles/2014/05/08/let-the-past-collapse-on-time.

Spongenberg, Helena. 2007. "Putin Speech Raises Alarm on EU-Russia Relations." EUobserver. February 12. https://euobserver.com/news/23471.

Standish, Reid. 2022. "Interview: How Russia's Intelligence Agencies Have Adapted After Six Months of War." Radio Free Europe. August 24. https://www.rferl.org/a/russia-intelligence-agencies-ukraine-war-six-months/32003096.html.

Stanovaya, Tatiana. 2022. "K diskussii o ratsional'nosti Putina" [On the Discussion of Putin's Rationality]. Telegram. November 3. https://t.me/stanovaya/1546.

Stalin, Joseph. 1945a. "Slava Nashemu Velikomu Narodu, Narodu-Pobeditelyu!" [Glory to Our Great Nation—the Victorious Nation!]. Istoria. May 8. https://histrf.ru/read/articles/slava-nashiemu-vielikomu-narodu-narodu-pobieditieliu.

———. 1945b. "Tost I.V. Stalina za 'zdorov'ye russkogo naroda': Vystupleniye na priyeme v Kremle v chest' komanduyushchikh voyskami Krasnoy Armii, 24 maya

1945 g" [The Toast of Joseph Stalin to the "Health of the Russian People": Address at a Reception in the Kremlin in Honor of the Commanders of the Red Army, May 24, 1945]. 100 Klyuchevykh dokumentov po rossiyskoy i sovetskoy istorii. May 24. https://www.1000dokumente.de/index.html?c=dokument_ru&dokument=0028_toa&object=translation&l=ru.

———. 1931. "O zadachakh khozaistvennikov" [On the Tasks of the Managers of the Economy]. https://fishki.net/anti/2754381-otstalyh-byjut-vyskazyvanie-ivstalina-v1931g-aktualyno-segodnja-kak-nikogda.html.

Stewart, Will. 2019. "Russian Children Marching as Putin's 'Youth Army' Tops Half a Million." Mail Online. May 8. https://www.dailymail.co.uk/news/article-7007211/Russian-children-taught-march-military-uniforms-Putins-youth-army-tops-half-million.html.

Stroitel'stvo. 2020. "Vo skol'ko oboshlos' stroitel'stvo khrama vooruzhyonnykh sil" [How Much Did the Construction of the Cathedral of the Armed Forces Cost?]. June 23. https://rcmm.ru/novosti/49570-vo-skolko-oboshlos-stroitelstvo-hrama-vooruzhennyh-sil.html.

Sukhankin, Sergey. 2016. "Russia's 'Youth Army': Sovietization, Militarization or Radicalization?" *Eurasia Daily Monitor* 13, no. 180 (November 9). https://jamestown.org/program/russias-youth-army-sovietization-militarization-radicalization.

Tagaeva, Lola. 2014. "Lev Gudkov: 'Yesli za vse otvechayet odin chelovek v strane, cherez kakoye-to vremya illyuzii v otnoshenii yego sposobnosti prevrashchayutsya v razdrazheniye'" [Lev Gudkov: "If Only One Man Is Responsible for Everything in the Country, After Some Time the Illusions About His Abilities Start to Irritate"]. Republic.ru. June 2. https://republic.ru/posts/41566.

Tarasov, Aleksei. 2019. "Detstvo—pod ruzhyo" [Childhood [Shoved] Under the Gun]. *Novaya Gazeta*. March 13. https://novayagazeta-vlad.ru/2019/03/13/3571/detstvo-pod-ruzhe.html.

TASS. 2022. "Lithuania's Russian-Speaking Population Shrinks to 5% in Past Decade." January 3. https://tass.com/world/1383623.

———. 2019a. "Shoigu nazval tsel' informatsionnoi voiny Zapada protiv Rossii" [Shoigu Identified the Goal of the West's Informational War Against Russia]. June 26. https://tass.ru/armiya-i-opk/6596144.

———. 2019b. "Yunarmeytsam dobavyat bally k EGE" [Yunarmiya Members Will Receive Additional Points in the Unified State Examination]. March 29. https://tass.ru/obschestvo/6273668.

———. 2015a. "Nravstennym orientirom dlya podrostkov dolzhna stat' lyubov k rodine" [Love of the Motherland Must Become the Moral Guideline for Teenagers]. October 8. https://tass.ru/obschestvo/2329167.

———. 2015b. "Putin Agrees with Emperor That Russia's Only Allies Are Army and Navy." April 16. https://tass.com/russia/789866.

Taylor, Brian. 2019. "Putin's Fourth Term: The Phantom Breakthrough." PONARS Eurasia. July 18. https://www.ponarseurasia.org/putin-s-fourth-term-the-phantom-breakthrough.

Teksty Pesen. 2018. "Kadety—Dyadya Vova my s tobou" [Uncle Vlad, We're with You]. November 27. http://teksti-pesenok.ru/en/10/kadety/tekst-pesni-Dyadya-Vova-my-s-toboy.

Teller Report. 2021. "Putin Unveiled a Monument to Emperor Alexander III in Gatchina." May 6. https://www.tellerreport.com/news/2021-06-05-putin-unveiled-a-monument-to-emperor-alexander-iii-in-gatchina.Hy9T6YFq_.html.

Tolstoy, Lev. 2006. "Khadzhi-Murat." In *Lev Nikolaevich Tolstoy: Povesti i rasskazy* [*Lev Nikolaevich Tolstoy, Novellas and Stories*], 558. Moscow, Russia: Eksmo.

Troianovski, Anton, and Matthew Bodner. 2018. "With Putin's Reelection, Expect Rising Tensions with the West." *Washington Post*. March 18. https://www.washingtonpost.com/world/europe/with-putins-re-election-expect-rising-tensions-with-the-west/2018/03/18/8430f69e-2abf-11e8-8dc9-3b51e028b845_story.html.

Tsipko, Alexander. 2020. "Istoki i sud'ba sakralizatsii vlasti Putina" [The Origins and the Fate of the Sacralization of Putin's Authority]. *Nezavisimaya Gazeta*. May 20. http://www.ng.ru/ideas/2020-05-20/7_7865_sacralization.html.

Tumakova, Irina. 2020. "Rossiya na izmene" [The Treasonous Russia]. *Novaya Gazeta*. July 10. https://novayagazeta.ru/articles/2020/07/09/86211-rossiya-na-izmene.

Unanyants, Vladimir. 2021. "Ul'timatim Putina: razgnevanniy Kiev, zataivshiisya Tbilisi" [Putin's Ultimatum: An Angry Kiev, and a Lurking Tbilisi]. Ekho Kavkaza. December 24. https://www.ekhokavkaza.com/a/31624923.html.

Union of Concerned Scientists. 2022. "Tactical Nuclear Weapons." June 1. https://www.ucsusa.org/resources/tactical-nuclear-weapons.

US Army. n.d. "82nd Airborne Division." https://home.army.mil/bragg/index.php/units-tenants/82nd-airborne-division.

US Embassy and Consulates in Russia. 2020. "World War II Allies: U.S. Lend-Lease to the Soviet Union, 1941–1945." May 10. https://ru.usembassy.gov/world-war-ii-allies-u-s-lend-lease-to-the-soviet-union-1941-1945.

US Energy Information Agency. 2021. "Europe Brent Spot Price." https://www.eia.gov/dnav/pet/hist/LeafHandler.ashx?n=PET&s=RBRTE&f=A.

———. 2020. "Crude Oil Prices Were Generally Lower in 2019 Than in 2018." January 7. https://www.eia.gov/todayinenergy/detail.php?id=42415.

V1.ru. 2017. "V Kremle prokommentirovali pesnyu Anny Kuvychko 'Dyadya Vova, my s toboy!'" [The Kremlin Commented on Anna Kuvychko's Song "Daddy Vova, We Are with You"]. November 15. https://v1.ru/text/gorod/2017/11/15/51500131.

Vandiver, John. 2023. "Army 10th Mountain, 101st Airborne Division Soldiers Deploying to NATO's Southeast Flank." *Stars and Stripes*. March 8. https://www.stripes.com/branches/army/2023-03-08/101st-airborne-10th-mountain-romania-9421840.html.

Veselov, Andrey. 2018. "Chto rasskazal Vladimir Putin strane i miru v poslanii Federal'nomu Sobraniyu" [What Putin Told the Country and the World in His Message to the Federal Assembly]. RIA Novost. March 1. https://ria.ru/20180301/1515574957.html.

Vesti. 2020. "V Detskom Sadu Poyavilis' Kaleendari s Okrovavlennymi Det'mi v Obraze Frontovikov" [Calendars with Bloodstained Children Dressed as Front-Line Soldiers Appeared in a Kindergarten]. February 12. https://www.vesti.ru/article/1272980.

———. 2017. "Putin nazhal na 'krasnuyu knopku'" [Putin Pressed the "Red Button"]. October 29. https://www.vesti.ru/article/1601485.

Vesti Obrazovanie. 2019. "Million detei v Yunarmiyu, po yacheike—v kazhduyu shkolu" [A Million Children in Yunarmiya—a Cell in Every School]. September 16. http://vogazeta.ru/articles/2019/9/16/upbringing/9398-million_detey_v_yunarmiyu_po_yacheyke__v_kazhduyu_shkolu.

Vitte, Sergei. *Vospominaniya* [*Memoirs*] (Moscow, Soviet Union: Socio-Economic Literature, 1960).

Vladimirov, Viktor. 2020. "Dmitrii Oreshkin: 'Triumf Besstydstva'" [Dmitry Oreshkin: "The Triumph of Shamelessness"]. Voice of America. July 3. https://www.golosameriki.com/a/putin-amendments-oreshkin-interview/5487913.html.

Volgodonskaya Diocese. 2015. "Chin Osvyashcheniya Samolyotov. g. Morozovsk" [Aircraft Consecration Ceremony in the Town of Morozovsk]. August 15. http://viseparchia.ru/2015/08/15/chin-osvyashheniya-samoleta-g-morozovsk.

Volkov, Denis. 2018. "The Popularity Paradox." Chatham House. June 8. https://www.chathamhouse.org/publications/the-world-today/2018-06/popularity-paradox.

Volkov, Denis, and Sergei Medvedev. 2021. "Vozvrashchenie generalissimusa" [The Return of the Generalissimos]. Radio Svoboda. September 12. https://www.svoboda.org/a/vozvraschenie-generalissimusa/31456588.html.

VPTs Vympel. n.d. "O VPTs 'Vympel'" [About the Military-Patriotic Center "Vympel"]. https://xn--b1aajydqc7c5b.xn--p1ai/o-nas.

Vympel Group Association. n.d. "Obrashchenie veteranov Gruppy 'Vympel' k molodyozhi" [Address to the Youth by the Veterans of the "Vympel" Group]. http://group-vympel.ru/index.php/press-sluzhba/stati/110-stati-v-press-byuro/511-obrashchenie-veteranov-gruppy-vympel-k-molodjozhi.

Walker, Shaun. 2015. "Vladimir Putin Opens Russian 'Military Disneyland' Patriot Park." *Guardian*. June 16. https://www.theguardian.com/world/2015/jun/16/vladimir-putin-opens-russian-military-disneyland-patriot-park.

Wall, Mike. 2022. "Russia Conducts 1st Full Flight Test of New 'Sarmat' Intercontinental Ballistic Missile." Space.com. April 22. https://www.space.com/russia-test-launch-sarmat-icbm.

Wall Street Journal. 2020. "Russia Cements Ties with Crimea, Freezing Conflict with West." March 18. https://www.wsj.com/articles/russia-cements-ties-with-crimea-freezing-conflict-with-west-11584523802.

Wezeman, Siemon. 2020. "Russia's Military Spending: Frequently Asked Questions." Sipri. April 27. https://www.sipri.org/commentary/topical-backgrounder/2020/russias-military-spending-frequently-asked-questions.

World Bank. 2022. "Current Health Expenditure (% of GDP)—Russian Federation, European Union." October 24. https://data.worldbank.org/indicator/SH.XPD.CHEX.GD.ZS?locations=RU-EU.

———. 2021a. "GDP Growth (Annual %)—Russian Federation." https://data.worldbank.org/indicator/NY.GDP.MKTP.KD.ZG?locations=RU.

———. 2021b. "GDP Per Capita (Current US$)," https://data.worldbank.org/indicator/NY.GDP.PCAP.CD?end=1991&most_recent_value_desc=true&start=1990.

———. 2021c. "Life Expectancy at Birth, Total (Years)." https://data.worldbank.org/indicator/SP.DYN.LE00.IN?most_recent_value_desc=false.

———. 2021d. "Military Expenditure (% of GDP)—Russian Federation, United Kingdom, China, United States, France, Germany, India, Japan, Korea, Rep., Brazil." https://data.worldbank.org/indicator/MS.MIL.XPND.GD.ZS?end=2020&locations=RU-GB-CN-US-FR-DE-IN-JP-KR-BR&most_recent_value_desc=true&start=2010.

———. 2020a. "GDP—Russian Federation: 1988–2020." https://data.worldbank.org/indicator/NY.GDP.MKTP.CD?locations=RU.

———. 2020b. "Survival to Age 65, Male (% of Cohort)—Russian Federation." https://data.worldbank.org/indicator/SP.DYN.TO65.MA.ZS?locations=RU&most_recent_year_desc=false.

Wrigley, Alan. 2012. "Plaque Commemorating Former Soviet Leader Yuri Andropov, Moscow." Alamy Stock Photo. https://www.alamy.com/stock-photo-plaque-commemorating-former-soviet-leader-yuri-andropov-moscow-51139949.html.

Yaffa, Joshua. 2014. "Dmitry Kiselev Is Redefining the Art of Russian Propaganda." *New Republic.* July 1. https://newrepublic.com/article/118438/dmitry-kiselev-putins-favorite-tv-host-russias-top-propogandist.

Yankovskiy, Alexander, and Inna Annitova. 2021. "Ot global'nikh pretenzii k samorealizatsii. [From Global Pretensions to Self-Realization]. Krym.Realii. July 6. https://ru.krymr.com/a/rossiya-putin-kreml-natsionalnaya-strategiya/31343919.html.

Yarovoy, Gleb. 2021. "'Narastayushchaya agressivnost. Sotsiolog Lev Gudkov o nastroyeniyakh rossiyan" ["Increasing Aggressiveness." Sociologist Lev Gudkov About the Attitudes of Russians]. Sever.Realii. July 7. https://www.severreal.org/a/sotsiolog-lev-gudkov-o-nastroeniyah-rossiyan/31343336.html.

Yurgens, Igor. 2014. "Razvernut' stranu nazad nevozmozhno" [Turning the Country Back Is Impossible]. *Novaya Gazeta.* November 14. https://novayagazeta.ru/articles/2014/11/14/61943-igor-yurgens-171-razvernut-stranu-nazad-nevozmozhno-hod-istorii-somnet-takoy-algoritm-187.

Yuzbashev, Viktor. 2007. "Moleben Yadernomu Oruzhiyu" [A Public Prayer for Nuclear Weapons]. *Nezavisimoie Voennoe Obrozrenie.* September 7. https://nvo.ng.ru/forces/2007-09-07/3_moleben.html?id_user=Y.

Zakharova, Olesya. 2020. "How Does Putin Justify Resetting His Term-Limit Clock?" Riddle. April 28. https://ridl.io/how-does-putin-justify-resetting-his-term-limit-clock.

Zubarevich, Natalia. 2022. "Natal'ya Zubarevich: 'Nado govorit' ne o gibeli, a o degradatsii nashey ekonomiki'" [Natalia Zubarevich: We Must Talk Not About the Death, but About the Degradation of Our Economy]. *Novaya Izvestia.* November 16. https://newizv.ru/news/2022-11-16/natalya-zubarevich-nado-govorit-ne-o-gibeli-a-o-degradatsii-nashey-ekonomiki-372647.

Zysk, Katarzyna. 2017. "Nonstrategic Nuclear Weapons in Russia's Evolving Military Doctrine." *Bulletin of the Atomic Scientists* 73, no. 5 (September 3): 322–27. https://doi.org/10.1080/00963402.2017.1362908.

Index

RESEARCH STAFF

SAMUEL J. ABRAMS
Nonresident Senior Fellow

BETH AKERS
Senior Fellow

J. JOEL ALICEA
Nonresident Fellow

JOSEPH ANTOS
Senior Fellow; Wilson H. Taylor Scholar in Health Care and Retirement Policy

LEON ARON
Senior Fellow

KIRSTEN AXELSEN
Nonresident Fellow

JOHN P. BAILEY
Nonresident Senior Fellow

CLAUDE BARFIELD
Senior Fellow

MICHAEL BARONE
Senior Fellow Emeritus

ROBERT J. BARRO
Nonresident Senior Fellow

MICHAEL BECKLEY
Nonresident Senior Fellow

ERIC J. BELASCO
Nonresident Senior Fellow

ANDREW G. BIGGS
Senior Fellow

MASON M. BISHOP
Nonresident Fellow

JASON BLESSING
Jeane Kirkpatrick Visiting Research Fellow

DAN BLUMENTHAL
Senior Fellow

KARLYN BOWMAN
Distinguished Senior Fellow Emeritus

HAL BRANDS
Senior Fellow

ELISABETH BRAW
Senior Fellow

ALEX BRILL
Senior Fellow

ARTHUR C. BROOKS
President Emeritus

RICHARD BURKHAUSER
Nonresident Senior Fellow

CLAY CALVERT
Nonresident Senior Fellow, Domestic Policy

JAMES C. CAPRETTA
Senior Fellow; Milton Friedman Chair

TIMOTHY P. CARNEY
Senior Fellow

AMITABH CHANDRA
Nonresident Fellow

LYNNE V. CHENEY
Distinguished Senior Fellow

JAMES W. COLEMAN
Nonresident Senior Fellow

MATTHEW CONTINETTI
Senior Fellow; Patrick and Charlene Neal Chair in American Prosperity

ZACK COOPER
Senior Fellow

KEVIN CORINTH
Senior Fellow, Domestic Policy

JAY COST
Gerald R. Ford Nonresident Senior Fellow

DANIEL A. COX
Senior Fellow

SADANAND DHUME
Senior Fellow

GISELLE DONNELLY
Senior Fellow

MICHAEL BRENDAN DOUGHERTY
Nonresident Fellow

ROSS DOUTHAT
Nonresident Fellow

COLIN DUECK
Nonresident Senior Fellow

MACKENZIE EAGLEN
Senior Fellow

NICHOLAS EBERSTADT
Henry Wendt Chair in Political Economy

MAX EDEN
Research Fellow

JEFFREY EISENACH
Nonresident Senior Fellow

ANDREW FERGUSON
Nonresident Fellow

JESÚS FERNÁNDEZ-VILLAVERDE
John H. Makin Visiting Scholar

JOHN G. FERRARI
Nonresident Senior Fellow

JOHN C. FORTIER
Senior Fellow

AARON FRIEDBERG
Nonresident Senior Fellow

JOSEPH B. FULLER
Nonresident Senior Fellow

SCOTT GANZ
Research Fellow

R. RICHARD GEDDES
Nonresident Senior Fellow

ROBERT P. GEORGE
Nonresident Senior Fellow

JOSEPH W. GLAUBER
Nonresident Senior Fellow

JONAH GOLDBERG
Senior Fellow; Asness Chair in Applied Liberty

BARRY K. GOODWIN
Nonresident Senior Fellow

SCOTT GOTTLIEB, MD
Senior Fellow

PHIL GRAMM
Nonresident Senior Fellow

WILLIAM C. GREENWALT
Nonresident Senior Fellow

SHEENA CHESTNUT GREITENS
Jeane Kirkpatrick Visiting Fellow

JIM HARPER
Nonresident Senior Fellow

WILLIAM HAUN
Nonresident Fellow

BLAKE HERZINGER
Nonresident Fellow

FREDERICK M. HESS
Senior Fellow; Director, Education Policy Studies

CAROLE HOOVEN
Nonresident Senior Fellow, Domestic Policy

BRONWYN HOWELL
Nonresident Senior Fellow

R. GLENN HUBBARD
Nonresident Senior Fellow

HOWARD HUSOCK
Senior Fellow

BENEDIC N. IPPOLITO
Senior Fellow

MARK JAMISON
Nonresident Senior Fellow

LYNNE KIESLING
Nonresident Senior Fellow, Domestic Policy

FREDERICK W. KAGAN
Senior Fellow; Director, Critical Threats Project

STEVEN B. KAMIN
Senior Fellow

LEON R. KASS, MD
Senior Fellow Emeritus

JOSHUA T. KATZ
Senior Fellow

KLON KITCHEN
Nonresident Senior Fellow

KEVIN R. KOSAR
Senior Fellow

ROBERT KULICK
Visiting Fellow

PAUL H. KUPIEC
Senior Fellow

DESMOND LACHMAN
Senior Fellow

Milton Keynes UK
Ingram Content Group UK Ltd.
UKHW050208301123
433462UK00009B/84/J

* 9 7 8 0 8 4 4 7 5 0 5 4 5 *